21世纪高水平职业教育改革成果系列教材

高等学校英语应用能力考试（A&B级）真题+模拟

主　编　段利莹　杨　佳
副主编　李丽春　李买燕　李　睿　余　娟

北京理工大学出版社
BEIJING INSTITUTE OF TECHNOLOGY PRESS

简　　介

《高等学校英语应用能力考试（A&B级）真题＋模拟》一书由8套真题和8套模拟题构成。真题部分为历年最新真题，模拟题部分难易适中。所有试题均提供参考答案。听力部分附录音原文。通过学习本书可以提高考生的A&B级通过率并掌握所学的基础知识。

版权专有　侵权必究

图书在版编目（CIP）数据

高等学校英语应用能力考试（A&B级）真题＋模拟／段利莹，杨佳主编．—北京：北京理工大学出版社，2019.8（2021.10重印）

ISBN 978-7-5682-7510-1

Ⅰ．①高… Ⅱ．①段… ②杨… Ⅲ．①大学英语水平考试－高等职业教育－习题集 Ⅳ．① H310.421-44

中国版本图书馆 CIP 数据核字（2019）第 191067 号

出版发行 / 北京理工大学出版社有限责任公司
社　　址 / 北京市海淀区中关村南大街5号
邮　　编 / 100081
电　　话 /（010）68914775（总编室）
　　　　　（010）82562903（教材售后服务热线）
　　　　　（010）68948351（其他图书服务热线）
网　　址 / http://www.bitpress.com.cn
经　　销 / 全国各地新华书店
印　　刷 / 三河市天利华印刷装订有限公司
开　　本 / 787毫米 × 1092毫米　1/16　　　　　　　责任编辑 / 武丽娟
印　　张 / 13.5　　　　　　　　　　　　　　　　　文案编辑 / 武丽娟
字　　数 / 320千字　　　　　　　　　　　　　　　　责任校对 / 刘亚男
版　　次 / 2019年8月第1版　2021年10月第2次印刷　责任印制 / 施胜娟
定　　价 / 39.80元

图书出现印装质量问题，请拨打售后服务热线，本社负责调换

前　言

教育部颁布的《高职高专教育英语课程教学基本要求（试行）》明确指出：高职高专院校应把高等学校英语应用能力考试 A 级作为学生达标要求，B 级作为过渡性要求。高等学校英语应用能力考试自 2014 年 12 月起开始采用新题型。新题型最大的变化是听力理解部分分值增多，难度加大；语法结构部分分值比例不变，题量减少，难度降低；翻译的英译汉部分分值比例减少，四选一改为三选一，难度大大降低。为了帮助考生进一步熟悉新题型的内容及难度，顺利通过考试，我们精心策划并编写了此书。在编写过程中，我们严格按照教育部高等教育司颁布的《高职高专英语课程基本要求》和《高等学校英语应用能力考试大纲》，本书适用于参加全国高等学校英语应用能力 A、B 级考试的所有考生。

本书具有以下特点：

1. 紧扣考纲、针对性强：本书的试卷内容、难易程度、覆盖面和试卷质量严格按照《高等学校英语应用能力考试大纲》（2014 年新大纲）编写，以帮助考生在短时间内掌握最新考试题型和解题技巧。

2. 选题新颖、实用性强：本书分别收录了 4 套最新的 A 级和 B 级实考试题及其录音原声，使考生能够了解有关考试的最新、最准确的信息和动向。另外还分别精选了 4 套 A 级和 B 级模拟题，供考生考前自测。考生使用本书进行复习训练有助于提高 A、B 级考试的通过率，同时掌握英语的实际应用本领以及语言交际能力。

本书是编者在长期研究高等学校英语应用能力 A、B 级考试的基础上编写的。恳请广大考生和同行提出宝贵的意见，以待再版时修订。

编　者

Contents

PRETCO (Level B)

2018年12月B级考试全真试题 ·· 1
2018年6月B级考试全真试题 ·· 11
2017年12月B级考试全真试题 ·· 21
2017年6月B级考试全真试题 ·· 31
Model Test One(Level B) ··· 41
Model Test Two(Level B) ··· 51
Model Test Three(Level B) ·· 61
Model Test Four(Level B) ·· 70

PRETCO (Level A)

2018年12月A级考试全真试题 ·· 80
2018年6月A级考试全真试题 ·· 90
2017年12月A级考试全真试题 ·· 100
2017年6月A级考试全真试题 ·· 110
Model Test One(Level A) ··· 120
Model Test Two(Level A) ··· 130
Model Test Three(Level A) ·· 139
Model Test Four(Level A) ·· 149
B级参考答案(Keys to the Tests) ··· 159
A级参考答案(Keys to the Tests) ··· 167
B级听力文稿(Scripts for the Tests) ·· 175
A级听力文稿(Scripts for the Tests) ·· 190
参考文献 ·· 205

2018年12月B级考试全真试题

Part I Listening Comprehension   （25 minutes）

Directions: *This part is to test your listening ability. It consists of 4 sections.*

Section A

Directions: *This section is to test your ability to give proper responses. There are 7 recorded questions in it. After each question, there is a pause. The questions will be spoken **two times**. When you hear a question, you should decide on the correct answer from the 4 choices marked A), B), C) and D) given in your test paper. Then you should mark the corresponding letter on the Answer Sheet with a single line through the center.*

Example: *You will hear:*

   You will read: A) I'm not sure.   B) You're right.
                C) Yes, certainly.   D) That's interesting.

*From the question we learn that the speaker is asking the listener to leave a message. Therefore, **C) Yes, certainly** is the correct answer. You should mark C) on the Answer Sheet with a single line through the center.*

[A] [B] [C] [D]

Now the test will begin.

1. A) Sorry, he's not in.   B) Here you are.
   C) Try again, please.   D) Thank you.

2. A) Nice to meet you.   B) See you later.
   C) No, I don't.   D) Take care.

3. A) See you next time.   B) No, thanks.
   C) You are welcome.   D) Press the button here.

4. A) Over there.   B) Yes, I do.
   C) I like Chinese food.   D) Tomorrow morning.

5. A) Never mind.   B) Certainly.
   C) Only a week.   D) My pleasure.

6. A) On the Internet.   B) She's very nice.
   C) By bus.   D) It's far away.

7. A) We are busy.   B) Take it easy.
   C) It's expensive.   D) He's very kind.

·1·

Section B

Directions: *This section is to test your ability to understand short dialogues. There are 7 recorded dialogues in it. After each dialogue, there is a recorded question. Both the dialogues and questions will be spoken* **two times.** *When you hear a question, you should decide on the correct answer from the 4 choices marked A), B), C) and D) given in your test paper. Then you should mark the corresponding letter on the Answer Sheet with a single line through the center.*

Now listen to the dialogues.

8. A) Earth Day.　　　　　　　　　　　　B) Mother's Day.
　 C) Father's Day.　　　　　　　　　　　D) Thanksgiving Day.
9. A) Flight number.　　　　　　　　　　B) Bus schedules.
　 C) Banking services.　　　　　　　　　D) Office hours.
10. A) How to book a flight.　　　　　　　B) Where to sign the name.
　　C) When to hand in the form.　　　　　D) Who to ask for help.
11. A) From newspapers.　　　　　　　　B) From the sales department.
　　C) From magazines.　　　　　　　　　D) From the website.
12. A) The development plan.　　　　　　B) The market share.
　　C) Sales of a new product.　　　　　　D) Costs of advertising.
13. A) When to get the orders.　　　　　　B) Where to obtain the price list.
　　C) How to pay for the goods.　　　　　D) Whom to contact.
14. A) It has over 500 employees.　　　　　B) It was started in 1998.
　　C) It has several branches.　　　　　　D) It is located in Beijing.

Section C

Directions: *In this section, there are 2 recorded conversations. After each conversation, there are some recorded questions. Both the conversations and questions will be spoken* **two times.** *When you hear a question, you should decide on the correct answer from the 4 choices marked A), B), C) and D) given in your test paper. Then you should mark the corresponding letter on the Answer Sheet with a single line through the center.*

Now listen to the conversations.

Conversation 1

15. A) Making a sales plan.　　　　　　　B) Preparing an annual report.
　　C) Doing a market survey.　　　　　　D) Writing a business letter.
16. A) It costs much less.　　　　　　　　B) It saves time.
　　C) Most old people like it.　　　　　　D) Most young people like it.

Conversation 2

17. A) He has got a summer job.　　　　　B) He has lost his job.

C) He has just visited a park.　　　　　D) He has been to the beach.
18. A) A sales person.　　　　　　　　　B) A tour guide.
　　C) A manager assistant.　　　　　　　D) A computer programmer.
19. A) Because the salary is too low.
　　B) Because the company is too small.
　　C) Because she has to travel abroad frequently.
　　D) Because a tour guide has to work long hours.

Section D

Directions: *In this section you will hear a recorded short passage. The passage is printed in the test paper, but with some words or phrases missing. The passage will be read **three times**. During the second reading, you are required to put the missing words or phrases on the Answer Sheet in order of the numbered blanks according to what you hear. The third reading is for you to check your writing.*

Now the passage will begin.

Good evening, ladies and gentlemen!

First of all, I'd like to __20__ a sincere welcome to you all, the new comers of our company. As you know, our company is one of the top 50 companies in the country and has a history of more than 100 years. I think you must __21__ being a member of such a great company. But we cannot __22__ tradition alone. We need new employees with new knowledge and creative __23__.

I would like to welcome you __24__, and from today, let's begin to work together.

Part II　Vocabulary & Structure　　　　　　　　　(10 minutes)

Directions: *This part is to test your ability to construct correct and meaningful sentences. It consists of 2 sections.*

Section A

Directions: *In this section, there are 10 incomplete sentences. You are required to complete each one by deciding on the most appropriate word or words from the 4 choices marked A), B), C) and D). Then you should mark the corresponding letter on the Answer Sheet with a single line through the center.*

25. If Mary had _____ the situation to Tom, he would have understood it.
　　A) supplied　　　　B) explained　　　　C) charged　　　　D) thrown

26. I'm pleased to receive your letter of April 10th, _____ for our catalogue and price-list.
　　A) ask　　　　　　B) asked　　　　　　C) to ask　　　　　D) asking

27. _____ your trip is short or long, we can work out a schedule for you.
　　A) Whether　　　　B) What　　　　　　C) How　　　　　　D) Which

28. The project team _____ people from different departments of the company.
　　A) falls into　　　　B) brings about　　　C) consists of　　　D) results from

29. In the survey, we asked the workers about things _____ made their work harder to do.
    A) what   B) that   C) who   D) this
30. We'd like to make an _____ with your manager to further discuss the contract.
    A) opportunity   B) influence   C) appointment D) experiment
31. About a quarter of American adults say that they _____ a book in whole in the past year.
    A) will not read B) do not read   C) would not read D) have not read
32. We would be _____ of cultural differences while doing foreign trade.
    A) aware   B) active   C) friendly   D) hopeful
33. This study has found some key factors _____ employees' stress in their work.
    A) turning down B) leading to   C) taking off   D) carrying out
34. The company can now focus its attention _____ developing its latest car model.
    A) in   B) with   C) at   D) on

Section B

Directions: *There are 5 incomplete statements here. You should fill in each blank with the proper form of the word given in brackets. Write the word or words in the corresponding space on the Answer Sheet.*

35. This App allows you (see)_____ the departures and arrivals of all the flights.

36. We assure you that your order will (deliver)_____ within 5 workdays.

37. If you choose not to receive those emails, please let us know by (send)_____ us a message.

38. We are responsible for the installation and repair of the (equip)_____.

39. If you find any product that is (cheap)_____ than ours in others stores, please contact us.

Part III Reading Comprehension   (35 minutes)

Directions: *This part is to test your reading ability. There are 5 tasks for you to fulfill. You should read the reading materials carefully and do the tasks as you are instructed.*

Task 1

Directions: *After reading the following passage, you will find 5 questions or unfinished statements, numbered 40 to 44. For each question or statement, there are 4 choices marked A), B), C) and D). You should make the correct choice and mark the corresponding letter on the Answer Sheet with a single line through the center.*

PowerShow.com is a leading presentation/slide shows（展示与放映幻灯片）sharing website. Whether your application is business, how-to, education, medicine, school, sales, marketing, online training or just for fun, *PowerShow.com* is a great resource. And, best of all, most of its cool features are free and easy to use.

You can use *PowerShow.com* to find and download sample *PowerPoint* presentations on just about any topic you can imagine, so you can learn how to improve your own slides and presentations for free.

For a small fee you can get the industry's best online privacy (网络隐私) or publicly promote your presentations and slide shows with top rankings (排名). But aside from that, it's FREE. We'll even change your presentations and slide shows into the Flash, including 2D and 3D effects, music or other audio. All for free. Most of the presentations and slide shows on *PowerShow.com* are free to view; many are even free to download. Check out *PowerShow.com* today— for FREE. There is truly something for everyone!

40. According to the first paragraph, *PowerShow.com* is a website which _____.
    A) offers advertising spaces   B) provides training courses
    C) shares slide shows   D) sells Apps
41. Most of *PowerShow.com*'s features are _____.
    A) convenient to develop   B) expensive to buy
    C) difficult to log in   D) easy to use
42. By using *PowerShow.com*, you can learn to _____.
    A) make you presentations better   B) create your personal website
    C) develop your own software   D) conduct an online survey
43. If you want to get the industry's best online privacy, you need to _____.
    A) sign a contract   B) pay a small fee
    C) ask for permission   D) register a new account
44. Which of the following could be the title of the passage?
    A) Introduction to PowerShow Website   B) Developing Presentation Skills
    C) Setting up a Personal Website   D) Future of *PowerShow.com*

Task 2

Directions: *The following is a poster. After reading it, you will find 3 questions or unfinished statements, numbered 45 to 47. For each question or statement, there are 4 choice marked A), B), C) and D). You should make the correct choice and mark the corresponding letter on the Answer Sheet with a single line through the center.*

PUBLIC ANNOUNCEMENT:

We would like to take this opportunity to thank our friends and customers for their loyal patronage for the past four years.

At this time and after careful consideration, we have decided to close our retail store in order to expand our wholesale business. The Vinjerud Family, however, does plan to open in a more convenient location in the future.

> If you have a gift card, please contact Olivia Costa at 508,910,200 or olivia@oceans-fleet.com between the hours of 9:30 a.m. and 1:30 p.m. to make an appointment to be reimbursed for the full remaining value.
>
> Again, we sincerely appreciate all the support we have received.
>
> Sincerely.
> The Management

Notes: 1. patronage 惠顾 2. reimburse 偿还

45. This announcement is to inform the public about _____.

   A) the awards and prize winners
   B) the closing of a retail store
   C) the seasonal sales
   D) the new arrivals

46. In the future, the Vinjerud Family intends to start its business _____.

   A) on a similar scale
   B) with more employees
   C) under better management
   D) in a more convenient place

47. What are people asked to do if they have a gift card?

   A) Contact the store for the remaining value.
   B) Shop in any other retail stores in the town.
   C) Exchange for gifts in the store.
   D) Keep it for future use.

Task 3

Directions: *Read the following passage. After reading it, you should complete the information by filling in the blanks marked 48 to 52 (**in no more than 3 words**) in the table below. You should write your answers on the Answer Sheet correspondingly.*

A sure way to grow your business is to get people excited about your products or services. Postcards, posters(海报), and brochures(小册子) are easy and effective ways to get the news out about sales, events and other promotions.

Postcards with discount information is a great way to attract customers to return. You can mail them out, add them to your packaging, leave them on your counter for customers to take and share.

Posters are eye-catching and easily seen. Show them outside to attract passerby(过路人), and hang them inside your store to guide and inform customers. Use bold, bright messaging and images to gain attention.

Brochures allow you to present more detailed information about your business. Use photos and clear messaging to tell potential customers everything you want them to know. These products have plenty of room for pricing, service lists and menus, too.

Ways to Grow Your Business

Postcards with discount information: 1. why: attract customers to ___48___
         2. how: 1) mail them out
            2) add them to ___49___
            3) leave them on the counter

Posters: 1. why: eye-catching and ___50___
    2. how: 1) show them outside to attract people
         2) hang them inside the store
         3) use bold, bright messaging and images

Brochures: 1. why: offer more ___51___ about the business
     2. how: use ___52___ and clear messaging

Task 4

Directions: *The following is a list of terms used for workplace safety. After reading it, you are required to find the items equivalent to those given in Chinese in the table below. Then you should mark the corresponding letters in order of the numbered blanks, 53 through 57, on the Answer Sheet.*

A—Avoid Loose Clothing   B—Install Safety Guards
C—Keep Workplace Clean   D—Know Evacuation Routes
E—Know How to Lift Heavy Loads   F—Know Machine Operating Procedure
G—Never Reach into Running Machines H—Place Trash in Proper Containers
I—Report Any Unsafe Conditions   J—Shut down Machines When Not in Use
K—Store Chemicals Correctly   L—Store Your Tools after Use
M—Turn off Machine in Between Jobs   N—Wash Hands
O—Wear Protective Uniform   P—Wear Safety Glasses
Q—Use Two-handed Operations

Examples: (D) 熟悉疏散路线   (F) 掌握机器操作程序

53. ( ) 保持工作区域清洁		( ) 工作间隙关闭机器	
54. ( ) 正确储存化学品		( ) 戴上防护眼镜	
55. ( ) 机器不用时请关闭		( ) 任何不安全状况须报告	
56. ( ) 勿穿宽松衣服		( ) 穿好防护制服	
57. ( ) 使用双手操作		( ) 了解如何提升重物	

Task 5

Directions: *Read the following passage. After reading it, you are required to complete the answers that follow the questions (NO.58 to No. 62). You should write your answers (**in no more than three words**) on the Answer Sheet correspondingly.*

Have your insurance card ready when you go to the doctor or to pick up a prescription(处方). Your card will have basic information on it, including the insurance provider, the policy number, and the expiration(到期) date.

Knowing your policy benefits can make a huge difference, especially if you are involved in a medical emergency. Before getting insurance, you will find out about what and how much your insurance covers. You can find this information on your insurance provider's website.

Also, stay update! Make sure you are aware of any changes in your insurance benefits.

Where to Start:

Look into finding a doctor that you can go to regularly for your check-ups and illness. Having one doctor who knows about many aspects of your health ensures you get the best care.

If your college has a clinic(诊所), that may be good a place to start. If this isn't a good choice for you, look into nearby clinics in the area. Be careful to check what insurance plans they accept. This is important because health care can be expensive.

58. What should you do before going to a doctor?
    You should have your _____ ready.
59. What information can be found on your insurance card?
    The insurance provider, _____, and the expiration date.
60. Where can you find the information about what your insurance covers?
    On your _____.
61. Why should you always stay updated?
    To be aware of _____ in the insurance benefits.
62. Why is it important to check what insurance plans the clinics accept?
    Because health care can be _____.

Part IV Translation—English into Chinese (25 minutes)

Directions: *This part, numbered 63 to 67, is to test your ability to translate English into Chinese. Each of the four sentences (No.63 to No.66) is followed by three choices of suggested translation marked A), B), and C). Make the best choice and write the corresponding letter on the Answer Sheet with a single line through the center. And then write your translation of the paragraph (No.67) in the corresponding space on the Translation/Composition Sheet.*

63. Before setting up the business, they conducted a market survey about production, sales and after-sales service.

    A) 如果要创业,他们得有一笔启动资金,并且要有销售渠道。

B）在创业前，他们对生产、销售和售后服务进行了市场调研。

C）在开展业务前，他们对该产品的售后服务进行了市场调查。

64. Many Americans understands the life-saving value of the seat belt—the national use rate of it is at 90.1%.

A）许多美国人懂得安全带的救生价值，全国安全带的使用率达到 90.1%。

B）许多美国人习惯于使用安全带，系安全带可以减少死亡率达到 90.1%。

C）许多美国人知道开车必须系安全带，90.1% 的人都自觉遵守这一规则。

65. We are building a network of business experts who are ready to help you when you need it.

A）我们正在筹建一个商业专家系统，他们可以向公众随时提供专业指导和帮助。

B）我们正在创办一个专家信息库，急需一些能够随时提供帮助的专家给予指导。

C）我们正在建立一个商务专家网络，当你需要帮助的时候，他们很乐于帮助你。

66. As our products have a good reputation both at home and abroad, their demand is increasing year by year.

A）我们的产品在国内外享有良好的声誉，所以其需求量正在逐年增加。

B）由于我们的产品质量非常好，它们在国内外的需求量一年超过一年。

C）因为国内外对我们产品的需求量都很大，所以我们每年都扩大生产。

67. We hope that you found the tips on this page helpful and can put them to use on your next vacation. Whether you plan to fly or drive, use our travel comparison tool for all your transportation and hotel needs. Please visit us again and sign up for our newsletter（业务通信）to keep getting the best deals and travel tips. By comparing hotel prices, you can save up to 70%.

Part V Writing   （25 minutes）

Directions: *This part is to test your ability to do practical writing. You are required to complete a Volunteer Application Form according to the following information given in Chinese. Remember to do your writing on the Translation / Composition Sheet.*

说明：假设你是陈大明，你想参加 Reading Together 志愿者组织，根据下列内容填写一份志愿者申请表。

手机号码：177××××8956

电子邮箱：chendm999@163.com

出生日期：1998 年 12 月 15 日

就读学校：东方技术学院

所在系部：计算机系

所学专业：计算机技术

申请原因：1. 对阅读很感兴趣；

2. 希望用自己所学的知识帮助乡村儿童；

3. 通过志愿者活动认识更多喜欢阅读的朋友；

4. 提高自己的阅读与沟通能力。

Volunteer Application Form

Thank you for your interest in volunteering with Reading Together

Personal Details

Name: ___(1)___ √ Mr.   ☐ Mrs.   ☐ Ms.
Mobile: ___(2)___
Email: ___(3)___
Birth Date: ___(4)___

College Information

College Name: Dongfang Technical College
Major: Computer Technology   Department: ___(5)___

Describe why you are interested in working as a volunteer with us.

_____
_____
_____
_____

2018年6月B级考试全真试题

Part I　Listening Comprehension　　　　（25 minutes）

Directions: *This part is to test your listening ability. It consists of 4 sections.*

Section A

Directions: *This section is to test your ability to give proper responses. There are 7 recorded questions in it. After each question, there is a pause. The questions will be spoken **two times**. When you hear a question, you should decide on the correct answer from the 4 choices marked A), B), C) and D) given in your test paper. Then you should mark the corresponding letter on the Answer Sheet with a single line through the center.*

Example: *You will hear*:

　　　　You will read:　A) I'm not sure.

　　　　　　　　　　　　B) You're right.

　　　　　　　　　　　　C) Yes, certainly.

　　　　　　　　　　　　D) That's interesting.

From the question we learn that the speaker is asking the listener to leave a message. Therefore, C) *Yes, **certainly*** is the correct answer. You should mark C) on the Answer Sheet with a single line through the center.

　　　　　　　　　　　　　　　　　　　　　　　　[A] [B] [C̶] [D]

Now the test will begin.

1. A) Oh, yes please.　　　　　　　　　B) I like it very much.
   C) Sit down please.　　　　　　　　　D) Fine, and you?

2. A) Take care.　　　　　　　　　　　B) My pleasure.
   C) It's great.　　　　　　　　　　　　D) This way, please.

3. A) See you tomorrow.　　　　　　　　B) OK, it doesn't matter.
   C) Sorry, all our rooms are booked.　　D) Here is the room key.

4. A) Have a nice day.　　　　　　　　　B) Yes, please.
   C) Don't do it.　　　　　　　　　　　D) Let's go.

5. A) Certainly. Is Friday OK?　　　　　B) So long.
   C) Hurry up.　　　　　　　　　　　　D) Mind your steps.

6. A) Coffee, please.　　　　　　　　　B) I'm fine, thank you.
   C) Your telephone number, please.　　D) Yes, here you are.

7. A）Don't worry.　　　　　　　　　　B）All right.
   C）Good luck!　　　　　　　　　　　D）Never mind.

Section B

Directions: *This section is to test your ability to understand short dialogues. There are 7 recorded dialogues in it. After each dialogue, there is a recorded question. Both the dialogues and questions will be spoken **two times**. When you hear a question, you should decide on the correct answer from the 4 choices marked A）, B）, C）and D）given in your test paper. Then you should mark the corresponding letter on the Answer Sheet with a single line through the center.*

Now listen to the dialogues.

8. A）By bus.　　　　　　　　　　　　B）On foot.
   C）By taxi.　　　　　　　　　　　　D）By bicycle.

9. A）A report.　　　　　　　　　　　B）A project.
   C）A plan.　　　　　　　　　　　　D）A design.

10. A）He is an engineer.　　　　　　　B）He is a doctor.
    C）He is a programmer.　　　　　　D）He is a manager.

11. A）Dealing with angry customers.　　B）Writing work reports.
    C）Giving presentations.　　　　　　D）Working on weekends.

12. A）To visit friends.　　　　　　　　B）To see a doctor.
    C）To take a holiday.　　　　　　　D）To do business.

13. A）It had a flat tire.　　　　　　　　B）Its front window was broken.
    C）It was out of fuel.　　　　　　　　D）The engine didn't work.

14. A）Attend a job fair.　　　　　　　　B）Read newspaper.
    C）Visit the website.　　　　　　　　D）Ask her friends for help.

Section C

Directions: *In this section, there are 2 recorded conversations. After each conversation, there are some recorded questions. Both the conversations and questions will be spoken **two times**. When you hear a question, you should decide on the correct answer from the 4 choices marked A）, B）, C）and D）given in your test paper. Then you should mark the corresponding letter on the Answer Sheet with a single line through the center.*

Now listen to the conversations.

Conversation 1

15. A）To order a meal.　　　　　　　　B）To report a case.
    C）To ask for sick leave.　　　　　　D）To book a hotel room.

16. A）Her passport.　　　　　　　　　B）Her smartphone.
    C）Her watch.　　　　　　　　　　D）Her computer.

Conversation 2

17. A) She has coughed a lot.　　　　　　　B) She has a higher fever.
    C) She has got a pain in the stomach.　　D) She has got a bad cold.
18. A) This morning.　　　B) This afternoon.
    C) Last night.　　　　D) Yesterday.
19. A) Take her blood pressure.　　　　　　　B) Give her some medicine.
    C) Perform an operation on her at once.　D) Send her to the emergency room.

Section D

Directions: *In this section you will hear a recorded short passage. The passage is printed in the test paper, but with some words or phrases missing. The passage will be read **three times**. During the second reading, you are required to put the missing words or phrases on the Answer Sheet in order of the numbered blanks according to what you hear. The third reading is for you to check your writing.*

Now the passage will begin.

Volunteers are our heart and soul. Please come and help us build homes for __20__ low-income families. There is no experience needed and we supply the __21__. Just volunteer for a day. It's fun, rewarding and you can learn some __22__!

If building isn't your thing, come and volunteer for one of our events or __23__.

You must be __24__ 14 years of age to volunteer and those 15 years and under must come with a parent.

Come and sign up now to volunteer your time.

Part II　Vocabulary & Structure　　　　　　　(10 minutes)

Directions: *This part is to test your ability to construct correct and meaningful sentences. It consists of 2 sections.*

Section A

Directions: *In this section, there are 10 incomplete sentences. You are required to complete each one by deciding on the most appropriate word or words from the 4 choices marked A), B), C) and D). Then you should mark the corresponding letter on the Answer Sheet with a single line through the center.*

25. Let's find people with computer skills to _____ a team for the project.
    A) look up　　　B) ring up　　　C) give up　　　D) make up
26. If I were you, I _____ the company's website for more detailed information.
    A) would visit　　B) will visit　　C) visit　　D) have visited
27. No company can afford to bear the _____ of customer confidence.
    A) stress　　　B) loss　　　C) worry　　　D) hurry

28. _____ she has been working in China for only two years, she speaks fluent Chinese.

　　A) When　　　　B) If　　　　C) Although　　　　D) Until

29. We have read this instruction many times and we are _____ with all the steps we should take.

　　A) similar　　　　B) useful　　　　C) helpful　　　　D) familiar

30. Employees would like to work under team leaders who _____ good examples.

　　A) turn　　　　B) put　　　　C) do　　　　D) set

31. Turn to us for legal advice at any time _____ you need it.

　　A) when　　　　B) how　　　　C) where　　　　D) why

32. Your pay raise will in part _____ your work experience and skills.

　　A) carry on　　　　B) take on　　　　C) depend on　　　　D) put on

33. Your are required to enter the name of the city in which your company _____.

　　A) locates　　　　B) located　　　　C) is locating　　　　D) is located

34. Tourists can get the latest information of our city _____ the help of our local tour guides.

　　A) on　　　　B) with　　　　C) under　　　　D) for

Section B

Directions: *There are 5 incomplete statements here. You should fill in each blank with the proper form of the word given in brackets. Write the word or words in the corresponding space on the Answer Sheet.*

35. Patients can be treated in many (difference) _____ setting with various approaches.

36. After taking the training course, they have performed their duties much (well) _____ than before.

37. Only by (create) _____ a clean environment can we truly encourage more tourists to come.

38. This research paper focuses on (health) _____ lifestyles for elderly people.

39. Our new manager (expect) _____ to deliver a speech at tomorrow's meeting.

Part III　Reading Comprehension　　　　（35 minutes）

Directions: *This part is to test your reading ability. There are 5 tasks for you to fulfill. You should read the reading materials carefully and do the tasks as you are instructed.*

Task 1

Directions: *After reading the following passage, you will find 5 questions or unfinished statements, numbered 40 to 44. For each question or statement, there are 4 choices marked A), B), C) and D). You should make the correct choice and mark the corresponding letter on the Answer Sheet with a single line through the center.*

Your home is the place you feel safe and secure. We understand the importance of your home and the things in it and can help you if something unexpected should happen. Our Home Solutions insurance offers buildings, contents or combined buildings and contents cover.

In an emergency

Call the 24-hour Emergency Homeline. We'll arrange for a repairman to carry out repairs, out of usual business hours. As long as the policy covers the damage, you don't need to pay for the repairs.

Lost keys

We'll pay for the full cost of replacing locks on external(外部的) doors if you lose your keys, if they are stolen or if the lock is accidentally damaged.

Important events

We automatically increase your valuables(贵重物品) limit by $3,000 at certain special times, such as your wedding or festival.

Alternative accommodation(住处)

We'll find somewhere for you and your pets to live if your home has been damaged by an insured event and you can't live there. With our building insurance we'll pay up to $30,000 for alternative accommodation, and up to $20,000 with contents insurance.

40. According to the insurance company, by buying Home Solutions, you can get help _____.
    A) when your vehicle breaks down on your way work
    B) when something unexpected happens to your home
    C) when anyone in your family gets hurt or sick
    D) when you want to move to a new house

41. When you call the Emergency Homeline, _____.
    A) a repairman will be sent to do the repairs
    B) they will pay you on the repairing cost first
    C) you have to send a photo of the damage
    D) you will be told to wait for a doctor

42. If you lose your keys to the external doors, the insurance company will _____.
    A) pay for the cost of replacing locks   B) deliver new locks to your home
    C) tell you where to buy new locks   D) refuse to pay for new locks

43. According to the passage, in a festival your valuables limit will be _____.
    A) reduced to a certain degree   B) re-checked within a week
    C) automatically increased   D) doubled upon request

44. What is the company likely to do if your home is damaged by an insured event?
    A) It will pay you more than $50,000.   B) It will help your build a new house.
    C) It will decrease your valuables limit.   D) It will find somewhere for you to live.

Task 2

Directions: *The following is a poster. After reading it, you will find 3 questions or unfinished statements, numbered 45 to 47. For each question or statement, there are 4 choices marked A), B),*

C) and D). You should make the correct choice and mark the corresponding letter on the Answer Sheet with a single line through the center.

NOTICE

Postponement of President's Cup 2016

Dear Golfers

We regret to inform that the President's Cup originally set to be on 20th August 2016 will be postponed to a later date due to an unforeseen change in our Club President's schedule.

Those who have signed up for the event may continue to play a social game at the usual member's rates. The golf game will commence at 13:15 with shotgun start.

We apologize for any inconvenience caused and thank you for your kind understanding.

SCC Management

12 August, 16

Notes: postpone 延期   commence 开始

45. The notice is to inform the golfers of _____.

   A) the application for Club membership

   B) the postponement of President's Cup

   C) the final result of President's Cup

   D) the activities of Club President

46. The change of the game date is due to _____.

   A) a lack of funding

   B) the absence of some golfers

   C) the terrible weather conditions

   D) a change in President's schedule

47. According to the Notice, the social game will start _____.

   A) in the morning   B) on August 30

   C) at 13:15   D) next week

Task 3

Directions: *The following passage is about a medicine company, Prime Medicine LIC. After reading it, you should complete the information by filling in the blanks marked 48 to 52 (**in no more than 3 words**) in the table below. You should write your answers on the Answer Sheet correspondingly.*

At Prime Medicine LIC, we have only one purpose—we help people to get the medicine they need to feel better and live well.

Our pharmacy (药店) experts are working hard to make your medicine cheaper, and your experience easier. Here are the ways of delivering our services.

PrimeMail

Order your long-term medicine from PrimeMail. Receive up to a 90-day supply of your medicine anywhere in the U.S.

Retail pharmacy

Prime offers a large national network of pharmacies—over 66,000. Just bring your prescription (药方) and member ID to a network pharmacy. (If you use a Pharmacy that is not in your network, you might need to pay more).

Special(特种药) pharmacy

Prime Therapeutics Specialty Pharmacy is a full-service delivery pharmacy. Our experienced professionals and staff focus on specialty medicines and the conditions they treat.

Prime

a medicine company

Aim:
1) to help you get your medicine
2) to make your medicine ___48___ and your experience easier

Ways of getting your medicine:
　　1) from PrimeMail, ordering your ___49___ medicine
　　2) from a large national ___50___ of pharmacies: bringing your prescription and ___51___
　　3) from Prime Therapeutics Specialty Pharmacy, a ___52___ pharmacy, for specialty medicines

---

Task 4

Directions: *The following is a list of public signs. After reading it, you are required to find the items equivalent to those given in Chinese in the table below. Then you should mark the corresponding letters in order of the numbered blanks, 53 through 57, on the Answer Sheet.*

　　A—School Zone　　　　　　　　　　　　B—Vendors Prohibited
　　C—Pass on Left　　　　　　　　　　　　D—Don't Step On
　　E—Keep Away for Safety　　　　　　　　F—Service Area
　　G—Administrative Area　　　　　　　　H—Watch Your Hand
　　I—Please Don't Leave Valuables Unattended　　J—Maintenance in Progress
　　K—Out of service　　　　　　　　　　　L—Stand on Right
　　M—Break Glass in Emergency　　　　　　N—Don't Touch
　　O—Keep Clear of the Door　　　　　　　P—Don't Exceed Speed Limit
　　Q—Icy Road

Examples: (E) 注意安全，请勿靠近　　　　　　(B) 禁止摆摊

53. (	) 当心夹手	(	) 请勿登踏
54. (	) 服务区	(	) 勿靠车门
55. (	) 严禁超速	(	) 正在检修
56. (	) 前方学校	(	) 靠右站立
57. (	) 路面结冰	(	) 紧急情况击碎玻璃

Task 5

Directions: *The following is a letter about a safety inspection. After reading it, you are required to complete the answers that follow the questions (NO.58 to No. 62). You should write your answers (**in no more three words**) on the Answer Sheet correspondingly.*

Please contact us to Arrange Safety Inspection.

Address: 246 N. High St., Columbus, Ohio 43215

Columbus Gas must perform a safety inspection at the address above.

We are required by federal law to inspect your service line and meter setting. Please call us at 1-800-344-4077, Monday through Friday, 7:00 a.m.-7:00 p.m.

If you have already arranged an inspection, there is no reason to call. Please ignore this letter. Please understand, communications will continue until the inspection has been completed.

This important safety inspection is part of promise to provide safe and reliable service to our customers.

We will make every effort to do the work at a date and time that is convenient to you.

If this inspection is not performed, we cannot continue your service. Please call us today to set up an inspection.

Thank you for your attention to this letter.

58. What is the gas company required to do by federal law?

    To inspect the letter receiver's _____ and meter setting.

59. In what case can the letter receiver ignore this letter?

    If he/she has already _____.

60. How long will the communications last?

    Communication will continue until _____ has been completed.

61. What has the gas company promised to do?

    To provide _____ service to its customers.

62. In what case will the gas company stop its service for its customers?

    If the inspection _____.

Part IV　Translation—English into Chinese　　(25 minutes)

Directions: *This part, numbered 63 to 67, is to test your ability to translate English into Chinese. Each of the four sentences (No.63 to No.66) is followed by three choices of suggested* translation marked A), B), and C). Make the best choice and write the corresponding letter on the Answer Sheet with a single line through the center. And then write your translation of the paragraph (No.67) in the corresponding space on the Translation/Composition Sheet.

63. The aim of our website is to control or reduce noise at work without stopping people from enjoying music.

   A) 本网站的方针是不断阻止或减少噪声，同时又能够使人们欣赏音乐。
   B) 本网站的目的是控制或减少工作中的噪声，却不妨碍人们欣赏音乐。
   C) 本网站的优势是用播放人们喜爱的音乐和方式，来缓解和抵消压力。

64. We have all been so impressed with your abilities and potential that we are pleased to offer you a position.

   A) 我们面试过的所有求职者中，你的能力最强，潜力最大。
   B) 我们都对你的能力和潜力印象深刻，乐于为你提供职位。
   C) 我们很欣赏你的能力和潜质，很高兴能有机会和你共事。

65. Anything you want to know can be found in seconds if you use the right keywords to search for it.

   A) 如你使用正确的关键词，就可以即刻搜索到你想要知道的任何事物。
   B) 你搜索的关键词如果准确，这样才能很快地找到你所想要的数据。
   C) 你先要知道使用关键词搜索的方法，才能从事你所做的研究工作。

66. We deal with a lot of foreign customers and are considered to be one of their most reliable agents.

   A) 我们同许多国外客户打过交道，被一致认为是国内外首屈一指的代理商。
   B) 我们与国外许多客户保持联系，而且我们为他们寻找国内最好的代理商。
   C) 我们与许多外国客户有业务往来，并被认为是他们最可靠的代理商之一。

67. If you're ready to take you next step in life we can offer help to make the most of your money. You can have an inform meeting with your account manager（客户经理）. The account manager will help you to find out a way to make your money work better. We'll also help you arrange your credit cards and loans. To book an appointment, call 0345-000-888.

Part V　Writing　　　　　　　　　　　　　　　（25 minutes）

Directions: *This part is to test your ability to do practical writing. You are required to complete a Memo according to the following information given in Chinese. Remember to do your writing on the Translation / Composition Sheet.*

说明：假设你是总经理秘书 Tom Brown 先生，发一份通知给各部门经理。

主题：讨论下半年销售计划

时间：2018 年 6 月 18 日

抄送（CC）：John Smith 先生

主要内容：市场部已制订了公司下半年的销售计划，现发给你们，见附件。总经理办公室于 6 月 20 日下午 2 点在公司会议室召开会议，讨论该计划，并听取各部门意见。请各部门经理参加会议。如无法到会，请提前告知总经理办公室。

Memo

To: （1）
From: （2）
Date: （3）
CC: （4）
Subject: （5）

_____
_____
_____
_____
_____
_____
_____

附件　attachment

2017年12月B级考试全真试题

Part I Listening Comprehension (25 minutes)

Directions: This part is to test your listening ability. It consists of 4 sections.

Section A

Directions: This section is to test your ability to give proper responses. There are 7 recorded questions in it. After each question, there is a pause. The questions will be spoken **two times**. When you hear a question, you should decide on the correct answer from the 4 choices marked A), B), C) and D) given in your test paper. Then you should mark the corresponding letter on the Answer Sheet with a single line through the center.

Example: You will hear:

You will read: A) I'm not sure.　　　B) You're right.
　　　　　　　　C) Yes, certainly.　　D) That's interesting.

From the question we learn that the speaker is asking the listener to leave a message. Therefore, C) **Yes, certainly** is the correct answer. You should mark C) on the Answer Sheet with a single line through the center.

[A] [B] [C] [D]

Now the test will begin.

1. A) It's over there.　　　　　　B) Sorry to hear that.
   C) That's all right.　　　　　　D) It's wonderful.

2. A) Here you are.　　　　　　　B) It doesn't matter.
   C) Yes, of course.　　　　　　 D) Thank you.

3. A) You're right.　　　　　　　 B) It's great.
   C) Here is my card.　　　　　　D) How are you.

4. A) It's far away.　　　　　　　B) Take care.
   C) On Monday.　　　　　　　　D) Sure.

5. A) Yes, please.　　　　　　　　B) Mind your steps.
   C) OK.　　　　　　　　　　　　D) Tomorrow morning.

6. A) No, thanks.　　　　　　　　 B) It's fine.
   C) Sorry, wrong number.　　　　D) Not at all.

7. A) Certainly.　　　　　　　　　B) Hurry up.
   C) Don't mention it.　　　　　　D) See you later.

Section B

Directions: *This section is to test your ability to understand short dialogues. There are 7 recorded dialogues in it. After each dialogue, there is a recorded question. Both the dialogues and questions will be spoken **two times**. When you hear a question, you should decide on the correct answer from the 4 choices marked A), B), C) and D) given in your test paper. Then you should mark the corresponding letter on the Answer Sheet with a single line through the center.*

Now listen to the dialogues.

8. A) His health.　　　　　　　　　　B) His exam.
   C) His presentation.　　　　　　　　D) His interview.
9. A) A local paper.　　　　　　　　　B) A price list.
   C) A movie ticket.　　　　　　　　　D) A name card.
10. A) Call John.　　　　　　　　　　　B) Visit the man.
    C) Ask for help.　　　　　　　　　　D) Write a report.
11. A) It is being painted.　　　　　　　B) It has been booked.
    C) It is too expensive.　　　　　　　D) It is small.
12. A) Satisfied.　　　　　　　　　　　B) Confident.
    C) Excited.　　　　　　　　　　　　D) Nervous.
13. A) He has got a job offer.　　　　　B) He failed his final exam.
    C) He will move to a new city.　　　D) He wants to rent an apartment.
14. A) The man will travel on business.
    B) The man has taken a computer test.
    C) The woman has passed a road test.
    D) The woman will take a language course.

Section C

Directions: *In this section, there are 2 recorded conversations. After each conversation, there are some recorded questions. Both the conversations and questions will be spoken **two times**. When you hear a question, you should decide on the correct answer from the 4 choices marked A), B), C) and D) given in your test paper. Then you should mark the corresponding letter on the Answer Sheet with a single line through the center.*

Now listen to the conversations.

Conversation 1

15. A) To make an appointment.　　　　B) To ask about the man's order.
    C) To confirm the delivery.　　　　　D) To complain about the service.
16. A) They are use-friendly.　　　　　　B) They are newly developed.
    C) They are popular abroad.　　　　D) They are of high quality.

Conversation 2

17. A) It wouldn't start. B) It ran out of gas.
    C) It was broken. D) It was missing.
18. A) It has to be charged. B) It is still new.
    C) It is of good quality. D) It was bought a year ago.
19. A) To recharge it. B) To repair it.
    C) To return it. D) To sell it.

Section D

Directions: *In this section you will hear a recorded short passage. The passage is printed in the test paper, but with some words or phrases missing. The passage will be read* **three times.** *During the second reading, you are required to put the missing words or phrases on the Answer Sheet in order of the numbered blanks according to what you hear. The third reading is for you to check your writing.*

Now the passage will begin.

I am Mike Wang, a real estate agent. I __20__ to sell this home in just 15 days. I would love to help you buy or sell. Properties in this area are __21__. If you have considered selling your home, I would love to speak with you and help you in any way __22__. If you are currently renting a home and would like to buy one, give me a call. Home ownership has many __23__ over renting and is not as difficult as many think. Call me today and let me help you make __24__.

Part II Vocabulary & Structure   (10 minutes)

Directions: *This part is to test your ability to construct correct and meaningful sentences. It consists of 2 sections.*

Section A

Directions: *In this section, there are 10 incomplete sentences. You are required to complete each one by deciding on the most appropriate word or words from the 4 choices marked A), B), C) and D). Then you should mark the corresponding letter on the Answer Sheet with a single line through the center.*

25. We regard customer complaints as opportunities to _____ our service.
    A) bring B) receive
    C) improve D) obtain
26. We took advantage of its sports facilities _____ staying at hotel.
    A) although B) while
    C) until D) unless
27. It has been decided that Mr. Li will _____ the company when the CEO retires.

A) put off B) call for
C) bring about D) take over

28. The study shows that some students have difficulty _____ long English texts.
A) reading B) read C) to read D) to be read

29. If you _____ your mind, please call me at this number before Saturday.
A) changed B) would change
C) had changed D) change

30. Having obtained the college diploma, he _____ a position in that company.
A) carried on B) took in
C) applied for D) put on

31. It is the management _____ has to make sure its staff are not overworked.
A) what B) that C) which D) whose

32. Most people in this region think that they should _____ heavy industry.
A) develop B) supply C) take D) make

33. _____ you are a first time buyer or not, we will offer you a good price today.
A) Whatever B) Whenever
C) Whether D) However

34. Our purchase decision are generally made _____ the basis of price, delivery dates, and after-sales service.
A) with B) over C) in D) on

Section B

Directions: *There are 5 incomplete statements here. You should fill in each blank with the proper form of the word given in brackets. Write the word or words in the corresponding space on the Answer Sheet.*

35. We promise (give) _____ you a reply within five workdays.

36. The bank loan has (great) _____ strengthened our financial position in the industry.

37. Photography has changed our way of _____ (view) the world.

38. That new model of the machine is not likely to go into (produce) _____ before late 2018.

39. Anyone applying for a visa to China (require) _____ to have finger prints taken.

Part III Reading Comprehension   (35 minutes)

Directions: *This part is to test your reading ability. There are 5 tasks for you to fulfill. You should read the reading materials carefully and do the tasks as you are instructed.*

Task 1

Directions: *After reading the following passage, you will find 5 questions or unfinished* statements, numbered 40 to 44. For each question or statement, there are 4 choices marked A), B), C) and D). You should make the correct choice and mark the corresponding letter on the Answer Sheet with a single line through the center.

Starting a business is exciting and frightening. To add the excitement and ease the fear, you should get prepared from the beginning.

Set both your short-term and long-term goals. After you have created your goals, make sure you have a plan for your business that will guide you along the way.

There are a number of legal considerations when you start a business. For example, you need to decide on the structure of your business, register (注册) a business name, obtain necessary licenses and permits, and plan for business taxes.

Money is a major concern when you start a business, especially if you have to give up a well-paid job and if your business has considerable start-up expenses (费用). You can start your business while continuing to work full time. Or you can work a part-time job until your business becomes established. You can also wait to start your business until you have saved enough money, and even apply for a bank loan when necessary.

40. According to the passage, one way to ease your fear while starting a business is to _____.

    A) look for partners   B) be prepared
    C) be creative   D) work hard

41. Before making your business plan, you are advised to _____.

    A) establish business relationships   B) consult experts in the industry
    C) set your own business goals   D) look for suitable employees

42. The third paragraph is mainly about _____.

    A) legal considerations   B) the business structure
    C) ways of borrowing money   D) the importance of a business name

43. According to the passage, the major concern for starting a business is _____.

    A) management   B) technology
    C) personnel   D) money

44. One way to overcome your difficulty in meeting business start-up expenses is to _____.

    A) look for a well-paid job   B) cut off operating costs
    C) apply for a bank loan   D) attract investors

Task 2

Directions: *The following is a poster. After reading it, you will find 3 questions or unfinished statements, numbered 45 to 47. For each question or statement, there are 4 choice marked A), B), C) and D). You should make the correct choice and mark the corresponding letter on the Answer Sheet with a single line through the center.*

Notes: 1. representative 代表　　　2. attendance 出席
　　　　　3. customized binding system 定制的绑定系统

45. The "coffee and cake" morning is to be held on _____.

　　A) Monday　　　B) Wednesday　　　C) Thursday　　　D) Friday

46. Who will be invited to give a speech at the event?

　　A) A representative of USB clients.

　　B) The president of Employers Advisory Service.

　　C) A guest speaker from Employers Advisory Service.

　　D) The chief engineer from United Business Centers Ltd.

47. You need to contact Debby or Elaine by phone or email to _____.

　　A) confirm your attendance　　　　B) book the pick-up service

　　C) ask for a registration form　　　D) get a free trial of the system

Task 3

Directions: *The following is an introduction of Group Term Life Insurance plans. After reading it, you should complete the information by filling in the blanks marked 48 to 52 (**in no more than 3 words**) in the table below. You should write your answers on the Answer Sheet correspondingly.*

Your life is in constant motion—do you have insurance that can keep up? At age 33, get up to $250,000 of Group Term Life Insurance for just $8.54 a month. That may be just a bit of your monthly cell phone bill.

The American Society of Civil Engineers (ASCE) is offering Expedited (快速的) Insurance to its members for Group Term Life Insurance plans. You may be able to obtain coverage（保额）of up to $250,000 quicker than ever before!

This life insurance coverage is portable, so it stays with you even if you change jobs. As long as your policy is in force, you will have peace of mind knowing you have strengthened your financial position and helped fulfill your loved one's future needs.

Visit *asceinsurance.com/group-term* to apply for coverage to today. If you have any questions, contact your local insurance agency at 800-846-3582.

Expedited Insurance

The plan: 　1）premium（保费）: $8.54 a month for people at age __48__ ;
　　　　　　 2）coverage: up to __49__ ;
　　　　　　 3）offered to: __50__ of ASCE for Group Term Life Insurance plans.
Advantage: portable as long as the policy is __51__
Application: visit asceinsurance.com/group-term
Contact: local __52__

Task 4

Directions: *The following is a list of terms related to travelling abroad. After reading it, you are required to find the items equivalent to those given in Chinese in the table below. Then you should mark the corresponding letters in order of the numbered blanks, 53 through 57, on the Answer Sheet.*

　　A—Country of Citizenship　　　　　　　B—Passport Number
　　C—Country of Origin　　　　　　　　　 D—Destination Country
　　E—City Where You Boarded　　　　　　F—City Where Visa Was Issued
　　G—Date of Issue　　　　　　　　　　　H—Date of Birth
　　I—Accompanying Number　　　　　　　J—Official Use Only
　　K—Business Visa　　　　　　　　　　　L—Tourist Visa
　　M—Arrival Lobby　　　　　　　　　　　N—Departure Lobby
　　O—Boarding Gate　　　　　　　　　　　P—Boarding Card
　　Q—Visa Type

Example:（J）官方填写　　　　　　　　（I）同行人数

53.（　）护照号牌	（　）登机口
54.（　）目的地国家	（　）签证签发地
55.（　）登机牌	（　）签证种类
56.（　）登机城市	（　）出生日期
57.（　）抵达大厅	（　）旅行签证

Task 5

Directions: *Read the following passage. After reading it, you are required to complete the answers that follow the questions (NO.58 to No. 62). You should write your answers (**in no more than three words**) on the Answer Sheet correspondingly.*

Grounds Maintenance Workers

What Grounds Maintenance（维护）Workers Do

Grounds Maintenance Workers ensure that the grounds of house, businesses, and parks are attractive, orderly, and healthy in order to provide a pleasant outdoor environment.

Work Environment

Many grounds maintenance jobs are seasonal, available mainly in the spring, summer, and fall. Most of the work is done outdoor in all weather conditions.

Most grounds maintenance workers need no formal education and are trained on the job.

Training

A short period of on-the-job training is usually enough to teach new hires the skill they need, which often include how to plant and maintain areas and how to use some tools and other equipment.

Pay

The hourly wage for grounds maintenance workers was $12.90 in May 2016.

58. What job is offered in the advertisement?
    _____.

59. What is the responsibility of the job?
    To provide a pleasant _____.

60. What is the working environment of the job?
    The work is mostly done outdoors in _____.

61. What kind of training will be provided?
    A short period of _____ training.

62. What was the hourly wage for grounds maintenance worker in May 2016?
    $_____.

Part IV Translation—English into Chinese (25 minutes)

Directions: *This part, numbered 63 to 67, is to test your ability to translate English into Chinese. Each of the four sentences (No.63 to No.66) is followed by three choices of suggested translation marked A), B), and C). Make the best choice and write the corresponding letter on the Answer Sheet with a single line through the center. And then write your translation of the paragraph (No.67) in the corresponding space on the Translation/Composition Sheet.*

63. I am writing to complain about the unfair treatment that I received in your restaurant last Friday.

A）就你们餐馆低劣的服务质量，我上周五已致信消协反映。

B）我在贵餐馆受到了不礼貌的待遇，我上周五已写信投诉。

C）我写此信是投诉上星期五在贵餐馆受到的不公平的待遇。

64. To show our goodwill, we would like to offer you a 5% discount on your next order with us.

A）为表现我们的善意，我们对贵方这次订货可以给予 5% 的优惠。

B）为体现我们的诚意，贵方下次订货时，我们愿给你 5% 的折扣。

C）为促进商品销售，我们决定即日起对本公司所有的产品让利 5%。

65. I'm sorry I won't be able to attend the business meeting scheduled for next Friday.

A）我无法出席拟于下星期五举行的业务会议。

B）不巧的很，我没有时间，下周五我已经安排了生意谈判。

C）不好意思，我实在来不及参加下周五进行的业务会谈。

66. Having trust in each other is very important because doing business requires good interpersonal relationship.

A）有了信誉才有助于搞好对别人的关系，也有助于企业的发展。

B）彼此之间的信任非常重要，因为做生意需要良好的人际关系。

C）建立良好的人际关系至关重要，因为做生意必须要相互信任。

67. Some people may find it difficult to visit this park due to old age. Now, our project provides free services for these people. We have trained volunteers to work as drives. They are familiar with the park's history. And this wonderful project is supported by donations（捐赠）from the community. We ask you to give your support to this project.

Part V Writing   （25 minutes）

Directions: *This part is to test your ability to do practical writing. You are required to complete the Field Trip Report according to the following information given in Chinese. Remember to do your writing on the Translation/Composition Sheet.*

说明：请根据所给信息，完成下列《现场考察报告》

写报告人：李俊杰

接受报告人：王晓琳

送交报告日期：2017 年 12 月 24 日

考察地点：JUK 工厂

考察时间：自 2017 年 12 月 4 日至 2017 年 12 月 8 日

参加考察人员：李俊杰及其团队成员

内容要点：为了了解水污染问题，我们去 JUK 工厂参观一周。我们了解了污染的主要来源。工程师们向我们介绍了几种废水处理的办法。这次参观对我们的研究工作很有帮助。

Field Trip Report

Report to: Mr./Ms. (1)
Report from: Mr./Ms. (2)
Date: (3)

Trip destination: (4)
Trip period: from December 4, 2017 to (5)
Participants: Li Junjie & His team members
Summary

_____
_____
_____
_____
_____

Words for reference:
废水处理 waste water treatment

2017年6月B级考试全真试题

Part I Listening Comprehension （25 minutes）

Directions: *This part is to test your listening ability. It consists of 4 sections.*

Section A

Directions: *This section is to test your ability to give proper responses. There are 7 recorded questions in it. After each question, there is a pause. The questions will be spoken* **two times.** *When you hear a question, you should decide on the correct answer from the 4 choices marked A）, B）, C） and D） given in your test paper. Then you should mark the corresponding letter on the Answer Sheet with a single line through the center.*

Example: *You will hear*:

You will read: A）I'm not sure.

B）You're right.

C）Yes, certainly.

D）That's interesting.

From the question we learn that the speaker is asking the listener to leave a message. Therefore, **C）Yes, certainly** *is the correct answer. You should mark   C） on the Answer Sheet with a single line through the center.*

[A][B][C̶][D]．

Now the test will begin.

1. A）Let's have a break.　　　　　　B）This way, please.
   C）Don't mention it.　　　　　　　D）No, thank you.
2. A）On Monday.　　　　　　　　　B）John Smith.
   C）Take it easy.　　　　　　　　　D）It's too late.
3. A）How do you do?　　　　　　　 B）It doesn't matter.
   C）Yes, please.　　　　　　　　　D）Mind your step.
4. A）I'm afraid not.　　　　　　　　B）Never mind.
   C）Hurry.　　　　　　　　　　　　D）Have a good time.
5. A）Go ahead, please.　　　　　　　B）Yes, I am.
   C）I'd love to.　　　　　　　　　　D）He's from China.
6. A）Oh, I see.　　　　　　　　　　B）Here it is.
   C）It's over there.　　　　　　　　D）Yes, of course.

7. A) Go on, please. B) Two dollars.
   C) Sure, I will. D) Here you are.

Section B

Directions: *This section is to test your ability to understand short dialogues. There are 7 recorded dialogues in it. After each dialogue, there is a recorded question. Both the dialogues and questions will be spoken* **two times.** *When you hear a question, you should decide on the correct answer from the 4 choices marked A), B), C) and D) given in your test paper. Then you should mark the corresponding letter on the Answer Sheet with a single line through the center.*

Now listen to the dialogues.

8. A) About 150 years ago. B) About 120 years ago.
   C) About 115 years ago. D) About 100 years ago.
9. A) Boring. B) Difficult.
   C) Interesting. D) Satisfactory.
10. A) Its location. B) Its development.
    C) Its population. D) Its history.
11. A) It is modern. B) It is crowded.
    C) It is small. D) It is quiet.
12. A) She is in poor health. B) She failed a test.
    C) She hasn't enough money. D) She hasn't got any offer.
13. A) Show his ID card. B) Fill in a form.
    C) Write a report. D) Pay some money.
14. A) She has her leg broken. B) She fell from a bicycle.
    C) She feels a back pain. D) She has got a headache.

Section C

Directions: *In this section, there are 2 recorded conversations. After each conversation, there are some recorded questions. Both the conversations and questions will be spoken* **two times.** *When you hear a question, you should decide on the correct answer from the 4 choices marked A), B), C) and D) given in your test paper. Then you should mark the corresponding letter on the Answer Sheet with a single line through the center.*

Now listen to the conversations.

15. A) An apartment with a good view. B) An apartment of two bedrooms.
    C) An apartment on the ground floor. D) An apartment with central heating.
16. A) Near a subway station. B) Near a hotel.
    C) In the downtown. D) In the suburbs.

Conversation 2

17. A) To have better opportunities. B) To improve his skills.

C) To work fewer hours. D) To get a higher salary.
18. A) For six years. B) For five years.
    C) For three years. D) For two years.
19. A) A professor. B) A manager.
    C) An engineer. D) A designer.

Section D

Directions: *In this section you will hear a recorded short passage. The passage is printed in the test paper, but with some words or phrases missing. The passage will be read **three times**. During the second reading, you are required to put the missing words or phrases on the Answer Sheet in order of the numbered blanks according to what you hear. The third reading is for you to check your writing.*

Now the passage will begin.

First of all, on behalf of all the people from our company, I would like to say "Thank you for __20__ us to such a wonderful party". I think the music is __21__, the food and wine are very nice, and the people here are all very kind. Also we're enjoyed meeting and __22__ you, sharing the comfortable time together. We have really enjoyed ourselves. I hope we will be able to maintain the __23__ and make next year another great one together. Thank you again for the party. We've really had __24__.

Part II   Vocabulary & Structure   (10 minutes)

Directions: *This part is to test your ability to construct correct and meaningful sentences. It consists of 2 sections.*

Section A

Directions: *In this section, there are 10 incomplete sentences. You are required to complete each one by deciding on the most appropriate word or words from the 4 choices marked A), B), C) and D). Then you should mark the corresponding letter on the Answer Sheet with a single line through the center.*

25. It was not until yesterday _____ they decided to re-open the business talk.
    A) when   B) which   C) that   D) as
26. We have to _____ the cost of setting up a new hospital in that area.
    A) work out   B) put on   C) fill up   D) carry on
27. We need to _____ an eye on all the activities to make sure that people stay safe.
    A) catch   B) keep   C) take   D) bring
28. The local government has always placed a strong emphasis _____ education and vocational training.
    A) with   B) for   C) on   D) to

29. Don't take the wrong turn before you _____ the railway station.
    A) have   B) run
    C) keep   D) reach

30. The team doesn't mind _____ at weekends as long as they can finish the task.
    A) worked   B) working
    C) to work   D) work

31. We are non-profit company _____ team members are from all over the country.
    A) whose   B) that
    C) which   D) what

32. The meeting room is so small that it can hold 20 people _____.
    A) at last   B) at first
    C) at most   D) at once

33. She gave us a detailed _____ of the local government's new health-care proposal.
    A) impression   B) explanation
    C) education   D) communication

34. Linda _____ her training in a joint company by the end of next month.
    A) finishes   B) has finished
    C) had finished   D) will have finished

Section B

Directions: *There are 5 incomplete statements here. You should fill in each blank with the proper form of the word given in brackets. Write the word or words in the corresponding space on the Answer Sheet.*

35. We were impressed by the (suggest) _____ you made at yesterday's meeting.

36. The (long) _____ Charles has lived in this city, the more he likes it.

37. If you want to learn some terms related to your field, you will find this book might be (help) _____.

38. No one is allowed (smoke) _____ in public building according to the new regulation.

39. The new president (ask) _____ some tough questions by the reporter in the interview yesterday.

Part III Reading Comprehension   (35 minutes)

Directions: *This part is to test your reading ability. There are 5 tasks for you to fulfill. You should read the reading materials carefully and do the tasks as you are instructed.*

Task 1

Directions: *After reading the following passage, you will find 5 questions or unfinished statements, numbered 40 to 44. For each question or statement, there are 4 choices marked A), B), C) and D). You should make the correct choice and mark the corresponding letter on the Answer*

Sheet with a single line through the center.

Notice of Baggage Inspection（检查）

To protect you and your fellow passengers, the Transportation Security Administration (TSA) is required by law to inspect all checked baggage. As part of this process, some bags are opened and inspected. Your bag was among those selected for inspection.

During the inspection, your bag and its contents may have been searched for prohibited（违禁的）items. After the inspection was completed, the contents were returned to your bag.

If the TSA security officer was unable to open your bag for inspection because it was locked, the officer may have been forced to break the locks on your bag. TSA sincerely regrets having to do this. However, TSA is not responsible for damage to your locks resulting from this necessary security measures.

For packing tips and suggestion on how to secure your baggage during your next trip, please visit: www.tsa.gov.

We appreciate your understanding and cooperation. If you have questions, comments, or concerns, please feel free to contact the TSA Contact Center.

40. According to the passage, TSA is required to inspect your baggage _____.

   A) with your written permission   B) at the request of police
   C) by airlines   D) by law

41. According to the Notice, the purpose of the inspection is to _____.

   A) find all overweight baggage   B) search for prohibited items
   C) charge customs duties   D) check damaged items

42. After the inspection, the contents in your bag would _____.

   A) be delivered to your address   B) be given to you in person
   C) be returned to your bag   D) be kept at the airport

43. If your bag is locked, The TSA security officer may have to _____.

   A) break the locks   B) hand it over to police
   C) give up the inspection   D) ask you to open the bag

44. If the locks of your bag are damaged because of the inspection, TSA will _____.

   A) pay for the damage   B) buy you a new lock
   C) not be responsible for it   D) not inspect it in your next trip

Task 2

Directions: *The following is a poster. After reading it, you will find 3 questions or unfinished statements, numbered 45 to 47. For each question or statement, there are 4 choice marked A), B), C) and D). You should make the correct choice and mark the corresponding letter on the Answer Sheet with a single line through the center.*

Seymour Marine Discovery Center at Long Marine Lab
2017 DOCENT TRAINING
Applications due January 7, 2017!

JOIN OUR DOCENT TRAINING PROGRAM AND MAKE A DIFFERENCE FOR THE OCEANS

Our dynamic 10-week education program, beginning January 11, 2017, will give you all the tools you need to interpret innovative marine science and conservation for the public.

BECOME A VOLUNTEER
- Gain experience in public speaking
- Work with animals at the seawater table and shark pool
- Interact with the Long Marine Lab community
- Participate in expanded and in-depth learning opportunities

APPLY NOW!

Applications are now being accepted and reviewed. To apply, download an application form at seymourcenter.ucsc.edu. Call (831) 459-3854 for more information. **Summer availability is a must.** Docents must be at least 18 years old by the start of training in January 2017.

(831) 459-3800
seymourcenter.ucsc.edu

The Seymour Center is dedicated to educating people about the role scientific research plays in the understanding and conservation of the world's oceans

100 Shaffer Road, Santa Cruz, CA 95060
End of Delaware Avenue

Notes: docent（博物馆等场所的）讲解员

45. How long does the docent training program last?
    A) Four weeks.　　　　　　　　B) Six weeks.
    C) Eight weeks.　　　　　　　　D) Ten weeks.

46. To apply for the program, you should _____.
    A) first download an application form　　B) be good at working with animals
    C) be an experienced public speaker　　　D) first pay a visit to the lab

47. To attend the program, you must be at least _____.
    A) 14 years old　　B) 16 years old　　C) 18 years old　　D) 20 years old

Task 3

Directions: *The following passage is about a survey conducted by Corvallis Clinic. After reading* it, you should complete the information by filling in the blanks marked 48 to 52 (**in no more than 3 words**) in the table below. You should write your answers on the Answer Sheet correspondingly.

Thank you for selecting the Corvallis Clinic (诊所) for your recent healthcare needs. To continue delivering the highest possible level of service, we survey our patients to learn about their experiences at our clinic. The comments and suggestions you provide about your visit will help us evaluate (评价) our services and improve our care.

This survey takes only a few minutes to complete. Your comments and suggestions are very important to us, and they will be kept confidential (保密). A postage-paid reply envelope is enclosed for your convenience. If you have any question about this survey, please call our Service Center at 541-754-1374.

Thank you for helping us as we continually try our best to improve the quality of medical care. Please drop your complete survey in the mail as soon as possible.

Patients' Survey

Survey conducted by: Corvallis clinic

Aim of the survey: to deliver the highest possible level of service

Values of patients' comments and suggestions:

1) helping to evaluate the clinic's ___48___ ;

2) helping to improve the clinic's ___49___ ;

Promise by the clinic: comments and suggestions to be kept ___50___

Enclosure: a ___51___ reply envelope

Contact: to call Service Center at ___52___

Task 4

Directions: *The following is a list of terms used in safety management. After reading it, you are required to find the items equivalent to those given in Chinese in the table below. Then you should mark the corresponding letters in order of the numbered blanks, 53 through 57, on the Answer Sheet.*

A—Warning Equipment   B—Accident Management

C—Protection Measures   D—Risk Assessment

E—Administrative Controls   F—Detection Technique

G—Failure Analysis   H—Responsible Person

I—Harmful Substances   J—Protection Devices

K—Accident Statistics   L—Safety Standards

M—Accident Prevention   N—Monitoring System

O—Special Operation   P—Medical Aid

Q—Emergency Rescue

Examples：（Q）应急救援　　　　　（D）风险评估

53.（　）事故系统		（　）检测技术	
54.（　）报警设备		（　）医疗救护	
55.（　）有害物质		（　）管理控制	
56.（　）保护措施		（　）责任人	
57.（　）特殊作业		（　）失效分析	

Task 5

Directions：*Read the following passage. After reading it, you are required to complete the answers that follow the questions (No. 58 to No. 62). You should write your answers (**in no more than three words**) on the Answer Sheet correspondingly.*

ITaP Instructional Lab Etiquette（守则）

• This lab is a study zone——please limit your noise. Cell phones and other electronic communication devices should be turned off while inside the lab.

• Group studying——limit group studying to non-busy times. Give chairs to others so they can use available computers.

• Log off from your computer——workstations left idle（空闲状态的）for more than 10 minutes will be reset to the log-in screen.

• Printouts are limited to 10-minute printing time——break large print jobs into smaller print jobs.

• Customer's forms or paper are not permitted in ITaP printers——this can damage the printers.

• Computers are available on a first-come-first-serve basis only during computer lab hours of operation and when no class are scheduled in the room.

58. What should you do with your cell phones while you are inside the lab?
　　You should _____ your cell phone.

59. When can you do your group studying in the lab?
　　At _____ times.

60. Why should you break large print jobs into smaller ones?
　　Because printouts are limited to _____ printing time.

61. Why are the customer's forms or paper not permitted in ITaP printers?
　　They can _____ .

62. When can you use the computer in the lab?
　　During the lab hours of _____ with no classes scheduled.

Part IV Translation—English into Chinese (25 minutes)

Directions: *This part, numbered 63 to 67, is to test your ability to translate English into Chinese. Each of the four sentences (No.63 to No.66) is followed by three choices of suggested translation marked A), B) and C). Make the best choice and write the corresponding letter on the Answer Sheet Answer with a single line through the center. And then write your translation of the paragraph (No.67) in the corresponding space on the Translation/Composition Sheet.*

63. The healthcare and social assistant sector will account for almost a third of the job growth from 2012 to 2022.

    A）从 2012 年至 2022 年，从事医疗保健工作的员工将占社会救助业的三分之一。

    B）从 2012 年至 2022 年，医疗保健和社会救助业几乎将占就业增长的三分之一。

    C）从 2012 年至 2022 年，医疗保健和社会救助业将会占到三分之一的就业岗位。

64. Regardless of your line of work, sending business invitations will certainly be something you will face from time to time.

    A）无论你从事哪个行业，发业务邀请函必然是你时不时要遇到的事情。

    B）只要你从事这个业务，就摆脱不了经常去处理商务函电等事项。

    C）不管从事的是哪一个行当，你经常要做的一件事情就是收发邀请函。

65. Our company makes a special effort to establish good communication and cooperative relationship between management and labor.

    A）本公司重视与管理层和服务人员的沟通，建立了良好的合作关系。

    B）本公司为已与我们建立了良好贸易合作关系的客户提供特殊的服务。

    C）本公司特别致力于建立管理层和员工之间良好的沟通与合作关系。

66. If you need any help in starting a business, our team will be right here for you.

    A）如果你需要创业，我们团队就可以在此给你提供帮助。

    B）你在创业中如需任何帮助，我们团队会随时为你提供。

    C）如果你创业失败，我们团队将会帮助你重新制订计划。

67. Many items may be dangerous goods and could cause serious accidents when mailed. It is your responsibility to ensure that your parcel does not contain any dangerous goods. With your cooperation, accidents can be prevented. You could be held responsible if an accident occurred. If you wish to know whether you can mail a certain item, please call Customers Service at 1-800-267-1177.

Part V Writing (25 minutes)

Direction: *This part is to test your ability to do practical writing. You are required to complete the Guest Experiences Card according to the following information given in Chinese. Remember to do your writing on the Translation/Composition Sheet.*

说明：假定你是张建林，根据所给内容填写下列顾客意见反馈表。

顾客姓名：张建林

顾客邮址：zhangjl1999@163.com

抵达日期：2017年6月15日

抵达时间：上午11:30

内容：酒店员工非常友好，提供了良好的服务，尤其是一位名叫John Chen的员工。酒店的房间干净整洁，餐厅的食物美味可口，住店的体验很不错。但是酒店离市中心较远，建议酒店增设从酒店到地铁站的班车（shuttle bus），为客人提供方便。

Guest Experience Card

we value your feedback

Name：_____(1)_____

Email address：_____(2)_____

Date of visit：_____(3)_____

Time of visit：_____(4)_____

Did our Team Members exceed your expectations? __Yes__ If yes,

Please provide their names：_____(5)_____

Comments：
_____
_____
_____
_____
_____

Thank you for choosing our hotel.

If you would like to talk to us about your experience today, please contact the Guest Services Department at 1-888-601-1616.

Model Test One (Level B)

Part I Listening Comprehension (25 minutes)

Directions: *This part is to test your listening ability. It consists of 4 sections.*

Section A

Directions: *This section is to test your ability to give proper responses. There are 7 recorded questions in it. After each question, there is a pause. The questions will be spoken **two times**. When you hear a question, you should decide on the correct answer from the 4 choices marked A), B), C) and D) given in your test paper. Then you should mark the corresponding letter on the Answer Sheet with a single line through the center.*

Example: *You will hear:*

You will read: A) I'm not sure.   B) You're right.
                C) Yes, certainly.   D) That's interesting.

From the question we learn that the speaker is asking the listener to leave a message. Therefore, **C) Yes, certainly** *is the correct answer. You should mark C) on the Answer Sheet with a single line through the center.*

Now the test will begin.

1. A) Doing homework.   B) Fine, thank you.
   C) Very good.   D) Writing a book.
2. A) I work hard.   B) I'm dancing.
   C) I've got a headache.   D) I like swimming.
3. A) The blue one.   B) In section 9.
   C) Size 10.   D) Jane likes Jeans.
4. A) Good idea.   B) Thank you.
   C) Yes, it's very hot.   D) That's all right.
5. A) It's Friday.   B) It matches me well.
   C) I bought it in the department store.   D) Sorry, I don't know.
6. A) Yes, we never overcharge.   B) I'm sorry. The price is fixed.
   C) It's 250 dollars.   D) Yes, you can take it.
7. A) No, you can use your credit card.   B) Yes, you can use your credit card.
   C) Yes, you cannot use your credit card. D) Yes, you can change it in cash.

Section B

Directions: *This section is to test your ability to understand short dialogues. There are 7 recorded dialogues in it. After each dialogue, there is a recorded question. Both the dialogues and questions will be spoken two times. When you hear a question, you should decide on the correct answer from the 4 choices marked A), B), C) and D) given in your test paper. Then you should mark the corresponding letter on the Answer Sheet with a single line through the center.*

8. A) Director.   B) Teacher.   C) Father.   D) Student.
9. A) 7:05.   B) 7:20.   C) 7:15.   D) 7:10.
10. A) The man is quiet.   B) The man is proud.
    C) The man is in a hurry.   D) The man is talkative.
11. A) To the shops.   B) Home.
    C) To her friend's house.   D) To school.
12. A) He doesn't like it.   B) He has to take care of her daughter.
    C) He will see a doctor.   D) He is ill.
13. A) The man's girlfriend.   B) A salesgirl.
    C) Customer.   D) A passer-by.
14. A) At a dry cleaning shop.   B) At a restaurant.
    C) At a museum.   D) At a clothing store.

Section C

Directions: *This section is to test your ability to understand short conversations. There are 2 recorded conversations in it. After each conversation, there are some recorded questions. Both the conversations and questions will be spoken two times. When you hear a question, you should decide on the correct answer from the 4 choices marked A), B), C) and D) given in your test paper. Then you should mark the corresponding letter on the Answer Sheet with a single line through the center.*

Now listen to the conversations.

Conversation 1

15. A) He is interested in his work.   B) He is proud of his work.
    C) He is tired of his work.   D) He is keen on his work.
16. A) He plans to go abroad.   B) He plans to start his own business.
    C) He plans to work in another bank.   D) He plans to venture with Kitty.
17. A) From the bank he is working for.   B) From his friend.
    C) From another bank.   D) From his office.

Conversation 2

18. A) Booking a theatre ticket.   B) Reserving a room.
    C) Booking an air ticket.   D) Reserving a seat.

19. A) Wife and husband. B) Teacher and student.
    C) Clerk and guest. D) Employer and employee.

Section D

Directions: *In this section you will hear a recorded short passage. The passage is printed on the test paper, but with some words or phrases missing. The passage will be read three times. During the second reading, you are required to put the missing words or phrases on the answer sheet in order of the numbered blanks according to what you hear. The third reading is for you to check your writing. Now the passage will begin.*

Old age has always been thought of as the worst age to be; but is not __20__ for the old to be unhappy. With old age should come wisdom and the ability to help others with __21__ wisely given. The old have the joy of seeing their children making progress in life; they can __22__ their grandchildren __23__ around them; and perhaps best of all, they can, if their life has been a useful one, feel the happiness of having come through the __24__ of life safely and having reached a time when they can lie back and rest, leaving others to continue the battle.

Part II Vocabulary & Structure (10 minutes)

Directions: *This part is to test your ability to use words and phrases correctly to construct meaningful and grammatically correct sentences. It consists of 2 sections.*

Section A

Directions: *There are 10 incomplete statements here. You are required to complete each statement by choosing the appropriate answer from the 4 choices marked A), B), C) and D). You should mark the corresponding letter on the Answer Sheet with a single line through the center.*

25. The train starts at 8:00, so you _____ better be at the station by 7:50.
    A) had   B) should   C) have   D) would

26. I'd like to _____ your essay with you when you have time.
    A) go for   B) go over   C) go after   D) go by

27. I don't think these books are _____ for young children.
    A) suitable   B) capable   C) reasonable   D) probable

28. In Britain the father is more involved with _____ children, often because the mother goes out to work.
    A) bringing out   B) bringing up
    C) bringing forth   D) bringing about

29. Such problems _____ air and water pollution have no limited boundaries.
    A) of   B) about   C) as   D) of

30. With the _____ of Mary, all the girl students are eager to go to the party.
    A) exhibition   B) exception   C) except   D) reception

31. He works in our university as a visiting _____, not as a formal faculty member.
    A) traditional   B) scholar   C) nurse   D) pilot
32. The girl _____ left him a few weeks ago.
    A) he fell in love with   B) whom he fell in love
    C) that he fell in love   D) with who he fell in love
33. _____ I arrived in South Africa, I was struck by the very great difference in the atmosphere of the country.
    A) Since the moment   B) During the time
    C) By that time   D) From the moment
34. Mr. Johnson suggested _____ before details are discussed.
    A) not to draw a conclusion   B) should not draw a conclusion
    C) to draw not a conclusion   D) not drawing a conclusion

Section B

Directions: *There are 5 incomplete statements here. You should fill in each blank with the proper form of the word given in the brackets. Write the word or words in the corresponding space on the Answer Sheet.*

35. It's much (easy) _____ to talk about your problems than it is to solve them.
36. (believe) _____, the little boy can speak three foreign languages.
37. Unless he (tell) _____ us who he is, we won't let him in.
38. I'd like to go with you, but with so much work to do today I'm (able) _____ to.
39. When we were young, we had already learnt that life (be) _____ dependent on air and water.

Part III Reading Comprehension   (35 minutes)

Directions: *This part is to test your reading ability. There are 5 tasks for you to fulfill. You should read the reading materials carefully and do the tasks as you are instructed.*

Task 1

Directions: *After reading the following passage, you will find 5 questions or unfinished statements, numbered 36 through 40. For each question or statement there are 4 choices marked A), B), C) and D). You should make the correct choice and mark the corresponding letter on the Answer Sheet with a single line through the center.*

There are many ways to learn about people of other lands. One way is to study the clothing other people wear.

For thousands of years, people in different parts of the world have worn very different types of clothing. There are four big reasons for this.

One reason might be religion. In many Moslem countries, women must wear veils to hide their faces. The veils must be worn in public. Veils are part of the Moslem religion.

The second reason is that different materials are used in different countries. For instance, in France the materials used in clothing may be cotton (棉), silk, wool, or many other man-made materials. Most people in China wear cotton.

The ways clothes are made are also very different. This is another reason why people dress differently. Western countries rely on machines to make most of their clothing. Someone living in India can use only hand power to make the clothing he needs.

World-wide differences in customs also lead to differences in clothing. A Mexican farmer wears a straw hat with a brim (帽沿) up. In China, a farmer wears a straw hat with a brim down. Both hats are used to protect the farmers from the sun. Some of these customs have come down through thousands of years.

40. If you want to learn about the differences about people in the world, you _____.
    A) should know the ways to study other lands
    B) should know the four big reasons given in the passage
    C) may study the different types of clothing people wear
    D) may be surprised by the ways people wear hats

41. In many Moslem countries, women have to _____ in public.
    A) wear more clothes than men   B) cover their faces with veils
    C) protect their faces from being hurt D) wear religious clothing

42. Which of the following is the reason for the differences in clothing?
    A) Materials used for clothes differ from country to country.
    B) Cotton is the common material for clothing.
    C) Man-made materials are invented to make clothes.
    D) Most people like silk clothes.

43. The third reason for difference in clothing is _____.
    A) different materials   B) different ways of making clothes
    C) different styles of dressing   D) different religions

44. The two examples of wearing hats are given in the last paragraph to show _____.
    A) the effect of customs on dressing style   B) the function of wearing straw hat
    C) the correct way of wearing straw hat   D) the long history of some customs

Task 2

Directions: *This task is the same as Task 1. The 3 questions or unfinished statements are numbered 45 through 47.*

We use both words and gestures to express our feelings, but the problem is that these words and gestures (手势) can be understood in different ways. It is true that a smile means the same thing in any language. So does laughter or crying. Fear is another emotion that is shown in much the same way all over the world. In Chinese and in English literature, a phrase like "he went pale and began to tremble" suggests that the man is either very afraid or he has just got a very big shock. However, "he opened his eyes wide" is used to suggest anger in Chinese whereas in English it means surprise.

In Chinese surprise can be described in a phrase like "they stretched out their tongues!" Sticking out your tongue in English is an insulting (侮辱) gesture or expresses strong dislike. Even in the same culture, people differ in their ability to understand and express feelings. Experiments in America have shown that women are usually better than men at recognizing fear, anger, love and happiness on people's faces. Other studies show that older people usually find it easier to recognize or understand body language than younger people do.

45. Which of the following is TRUE according to the passage?
    A) It is difficult to tell what people's words or gestures really mean.
    B) Gestures can be understood by most people but words cannot.
    C) Body language can be better understood by older people.
    D) We can easily understand what people's gestures mean.

46. People's facial expressions may be misunderstood because _____.
    A) people of different sexes may understand a gesture differently
    B) people speaking different languages have different facial expressions
    C) people from different cultures use different facial expressions
    D) people of different ages may have different interpretations

47. In the same culture, people _____.
    A) hardly fail to understand each other's ideas and feelings
    B) are equally intelligent even if they have different backgrounds
    C) almost have the same understanding of the same thing
    D) may have different abilities to understand and express feelings

Task 3

Directions: *The following is a letter about the arrangement for a conference. After reading it, you should complete the information by filling in the blanks marked 48 through 52 (**in no more than 3 words**) in the table below.*

Dear Nancy,

Now I am sending you a copy of the final program schedule of the Conference, together with a map of the location of St. Martin's College.

Please note also that there has been an exchange between meetings. Those meetings for Friday morning will be replaced by those for Saturday afternoon. I hope this will not cause you any problem.

If you are going to present a paper, please let me have an abstract (摘要) of it as soon as possible. The deadline for the abstract is Monday 23 September.

The entire Conference fee (3 days) is $120. You may send the fee to the Conference organizer according to the above address or just pay on arrival.

Looking forward to meeting you soon.

Yours sincerely,
Dr. Johnson
Professor of Collins University & Organizer of the Conference

---

Information about a Conference at Collins University

Place of the Conference: __48__

Change in the schedule: Meeting for Friday morning will be held on __49__

The time for receiving an abstract: no later than __50__

Conference fee: __51__

Receiver of the Conference fee: __52__

Task 4

Directions: *The following are some expressions in a computer menu. After reading it, you are required to find the items equivalent（与……等同）to those given in Chinese in the list below. Then you should put the corresponding letters in brackets on the Answer Sheet, numbered 53 through 57.*

A—to Select Power Management Mode
B—to Show Hidden Files
C—to Select the Path Name for the File
D—to Rename an Existing File
E—to Complete a Document
F—to Select the Text You Want to Print
G—to Move to the start of the Current Line
H—to Delete the Current Line
I—to Delete the Current Selection
J—to Open Second Edit Window
K—to Close Second Edit Window
L—to Open the Ffile in Read-only Mode
M—to Click the Item You Want to Change
N—to Display Information About Edit
O—to Confirm Each Replacement

Examples：（E）完成一个文档　　　　　　　　（M）点击想更改的项目

53.（　）显示编辑资料　　　　　　　　（　）关闭第二个编辑窗口
54.（　）选择你想打印的文本　　　　　（　）删除当前选项
55.（　）选择电源管理模式　　　　　　（　）以只读模式打开文件
56.（　）移动光标到当前行的开头　　　（　）给一个已存在的文件重命名
57.（　）显示隐藏文件　　　　　　　　（　）给当前文件选择一个路径名

Task 5

Directions: *Read the following advertisement and the application. After reading them, you are required to complete the statements that follow the questions（No.58 to No.62）. You should write your answers（**in no more than 3 words**）on the Answer Sheet correspondingly.*

A Job Wanted Ad

CASTLE HOTEL

Assistant Manager

We are looking for an enthusiastic person to assist in the expansion of the hotel.

The successful applicant（申请人）will have experience of overall hotel work and at least one year's experience as an Assistant Manager.

Applicants need good knowledge of English and possibly two other languages.

Good salary, bonus（奖金）, good holidays and excellent prospects for promotion（晋升）within the group.

Apply in confidence with a full resume and a recent photograph to:

Mr. Gerry Bateman, Castle Hotel, Green Street, Barton BR7 7QT.

An Application Letter

136 Brownless Road

Catford, PL4 2 EB

August 19, 2000

Dear Mr. Bateman,

I saw your advertisement for an Assistant Manager in this week's issue of The Hotelier and I should like to apply for the position.

I am enclosing my resume and a recent photograph. As you see I have been Assistant Manager at the Granada Hotel in Madrid for a year and I would very much like to have experience of hotel work in England.

I am at present on holiday in England and staying with friends at the above address. I shall be returning to Spain at the end of the month.

Yours sincerely,

Maria Sanchez

58. Where did the applicant find the advertisement?

  In _____ of The Hotelier.

59. What other experience should the applicants have besides being an Assistant Manager?

  They should have experience of _____.

60. What are the applicants required to send to Mr. Gerry Bateman?

  A full resume and _____.

61. What is Maria Sanchez's present job?

  She is _____.

62. What is Maria Sanchez doing in England now?

  She is _____ there.

Part IV Translation—English into Chinese   (25 minutes)

Directions: *This part, numbered 63 to 67, is to test your ability to translate English into*

Chinese. Each of the four sentences (No.63 to No.66) is followed by four choices of suggested translation marked A), B), C) and D). Make the best choice and write the corresponding letter on the Answer Sheet. Write your translation of the paragraph (No. 67) in the corresponding space on the Translation/Composition Sheet.

63. Today's young people generally have more purchasing power than their parents and they are more prepared to use it.

　　A）如今年轻人的购买力一般超过他们的父母，而且更乐意消费。
　　B）总体上今天的年轻人赚的钱比父母多，而且他们时刻准备消费掉。
　　C）如今年轻人在消费上大都比父母大方，而且他们更做好了花钱的准备。
　　D）今天的年轻人大都认为他们需要比父母多买东西，而且时刻准备这么做。

64. Every employer wants and needs employees who can suggest improvements in an honest and constructive manner.

　　A）每位雇主都以诚实和建设性的方法要求雇员提出改进意见。
　　B）每位雇主都希望能有以诚实积极的态度提出改进意见的雇员。
　　C）每位雇主都要求雇员能够提出诚实积极的改进意见。
　　D）每位雇主都需要他们的雇员能够诚实而富有建设性。

65. The increase in international business has created a need for managers with skills in cross-cultural communication.

　　A）国际贸易增加了跨文化交流的机会，也提高了经理的技能。
　　B）国际贸易提高了对经理掌握跨文化交流技能的要求。
　　C）国际贸易的增加需要具有跨文化交流技能的经理。
　　D）国际贸易增加了对经理跨文化交际能力的需求。

66. Scientists are eager to talk with other scientists working on similar problem.

　　A）科学家热衷于与从事类似课题研究的其他科学家交流。
　　B）科学家更容易与其他科学家谈话来解决相同的问题。
　　C）科学家很乐意在解决类似问题时同其他科学家交流。
　　D）科学家更容易就雷同的问题与其他科学家交谈。

67. Financial management includes the search for adequate sources of capital and the management of the capital already invested. It requires estimating the amount of cash that the company will need in its operations, deciding whether to use short-term or long-term credit, choosing the right time to issue stock or sell bonds, etc.

_____
_____
_____

Part V　Writing　　　　　　　　　　（25 minutes）

Directions: *This part is to test your ability to do practical writing. You are required to write a*

Notice according to the information given below. Remember to write it on the Translation/Composition Sheet.

1. 事宜：关于计算机的用途以及如何利用 Internet 进行学习的讲座。
2. 讲座人：武汉大学计算机系申蓝教授。
3. 时间：12月26日，星期六，下午2:00。
4. 地点：图书馆208室。
5. 参加对象：计算机爱好者。
6. 组织者：学生会。
7. 通知时间：12月19日。

Model Test Two (Level B)

Part I Listening Comprehension (25 minutes)

Directions: *This part is to test your listening ability. It consists of 4 sections.*

Section A

Directions: *This section is to test your ability to give proper responses. There are 7 recorded questions in it. After each question, there is a pause. The questions will be spoken **two times**. When you hear a question, you should decide on the correct answer from the 4 choices marked A), B), C) and D) given in your test paper. Then you should mark the corresponding letter on the Answer Sheet with a single line through the center.*

Example: *You will hear:*

    You will read: A) I'm not sure.   B) You're right.
                     C) Yes, certainly.   D) That's interesting.

From the question we learn that the speaker is asking the listener to leave a message. Therefore, **C) Yes, certainly** *is the correct answer. You should mark C) on the Answer Sheet with a single line through the center.*

Now the test will begin.

1. A) Yes, I'd love to.   B) I'm afraid not.
   C) Please do it for me.   D) I don't know.
2. A) Yes, I'm ill.   B) No, I don't think so.
   C) Yes, he's very well.   D) I agree with you.
3. A) It's small but beautiful.   B) I like it.
   C) I don't like it.   D) I like teachers there.
4. A) Yes, it is.   B) It doesn't matter.
   C) So do I.   D) No, that's not good.
5. A) I'm not in the office.   B) No, I am.
   C) I have homework to do.   D) I'm a student.
6. A) Both, too.   B) Volleyball.
   C) Either.   D) Neither.
7. A) Hold on the line, please.   B) Yes, you may.
   C) No, you can't.   D) Don't mention it.

Section B

Directions: *This section is to test your ability to understand short dialogues. There are 7 recorded dialogues in it. After each dialogue, there is a recorded question. Both the dialogues and questions will be spoken two times. When you hear a question, you should decide on the correct answer from the 4 choices marked A), B), C) and D) given in your test paper. Then you should mark the corresponding letter on the Answer Sheet with a single line through the center.*

Now listen to the dialogues.

8. A) Strangers. B) Colleagues.
   C) Interviewer and interviewees. D) Classmate.
9. A) $3.00. B) $4.00.
   C) $7.00. D) $10.00.
10. A) She is afraid. B) She has never taken the bus before.
    C) She is new here. D) She does not want to tell him.
11. A) He was asked to hand in his paper. B) He didn't hand in his paper on time.
    C) He handed in his paper earlier. D) The teacher liked his paper very much.
12. A) She needs a quiet place. B) She likes moving around.
    C) She wants a bigger house. D) She likes playing the violin.
13. A) The flight will leave at 2:30. B) The flight will be late.
    C) The man will leave by flight at 4:30. D) The man will leave at once.
14. A) In a bank. B) In a post office.
    C) At a stop. D) At the school gate.

Section C

Directions: *This section is to test your ability to understand short conversations, There are 2 recorded conversations in it. After each conversation, there are some recorded questions. Both the conversations and questions will be spoken two times. When you hear a question, you should decide on the correct answer from the 4 choices marked A), B), C) and D) given in your test paper. Then you should mark the corresponding letter on the Answer Sheet with a single line through the center.*

Now listen to the conversations.

Conversation 1

15. A) 8:30 in the morning, Tuesday. B) 8:30 in the evening, Tuesday.
    C) 8:30 in the morning, Monday. D) 8:30 in the evening, Monday.
16. A) Because he wants to visit her.
    B) Because he wants to discuss her suggestion with her.
    C) Because he wants to offer a proposal.
    D) Because he wants to date her.

Conversation 2

17. A) At Leech's school. B) In the police station.
    C) On the phone. D) At Mrs. Smith's home.
18. A) Two days. B) The whole afternoon.
    C) A whole day. D) The whole morning.
19. A) Yellow and white. B) Blue and green.
    C) Green and black. D) Blue and black.

Section D

Directions: *In this section you will hear a recorded short passage. The passage is printed on the test paper, but with some words or phrases missing. The passage will be read three times. During the second reading, you are required to put the missing words or phrases on the answer sheet in order of the numbered blanks according to what you hear. The third reading is for you to check your writing. Now the passage will begin.*

The word horsepower was first used two hundred years ago. James Watt had made the world's first __20__ used steam engine. He had no way of telling people __21__ how powerful it was, for at that time there were no units for measuring power. Watt decided to __22__ how much work one __23__ horse could do in one minute. He called that unit one horsepower. With this unit he could measure the work his steam engine could do. He __24__ that a horse could lift a 3,300-pound weight 10 feet into the air in one minute. His engine could lift a 3,300 pound weight 100 feet in one minute. Because his engine did ten times as much work as the horse, Watt called it a ten-horsepower engine.

Part II Vocabulary & Structure   (10 minutes)

Directions: *This part is to test your ability to use words and phrases correctly to construct meaningful and grammatically correct sentences. It consists of 2 sections.*

Section A

Directions: *There are 10 incomplete statements here. You are required to complete each statement by choosing the appropriate answer from the 4 choices marked A), B), C) and D). You should mark the corresponding letter on the Answer Sheet with a single line through the center.*

25. An object remains still or in a straight line motion _____ a force acts upon it.
    A) unless   B) because   C) when   D) if
26. The book is _____ more difficult than the one I recommend to you.
    A) rather   B) much   C) very   D) so
27. The committee members propose that the plan _____ postponed for a few days.
    A) being   B) been   C) to be   D) be
28. They stood in the rain for two hours, but they _____ for Mr. Ying, because he didn't

come at all.

  A) mustn't have waited   B) may not have waited
  C) can't have waited   D) needn't have waited

29. There is a nice-looking car there. I wonder _____.

  A) whom it belongs to   B) whom does it belong to
  C) it belongs to whom   D) whom does it belong

30. _____ the population is too large, we have to take measures to control the birth rate.

  A) Although   B) Since   C) If   D) Until

31. He said, "I _____ a lot of new poems by the end of last year."

  A) had already learnt   B) have already learnt
  C) would have already learnt   D) already learnt

32. Only in this way _____ catch up with your brothers.

  A) do you can   B) can you   C) you can   D) you do can

33. Mr. John has decided that he will _____ the branch company set up in the small town.

  A) take over   B) hand in   C) put in   D) lead to

34. The town lacks _____ facilities such as a swimming pool or a bowling alley.

  A) pleasure   B) measure   C) leisure   D) treasure

Section B

Directions: *There are 5 incomplete statements here. You should fill in each blank with the proper form of the word given in the brackets. Write the word or words in the corresponding space on the Answer Sheet.*

35. The old couple had never been to such a big party, so they felt (comfort)_____ and kept quiet.

36. It was suggested that a team of five (set)_____ up to investigate the matter.

37. The little boy was afraid of being asked to sing the song, for he (not prepare)_____ for it.

38. All the members of the company were present when the manager (elect)_____ last week.

39. We should read more and see more in order to (wide)_____ our horizons.

Part III Reading Comprehension   (35 minutes)

Directions: *This part is to test your reading ability. There are 5 tasks for you to fulfill. You should read the reading materials carefully and do the tasks as you are instructed.*

Task 1

Directions: *After reading the following passage, you will find 5 questions or unfinished statements, numbered 40 through 44. For each question or statement there are 4 choices marked A), B), C) and D). You should make the correct choice and mark the corresponding letter on the*

Answer Sheet with a single line through the center.

Doctors believe that second-hand smoke may cause lung cancer in people who do not smoke. Nonsmokers often breathe in the smoke from other people's cigarettes. This is second-hand smoke. The U.S. Environmental Protection Agency（美国环保局）reports that about fifty-three thousand people die in the United States each year as a result of exposure（暴露）to second-hand smoke.

It is harder for children to avoid second-hand smoke. In the United States, nine million children under the age of five live in homes with at least one smoker. Research shows that these children are sick more often than children who live in homes where no one smokes. The damaging effects of second-hand smoke on children also continue as they grow up. The children of smokers are more than twice as likely to develop lung cancer when they are adults as children of nonsmokers. The risk is even higher for children who live in homes with both parents smoking.

People are becoming very aware of the danger of second-hand smoke. As a result, they have passed laws that prohibit people from smoking in many public places. Currently, 45 states in the United States have laws that restrict, or limit smoking. The most well-known law doesn't allow people to smoke on short native airline flights, i.e. flights within the country.

40. Compared with nonsmokers' children, the children whose parents both smoke are likely to _____.

   A) grow up slowly
   B) be sick under the age of five
   C) develop lung cancer more often
   D) become smokers more easily

41. Why are there laws against smoking in public places in the U.S.?

   A) Because people have realized the danger of second-hand smoke.
   B) Because more and more people don't like smoking now.
   C) Because parents don't want their children to become smokers.
   D) Because the government wants to limit the production of cigarettes.

42. Which of the following statements is TRUE?

   A) The number of smokers' children is twice greater than that of nonsmokers' children.
   B) People are now allowed to smoke on airline flights in the U.S.
   C) Adults whose parents smoked when they were children get cancer more frequently.
   D) Second-hand smoke is not as dangerous as first-hand smoke.

43. From the passage we can conclude that _____.

   A) the main cause of lung cancer is second-hand smoke
   B) most places know nothing about the danger of second-hand smoke
   C) public places are dangerous for people to stay
   D) children suffer most from second-hand smoke

44. This passage is mainly about _____.

   A) how people get cancer
   B) who can get cancer easily
   C) what should be done with smoking in public

D) whether second-hand smoking can be harmful

Task 2

Directions: *This task is the same as Task 1. The 3 questions or unfinished statements are numbered 45 through 47.*

As working women continue to receive better and better wages, housewives still work at home without receiving paycheck. Should a woman who works at home, doing the housework and caring for children, be paid for her services? In a 1986 study at Cornell University, it was found that the value of the services of a housewife averaged $11,600 a year. This rate was based on a family composed of a husband, wife and three young children. The $11,600 is what the husband would have to pay if he hired others to take over his wife's household work. The researchers concluded that it would be fair for husbands to pay wives according to government guidelines (方针) for least amounts of wages.

Another plan for rewarding women who work at home has been suggested by Dr. Johnson, a former Secretary of Health and Human Services. He says that full-time housewives should be allowed to pay social security taxes (社会保障金), with their employers (that is, their husbands) offering part to the payment. He feels that present system is unfair. He said, "If you work in a store you can qualify for Social Security, but if you stay at home and raise a family, you can't qulaity for it."

45. Now in the U.S. the women working outside home can get _____.
    A) the same pay as those doing housework
    B) as much as their husbands
    C) an average payment of $11,600 a year
    D) more and more money

46. The researchers at Cornell University suggest that _____.
    A) husbands hire others to do their housework
    B) husbands pay their wives for their work at home
    C) policies be worked out on women's wages
    D) women go out to work instead of working at home

47. The expression "full-time housewives" in paragraph 2 means _____.
    A) wives who can't do any housework
    B) wives who don't like to stay at home
    C) wives staying at home doing housework
    D) wives working outside home sometimes

Task 3

Directions: *The following is a short essay. After reading it, you should complete the information by filling in the blanks marked 48 through 52 (**in no more than 3 words**) in the table below.*

If a writer is going to write an article or other writings, he should go through some common stages in the writing process, from the preliminary (初步的) stage of brainstorming ideas all the way to the highly polished final draft, which is the last stage in writing before going to press.

After the initial stage of generating ideas, a rough plan or outline usually follows in the form of a mind map. This can then be transformed into the next stage, which is a more tightly structured written outline. At this point, the writer will now be ready to compose a rough or first draft.

The writer will then arrive at the revision stage of writing, and may ask for guidance or suggestions from other writers. After some deliberation the second draft is written in the subsequent stage. This in turn goes through to the final revision or proof-reading stage. After everything has been checked through carefully, the piece of writing reaches the final stage.

Process of Writing

Process of writing is made up of some important stages. The initial stage is brainstorming, or __48__ and then the writer begins the rough plan and makes it into a __49__. After that, a rough or __50__ is composed. After the revising stage of writing, __51__ is written. When at last the final revision is done the piece of writing reaches __52__ ready for publishing.

Task 4

Directions: *The following is a list of college courses. After reading it, you are required to find the Chinese equivalents in the table below. Then you should put the corresponding letters in the brackets on the Answer Sheet, numbered 53 through 57.*

A — Business Management
B — Marketing Management
C — International Business Law
D — Management Information Systems
E — Financial Management
F — International Business and World Environment
G — Managerial Economics and Decision Models
H — Operations Management
I — Human Resource Management
J — Managerial Accounting
K — Economic Law
L — Currency Banking Science
M — Practical International Trade
N — Equipment Management
O — Western Economics

Examples: (H) 生产管理　　　　　　　　　　(O) 西方经济学

53. (	) 跨国企业与全球环境	(	) 人力资源管理
54. (	) 企业管理	(	) 管理信息系统
55. (	) 财务管理	(	) 设备管理
56. (	) 管理会计	(	) 营销管理
57. (	) 国际商法	(	) 管理经济学与决策模式

Task 5

Directions: *There are two BUSINESS LETTERS below here. After reading the letters you should* give brief answers to the 5 questions (No.58 through No.62) that follow. The answers should be written after the corresponding numbers on the Answer Sheet.

Letter One

Jan. 25, 2001

Dear Mr. Guan Li,

From your advertisements we know that you are making transformers (变压器) in a variety of types. We are interested in your products. Would you please send us the details of your products? If possible, please send us some pictures of the products.

Looking forward to your early reply.

Yours sincerely,
Louis Smith

Letter Two

Feb. 14, 2001

Dear Mr. Louis Smith,

It's our pleasure to submit the attached quotation (报价) for your review and consideration. Here enclosed are some pictures of our latest types of transformers. This quotation package consists of the following:

Section 1 Price list for transformers

Section 2 Types of transformers

Section 3 Technical specification

In the price list you can see we are giving you the lowest prices and offer our best goods. We also think it better to offer you a 5% discount on purchases of more than 10 units.

Please advise if you have additional questions.

Yours sincerely,
Guan Li

58. What products are the two letters dealing with?
_____.

59. What does Mr. Louis Smith ask for in his letter?
_____ and pictures of the goods.

60. Apart from a price list of the goods, what else does Mr. Guan Li offer in his quotation package?
Types of the goods and _____.

61. How many transformers must Mr. Louis Smith buy to get a discount of 5%?
_____ of them.

62. What are also included in Guan Li's letter apart from the quotation package?
Some _____.

Part IV Translation—English into Chinese   (25 minutes)

Directions: *This part, numbered 63 to 67, is to test your ability to translate English into Chinese. Each of the four sentences (No.63 to No.66) is followed by three choices of suggested translation marked A), B) and C). Make the best choice and write the corresponding letter on the Answer Sheet. Write your translation of the paragraph (No. 67) in the corresponding space on the Translation/Composition Sheet.*

63. Women are going after equality themselves instead of waiting for organizations to deliver it.

    A) 妇女正在追求属于自己的平等，而不是组织机构给予的平等。

    B) 妇女在等待组织机构带来平等，相反地自己则在后面跟随。

    C) 妇女正在自己追求平等而不是等待组织机构赐予平等。

64. It's still unusual to get a job without a face-to-face contact with your boss-to-be.

    A) 不和你未来的老板面对面地签订合同就找到工作，这是非同寻常的。

    B) 未经与你的未来老板面对面接触就能得到一份工作，这依然是很罕见的。

    C) 找到一份工作就不想和你的老板见面，这是不常见的。

65. No one can use cell phones in anywhere at the hospital where equipment might be affected by the influence from cell phones.

    A) 在医院的任何区域都不得使用手机，因为会受到设备的干扰。

    B) 在医院的任何区域，手机会影响设备的使用，任何人不得使用。

    C) 医院内，在可能干扰设备使用的任何区域，禁止使用手机。

66. China's consumer price index in July dropped by 0.9 percent from a year earlier, against a decline of 0.8 percent in June.

    A) 七月份中国消费物价指数与去年同期相比下降了0.9%，而六月份该指数下降了0.8%。

    B) 中国消费物价七月份下降至前一年的0.9%，比六月份只下降了0.8%。

    C) 七月份中国消费物价指数比一年前下降了0.9%，比六月份下降了0.8%。

67. Many of the world's languages are disappearing as modern communications, migration (人口迁移) and population growth end the isolation of ethnic groups. At least half the world's 6,000 languages will likely die out in the next century and only 5 percent of languages are safe meaning they are spoken by at least 1 million people and receive state backing, experts say.

_____
_____
_____
_____

Part V Writing   (25 minutes)

Directions: *This part is to test your ability to do practical writing. You are required to write an*

Announcement of Removal according to the following instruction given in Chinese. Remember to write it on the Translation/Composition Sheet.

说明：请以总经理秘书（General Secretary）Clare Tao 的名义通知客户，公司因为开发新业务将迁至新地址，并为因此带来的不便表示歉意。同时借此机会感谢客户多年来的支持，表达期望长期合作的愿望。

具体信息如下：

迁址时间：2009 年 12 月 10 日

公司新址：中山路 17 号中信大厦 2022 室

公司新电话，传真：025-83321145；025-83326542

Model Test Three (Level B)

Part I Listening Comprehension   (25 minutes)

Directions: *This part is to test your listening ability. It consists of 4 sections.*

Section A

Directions: *This section is to test your ability to give proper responses. There are 7 recorded questions in it. After each question, there is a pause. The questions will be spoken **two times**. When you hear a question, you should decide on the correct answer from the 4 choices marked A), B), C) and D) given in your test paper. Then you should mark the corresponding letter on the Answer Sheet with a single line through the center.*

Example: *You will hear:*

    You will read: A) I'm not sure.   B) You're right.
                         C) Yes, certainly.   D) That's interesting.

From the question we learn that the speaker is asking the listener to leave a message. Therefore, **C) Yes, certainly** *is the correct answer. You should mark C) on the Answer Sheet with a single line through the center.*

Now the test will begin.

1. A) About 3 miles.   B) You can take the No. 2 bus.
   C) In half an hour.   D) It's very near.
2. A) No, I don't.   B) Yes, I don't.
   C) No, I do.   D) I don't like her.
3. A) By bus.   B) I work from Monday to Friday.
   C) It's very near.   D) I work in a hospital.
4. A) I know.   B) I see.
   C) You're welcome.   D) Our team.
5. A) By taking a course.   B) Very well.
   C) In the morning.   D) In the library.
6. A) Yes, they call me.   B) Yes, several times.
   C) Yes, I went to see you, but you were out.   D) OK, I will call you.
7. A) We start at 2:00 a.m.   B) Usually we start at 6:30 p.m.
   C) We start at 12:00 at noon.   D) Usually we start at 11:30 p.m.

Section B

Directions: *This section is to test your ability to understand short dialogues. There are 7 recorded dialogues in it. After each dialogue, there is a recorded question. Both the dialogues and questions will be spoken two times. When you hear a question, you should decide on the correct answer from the 4 choices marked A), B), C) and D) given in your test paper. Then you should mark the corresponding letter on the Answer Sheet with a single line through the center.*

Now listen to the dialogues.

8. A) Waiter and customer.　　　　　　B) Patient and doctor.
   C) Wife and husband.　　　　　　　D) Director and pupil.
9. A) Twenty minutes.　　　　　　　　B) Fifty minutes.
   C) Half an hour.　　　　　　　　　D) Eighty minutes.
10. A) Go home at 5 o'clock.　　　　　B) Work together with Mr. Golden.
    C) Type some letters.　　　　　　D) Help the woman.
11. A) She doesn't want to go to France.
    B) She doesn't want to get the visa.
    C) She's not sure when she can leave for France.
    D) She doesn't know how to get the visa.
12. A) She has got a driver's license.
    B) She was accepted by a college.
    C) She is going to another country.
    D) She got a good job.
13. A) She wants to know when they can eat breakfast.
    B) She wonders if they can eat a meal there quickly.
    C) She doesn't think they serve breakfast in the dining room.
    D) She doesn't think the service is very good there.
14. A) Doctor and patient.　　　　　　B) Customer and waiter.
    C) Shop-assistant and customer.　　D) Conductor and passenger.

Section C

Directions: *This section is to test your ability to understand short conversations. There are 2 recorded conversations in it. After each conversation, there are some recorded questions. Both the conversations and questions will be spoken two times. When you hear a question, you should decide on the correct answer from the 4 choices marked A), B), C) and D) given in your test paper. Then you should mark the corresponding letter on the Answer Sheet with a single line through the center.*

Now listen to the conversations.

Conversation 1

15. A) IBM.　　　　　　　　　　　　B) A supermarket.

C) ABC Company. D) A bookstore.
16. A) Dress. B) Computers.
    C) Shoes. D) Engines.

Conversation 2

17. A) Comedies. B) Horror films.
    C) Mystery films. D) Crime films.
18. A) Unreasonable. B) Horrible.
    C) Frightening. D) Stupid and unbelievable.
19. A) To ring up the ABC and find out what's on.
    B) To watch TV because there is a good musical on.
    C) To read an evening paper and find out what's on.
    D) To stay at home because there are no good films.

Section D

Directions: *In this section you will hear a recorded short passage. The passage is printed on the test paper, but with some words or phrases missing. The passage will be read three times. During the second reading, you are required to put the missing words or phrases on the Answer Sheet in order of the numbered blanks according to what you hear. The third reading is for you to check your writing. Now the passage will begin.*

Fish are animals that live in water. They live in almost any place __20__ there is water. Some are found in lakes, other fish live in the sea. Most fish never __21__ water. There are about 21,000 kinds of fish. One kind might not look like another. Some fish are very small. The smallest one is no bigger than a fly. Others are very big. The biggest fish can __22__ to 60 feet. One kind of fish looks __23__ it has a little horse's head. It is called a sea horse. It doesn't swim very well. A sea horse is mostly pushed along by the __24__ water. What does it do when it wants to stay in one place? It takes hold of plants with its little tail.

Part II Vocabulary & Structure   (10 minutes)

Directions: *This part is to test your ability to use words and phrases correctly to construct meaningful and grammatically correct sentences. It consists of 2 sections.*

Section A

Directions: *There are 10 incomplete statements here. You are required to complete each statement by choosing the appropriate answer from the 4 choices marked A), B), C) and D). You should mark the corresponding letter on the Answer Sheet with a single line through the center.*

25. While staying in America, the young journalist _____ some English.
    A) took away   B) took on

C) picked up D) carry up

26. It is better to avoid _____ downtown during the rush hour.
    A) to drive B) having driven
    C) to be driving D) driving

27. The most important outcome of education is to help students become independent _____ formal education.
    A) from B) of C) on D) in

28. By the end of this month, we surely _____ a satisfactory solution to the problem.
    A) will have found B) will be finding
    C) have found D) are finding

29. _____ the pupils have learned more than 4,000 English words, they can talk with the native speakers.
    A) Now that B) In case
    C) Unless D) Even though

30. Look! A heavy rain is _____. Let's hurry up.
    A) making the way B) on the way
    C) by the way D) in the way

31. You _____ your room before you left, now you find your money stolen.
    A) must have locked B) ought to lock
    C) ought to have locked D) needed to lock

32. It is requested that every man _____ the law.
    A) should obey B) to should obey
    C) should not to obey D) should not obey

33. Water is the first thing constructors consider when _____ to build a house.
    A) planning B) planed
    C) to plan D) having planed

34. It was yesterday _____ I met you on the street.
    A) what B) which
    C) where D) that

Section B

Directions: *There are 5 incomplete statements here. You should fill in each blank with the proper form of the word given in the brackets. Write the word or words in the corresponding space on the Answer Sheet.*

35. He was very busy yesterday, otherwise he (come) _____ to the meeting.

36. The girl was very sure of herself. She is always (confidence) _____ that she is right.

37. The man told me that the (equip) _____ would arrive in three days.

38. It is difficult for a foreigner (learn) _____ Chinese.

39. She will go to work next week if she (be) _____ well.

Part III Reading Comprehension (35 minutes)

Directions: *This part is to test your reading ability. There are 5 tasks for you to fulfill. You should read the reading materials carefully and do the tasks as you are instructed.*

Task 1

Directions: *After reading the following passage, you will find 5 questions or unfinished statements, numbered 40 to 44. For each question or statement there are 4 choices marked A), B), C) and D). You should make the correct choice and mark the corresponding letter on the Answer Sheet with a single line through the center.*

Online advertising is the means of selling a product on the Internet. With the arrival of the Internet, the business world has become digitalized (数字化) and people prefer buying things online, which is easier and faster. Online advertising is also known as e-advertising. It offers a great variety of services, which cannot be offered by any other way of advertising.

One major benefit of online advertising is the immediate spread of information that is not limited by geography or time. Online advertising can be viewed day and night throughout the world. Besides, it reduces the cost and increases the profit of the company.

Small businesses especially find online advertising cheap and effective. They can focus on their ideal customers and pay very little for the advertisements.

In a word, online advertising is a cheap and effective way of advertising, whose success has so far fully proved its great potential (潜力).

40. According to the first paragraph, buying things online is more _____.
    A) convenient   B) fashionable
    C) traditional   D) reliable

41. Compared with any other way of advertising, online advertising _____.
    A) attracts more customers   B) displays more samples
    C) offers more services   D) makes more profits

42. Which of the following statements is TRUE of online advertising?
    A) It has taken the place of traditional advertising.
    B) It will make the Internet technology more efficient.
    C) It can help sell the latest models of digitalized products.
    D) It can spread information without being limited by time.

43. Who can especially benefit from online advertising?
    A) Local companies.   B) Small businesses.
    C) Government departments.   D) International organizations.

44. This passage is mainly about _____.
    A) the function and the use of the Internet   B) the application of digital technology
    C) the development of small businesses   D) the advantages of online advertising

Task 2

Directions: *This task is the same as Task 1. The 3 questions or unfinished statements are numbered 45 to 47.*

During our more than 60-year history, with our vast knowledge and experience, Trafalgar has created perfectly designed travel experiences and memories.

Exceptional value

Traveling with Trafalgar can save you up to 40% when compared with traveling independently. We can find you the right hotels, restaurants, and our charges include entrance fees, tolls（道路通行费）, etc. Because we're the largest touring company with great buying power, we can pass on our savings to you.

Fast-track entrance

Traveling with us means no standing in line（排队）at major sights. Trafalgar takes care of all the little details, which means you are always at the front of the line.

Travel with like-minded friends

Because we truly are global, you will travel with English-speaking people from around the world, and that leads to life-long friendships.

Great savings

We provide many great ways to save money, including Early Payment Discount（折扣）, Frequent Traveler Savings and more.

Fast check-in

Once your booking has been made, you are advised to check in online at our website and meet your fellow travelers before you leave.

45. Because of its great buying power, Trafalgar _____.
    A) can find the cheapest restaurants   B) can pass on its savings to tourists
    C) takes tourists to anywhere in the world   D) allows tourists to travel independently

46. Traveling with Trafalgar, tourists do not have to _____.
    A) bring their passports with them   B) pay for their hotels and meals
    C) stand in line at major sights   D) take their luggage with them

47. Traveling with Trafalgar, tourists may _____.
    A) meet tour guides from different countries
    B) make new friends from around the world
    C) win a special prize offered by the company
    D) have a good chance to learn foreign languages

Task 3

Directions: *The following is a letter of complaint. After reading it, you are required to complete the outline below it（No.48 through No.52）. You should write your answer briefly（in no more than 3 words）on the Answer Sheet correspondingly.*

Dear Sirs,

I'm writing to tell you that your latest shipment (装运) of apples is not up to the standard we expected from you. Many of them are bruised (擦伤), and more than half are covered with little spots. They are classed as Grade A, but I think there must have been some mistake, as they are definitely not Grade A apples.

We have always been satisfied with the quality of your produce (农产品), which makes this case all the more puzzling. I would be grateful if you could look into the matter. We would be happy to keep the apples and try to sell them at a reduced price, but in that case we would obviously need a credit (部分退款) from you. Alternatively, you could collect them and replace them with apples of the right quality. Would you please phone me to let me know how you want to handle it?

Yours faithfully,

Fiona Stockton

Purchasing Manager

A letter of Complaint

Produce involved: Grade A ___48___.

Causes of complaint:

1. many of the apples are bruised
2. more than half of the apples are covered with ___49___

Suggested solutions:

1. allow to sell at ___50___ and give ___51___, or
2. collect them and replace them with apples of ___52___.

Task 4

Directions: *The following is a list of terms related to warning signs. After reading it, you are required to find the items equivalent to (与……等同) those given in Chinese in the table below. Then you should put the corresponding letters in the brackets on the Answer Sheet, numbered 53 through 57.*

A—Guard against Damp. B—Handle with Eare.
C—Keep Away from Heat. D—Keep Away from Cold.
E—Keep Dry. F—Keep Flat.
G—No Naked Fire. H—No Use of Hooks.
I—Not to Be Thrown Down. J—Open Here.
K—Open in Dark Room. L—Protect against Breakage.
M—Poison. N—Take Care.
O—This Side up. P—To be Kept Upright.
Q—Use No Knives.

Examples: (G) 严禁明火   (H) 禁用吊钩

53. (	) 远离热源	(	) 请勿用刀
54. (	) 此面朝上	(	) 此处开启
55. (	) 竖立安放	(	) 暗室开启
56. (	) 小心轻放	(	) 注意平放
57. (	) 不可抛掷	(	) 保持干燥

Task 5

Directions: *Here is a letter. After reading it you are required to complete the answers that follow the questions（No.58 to No.62）. You should write your answers（**in no more than 3 words**）on the Answer Sheet correspondingly.*

Dear Mr. Sampson,

    I want to thank you very much for interviewing me yesterday for the position of design engineer. I enjoyed meeting with you and learning more about your research and design work.

    The interview made me all the more interested in the position and working for XELL Company. I believe my education and work experiences fit nicely with the job requirements, and I am certain I could make a significant contribution（贡献）to the company over time.

    I would like to re-emphasize my strong desire for the position and working with you and your staff. You provide the kind of opportunity I seek. Please feel free to call me at the following phone number if I can provide you with any additional information：0811-8222-5555.

    Again, thank you for the interview and for your consideration.

Sincerely,
Mary Cruz

58. Why did Mary Cruz write this letter?
    To give thanks to Mr. Sampson for _____ her yesterday.

59. What position did Mary Cruz apply for?
    The position of _____.

60. Which company does the writer wish to work for?
    _____.

61. Why is the writer strongly interested in the position?
    Because the company provides the kind of _____ she seeks.

62. How can the writer be contacted?
    By calling her at _____.

Part IV Translation—English into Chinese （25 minutes）

Directions: *This part, numbered 63 to 67, is to test your ability to translate English into Chinese. Each of the four sentences（NO.63 to No.66）is followed by four choices of suggested translation marked A）, B）and C）. Make the best choice and write the corresponding letter on the*

Answer Sheet. Write your translation of the paragraph (No. 67) in the corresponding space on the Translation/Composition Sheet.

63. The boss told us not to use more material than it is necessary.

   A) 老板让我们按需要用料，别多用材料。

   B) 老板让我们不要多用材料，这没必要。

   C) 老板没让我们用必须要有的材料。

64. The little boy admitted his mistakes in the presence of the whole class.

   A) 这个小男孩站在同学面前承认了他的错误。

   B) 这个小男孩面对全体同学忏悔自己的错误。

   C) 这个小男孩当着全班同学的面承认了错误。

65. My first twenty years were spent in the countryside.

   A) 我的第一个20年花费在国家事务上。

   B) 我的前20年是在农村度过的。

   C) 我的前20年是在这个国家里度过的。

66. He is too clever not to solve this problem.

   A) 他太笨了，不会解决这个问题。

   B) 他有点聪明，能解决这个问题。

   C) 他非常聪明，不会不能解决这个问题。

67. Welcome to buy our books. We have a membership plan, which you can join now only by buying any one of our books. Membership costs one hundred Yuan and lasts for a period of one year. If you are a member, you can get a discount. It is a really a good deal especially if you intend to buy a lot of books.

Part V Writing (25 minutes)

Directions: *This part is to test your ability to do practical writing. You are required to write a letter to book a plane ticket. Remember to write it on the Translation/Composition Sheet.*

日期：2012年9月10日

订票人：David Smith

订票处：中国南方航空公司售票处

内容：

兹因急事，需尽快赶往香港，请代留明晨6点钟飞往香港的航班座位一个。机票可送到我下榻的白云宾馆第1903号房。不胜感谢。

Model Test Four (Level B)

Part I Listening Comprehension   (25 minutes)

Directions: *This part is to test your listening ability. It consists of 4 sections.*

Section A

Directions: *This section is to test your ability to give proper responses. There are 7 recorded questions in it. After each question, there is a pause. The questions will be spoken **two times**. When you hear a question, you should decide on the correct answer from the 4 choices marked A), B), C) and D) given in your test paper. Then you should mark the corresponding letter on the Answer Sheet with a single line through the center.*

Example: *You will hear*:

You will read: A) I'm not sure.   B) You're right.
                C) Yes, certainly.   D) That's interesting.

*From the question we learn that the speaker is asking the listener to leave a message. Therefore, **C) Yes, certainly** is the correct answer. You should mark C) on the Answer Sheet with a single line through the center.*

Now the test will begin.

1. A) Of course not.   B) Please close the door.
   C) Is it cold?   D) Please don't close the door.
2. A) No, it's too expensive.   B) I like it very much.
   C) It's about a love story.   D) No, I don't think I need it.
3. A) About 20 hours.   B) So long.
   C) Very fast.   D) I usually go home by air.
4. A) Here you are.   B) It is here.
   C) Yes, I would.   D) I've got some money.
5. A) That's all right.   B) I'm going to Shanghai.
   C) I'm fine. Thank you.   D) Everything is going well.
6. A) Really? Congratulations.   B) What's wrong with you?
   C) Oh, I'm sorry to hear that.   D) That's nothing.
7. A) The supermarket is near here.   B) You can go another day.
   C) You can ask somebody for help.   D) It's 10 kilometers far away.

Section B

Directions: *This section is to test your ability to understand short dialogues. There are 7 recorded dialogues in it. After each dialogue, there is a recorded question. Both the dialogues and questions will be spoken two times. When you hear a question, you should decide on the correct answer from the 4 choices marked A), B), C) and D) given in your test paper. Then you should mark the corresponding letter on the Answer Sheet with a single line through the center.*

Now listen to the dialogues.

8. A) Teacher and student.   B) Nurse and patient.
   C) Lawyer and client.   D) Boss and secretary.
9. A) Playing basketball.   B) Cleaning.
   C) Shopping around.   D) Planning his work.
10. A) At a bus station.   B) At an airport.
    C) At a cafeteria in the railway station.   D) At a railway station.
11. A) The man was quite all right.
    B) The woman was late for coming.
    C) The woman asked the man to wait.
    D) The man was annoyed by her late coming.
12. A) She'll type the report for him.
    B) She'll teach the man how to type.
    C) She has no idea where Diana is.
    D) She doesn't know how to use the machine.
13. A) A hotel.   B) Yes, it's very far.
    C) No, it's very near here.   D) A bank.
14. A) She is going downtown.
    B) She is going to her mother's in the town.
    C) She is going shopping with her mother.
    D) She is going to see her friend.

Section C

Directions: *This section is to test your ability to understand short conversations. There are 2 recorded conversations in it. After each conversation, there are some recorded questions. Both the conversations and questions will be spoken two times. When you hear a question, you should decide on the correct answer from the 4 choices marked A), B), C) and D) given in your test paper. Then you should mark the corresponding letter on the Answer Sheet with a single line through the center.*

Now listen to the conversations.

Conversation 1

15. A) Personnel manager.   B) Engineer.

C) Secretary to General Manager.　　D) Salesman.
16. A) General manager.　　B) Salesman.
　　C) Personnel manager.　　D) Secretary.
17. A) Two years.　　B) Half a year.
　　C) One and a half years.　　D) One year.

Conversation 2

18. A) In 1840.　　B) In 1820.　　C) In 1804.　　D) In 1890.
19. A) The British government.
　　B) The individual post offices.
　　C) Either the sender or the receiver of a letter.
　　D) The local government.

Section D

Directions: *In this section you will hear a recorded short passage. The passage is printed on the test paper, but with some words or phrases missing. The passage will be read three times. During the second reading, you are required to put the missing words or phrases on the Answer Sheet in order of the numbered blanks according to what you hear. The third reading is for you to check your writing. Now the passage will begin.*

New Zealand is famous for its agriculture. Most of the exports come from the farms. Yet only about 10% of the labor force work in agriculture, 25% of the labor force work in factories. Today the factories make clothes and shoes and __20__ other consumer goods. Most of the __21__ machinery has to be imported. Mining is not __22__, but New Zealand has plenty of power. 85% of the electricity is produced by water. There is a lot of rain during the year, and there are many __23__ and fast rivers in the mountains. Water power is cheaper than power from coal or oil. New Zealanders __24__ have the cheapest electricity in the world.

Part II　Vocabulary & Structure　　　　　（10 minutes）

Directions: *This part is to test your ability to use words and phrases correctly to construct meaningful and grammatically correct sentences. It consists of 2 sections.*

Section A

Directions: *There are 10 incomplete statements here. You are required to complete each statement by choosing the appropriate answer from the 4 choices marked A), B), C) and D). You should mark the corresponding letter on the Answer Sheet with a single line through the center.*

25. They often give the seats to _____ comes first.
　　A) whoever　　　　　　　　　　B) whom
　　C) whomever　　　　　　　　　D) whichever

26. They are interested in _____.
   A) he comes   B) he coming
   C) he's coming   D) his coming

27. The film was so _____ that they were too _____ to fall asleep.
   A) exciting; excited   B) excited; exciting
   C) exciting; exciting D) excited; excited

28. It was four years ago _____ my sister graduated from Beijing University.
   A) when   B) since
   C) that   D) since then

29. I don't mind _____ to Mary's birthday party.
   A) being not invited   B) not being invited
   C) not to be invited   D) not inviting

30. If it _____ the day after tomorrow, I will not go shopping with you.
   A) snows   B) is snowing
   C) snowed   D) will snow

31. Does he have any difficulty _____ English?
   A) to speak   B) speak
   C) speaking   D) spoke

32. He had nothing to do but _____ to see a film.
   A) go   B) to go
   C) went   D) to be going

33. The teacher always tells us never to _____ the things you want to do.
   A) give up   B) put off
   C) turn on   D) give out

34. The number of people invited _____ fifty, but a number of them _____ absent for different reasons.
   A) were; was   B) was; was
   C) was; were   D) were; were

Section B

Directions: *There are 5 incomplete statements here. You should fill in each blank with the proper form of the word given in the brackets. Write the word or words in the corresponding space on the Answer Sheet.*

35. I couldn't help (laugh) _____ when I heard the joke.
36. You are twenty now. It's time you (make) _____ up your mind.
37. (complete) _____ the hard work, the two girls felt tired out.
38. I suggest that you (go) _____ first.
39. It took me a lot of time (look) _____ up materials for my paper in the library.

Part III Reading Comprehension (35 minutes)

Directions: *This part is to test your reading ability. There are 5 tasks for you to fulfill. You should read the reading materials carefully and do the tasks as you are instructed.*

Task 1

Directions: *After reading the following passage, you will find 5 questions or unfinished statements, numbered 40 through 44. For each question or statement there are 4 choices marked A), B), C) and D). You should make the correct choice and mark the corresponding letter on the Answer Sheet with a single line through the center.*

People today are still talking about the generation gap（代沟）. Some parents complain that their children do not show them proper respect, while children complain that their parents do not understand them at all.

What has gone wrong? Why has the generation gap appeared?

One important cause is that young people want to choose their own life style. In more traditional societies, when children grow up, they are expected to live in the same area as their parents, to marry people that their parents like, and often to continue the family occupation.

Parents often expect their children to do better than they do, to find better jobs, to make more money, and to do all the things that they were unable to do. Often, however, the high wishes that parents place on their children are another cause of the generation gap.

Finally, the high speed of social changes deepens the gap. In a traditional culture, people are valued for their wisdom, but in our society today the knowledge of a lifetime may be out of use overnight（隔夜）.

40. According to the passage, children today expect their parents to _____.

  A) give them more independence B) choose a good job for them
  C) live together with them D) make more money

41. Parents often hope that their children will _____.

  A) make as much money as they do
  B) be more successful than they are
  C) choose jobs according to their own will
  D) avoid doing what their parents can't do

42. The generation gap has become wider than before because of _____.

  A) the increasing dependence of children on parents
  B) the influence of traditional culture on children
  C) the rapid changes of modern society
  D) the missing of lifelong occupation

43. In today's society, the knowledge of a lifetime _____.

  A) is still very much valued

B) becomes out of date quickly

C) is essential for continuing family occupations

D) helps the young generation to find a better job

44. A proper title for this passage would be _____.

A) Parents' Viewpoints on Generation Gap

B) Relationship between Family Members

C) Generation Gap between the Young and the Old

D) Difference between Traditional Culture and Modern Knowledge

Task 2

Directions: *This task is the same as Task 1. The 3 questions or unfinished statements are numbered 45 through 47.*

For some employers, the policy of lifelong employment is particularly important because it means that they can put money and effort into their staff (职员) training and make them loyal to the company. What they do is to select young people who have potential (潜能) and who can be trained. They then give the young people the kinds of skills that will make them suitable employees for the company. In other words, they adjust their training to their particular needs.

One recently employed graduate says that she is receiving a great deal of valuable training from the company. "This means that I will be a loyal employee," she says. "And it also means that the company will want to keep me, I am an important investment for them. So the policy is a good one because it benefits both the employer and the employee."

Recently, however, attitudes towards lifelong employment are beginning to change. Employees are slowly beginning to accept the idea that lifelong employment is not always in their best interest and that changing firms can have career advantages.

45. The purpose of lifelong employment is to _____.

A) adjust the needs of the company to its employees

B) make employees loyal to their company

C) select the best skilled young employees

D) keep the skilled staff satisfied

46. By training its employees, a company can make them _____.

A) do their work more easily

B) more interested in their work

C) willing to invest money into the company

D) possess the necessary qualities for the job

47. Talking about the training she has received, a recently employed graduate has the view that _____.

A) it is still well-received by all the staff members today

B) it is valuable to the employer and the employees

C) it is helpful for attracting young employees

D) it is both useful and interesting

Task 3

Directions: *The following is a general introduction to Hawaii. After reading it, you are required to complete the outline below it（No.48 through No.52）. You should write your answer briefly（**in no more than 3 words**）on the Answer Sheet correspondingly.*

Over a million people visit Hawaii(夏威夷)each year because of its beautiful weather and wonderful scenery(景色)! The Hawaiian Islands have very mild temperatures. For example, August, the hottest month, averages 78.4 °F, while February, the coldest month, averages 71.9 °F. In addition, the rainfall in Hawaii is not very heavy because mountains on the northern side of each island stop incoming storms; for instance, Honolulu averages only 23 inches of rain per year.

This beautiful weather helps tourists to enjoy Hawaii's wonderful natural scenery, from mountain waterfalls to fields of flowers and fruits. And Hawaii's beautiful beaches are everywhere from the lovely Mona coast beaches on the large island of Hawaii to Waikiki Beach on Oahu. Warm sunshine and beautiful beaches—it is not surprising that so many people visit Hawaii each year. Are you going to join us? Don't miss the chance!

Hawaii

Famous for its   48   and   49
Average Temperature: ranging from   50   to 78.4 °F
Annual rainfall in Honolulu: 51
Attractions for tourists: 52   and beautiful beaches

Task 4

Directions: *The following is a part of the contents of office practice. After reading it, you are required to find the items equivalent to those given in Chinese in the list below. Then you should put the corresponding letters in brackets on the Answer Sheet, numbered 53 through 57.*

A—Answer Phone   B—Burglar Alarm
C—Date-stamp   D—Electronic Display Material
E—Headed Paper   F—Office Information System
G—Shorthand   H—Annual Report
I—Registered Delivery   J—Office Automation
K—Time Sheet   L—Computer Package
M—Handbook   N—Waste Basket
O—Card-index   P—Blueprint

Example:（P）蓝图   （G）速记

53. (	) 年度报告	(	) 电子显示资料
54. (	) 计算机程序包	(	) 邮戳日期
55. (	) 办公自动化	(	) 废纸篓
56. (	) 印有信头的信纸	(	) 录音电话
57. (	) 挂号邮件	(	) 办公室信息系统

Task 5

Directions: *There is an advertisement below. After reading it, you should give brief answers to the 5 questions (No.58 through No.62) that follow. The answers (**in no more than 3 words**) should be written after the corresponding numbers on the Answer Sheet.*

APPOINTMENTS

YOUNG Italian girl, student, speaks English and French, seeks post in a school or family, giving lessons or looking after children. — Write Box L1367, The Daily, London, E.C.

YOUNG man, once an officer, tired of uninteresting office work, is willing to go to any part of the world and to do anything legal; speaks several languages; drives all makes of cars; exciting work more important than salary, — Write Box E238, The Daily, London, E.C.

MARRIED couple wanted Gardener; country house 2 miles from Oxford, good bus service; family three adults, five children; wages £9; comfortable rooms with central heating. — Write Box S754, The Daily, London, E.C.

58. What kind of work is suitable for the Italian girl?
   Teach classes or _____.

59. What foreign languages does the Italian girl know?
   She knows _____.

60. Why is the young man tired of his office work?
   Because it is _____.

61. What does the young man think of salary?
   He thinks that salary is _____ than exciting work.

62. What kind of helper is the married couple trying to find?
   They are trying to find _____.

Part IV   Translation—English into Chinese   (25 minutes)

Directions: *This part, numbered 63 to 67, is to test your ability to translate English into Chinese. Each of the four sentences (NO.63 to No.66) is followed by three choices of suggested translation marked A), B) and C). Make the best choice and write the corresponding letter on the Answer Sheet. Write your translation of the paragraph (No. 67) in the corresponding space on the Translation/Composition Sheet.*

63. In early times, most people were too busy making a living to have any hobbies.
   A) 从前，大多数人都忙于工作，忽略了业余爱好的培养。
   B) 从前，大多数人都忙于赚钱，以便能多发展自己的业余爱好。
   C) 过去，大多数人忙于谋生，没有时间从事业余爱好。

64. The newly-built bridge is twice the length of the one built last year.
   A) 这座新建的桥比去年建的那座长两倍。
   B) 这座去年建的桥是那座新建的一倍。
   C) 这座新建的桥比去年建的那座长一倍。

65. Having been given such a good chance, how could she let it get away?
   A) 当机会到来的时候，她为什么要让它溜走？
   B) 人家给了她这样一个好机会，她怎么能轻易放过？
   C) 遇到这样一个好机会，她怎会独自一个人静悄悄地离开？

66. Traffic in Shanghai is quite a serious problem. The same is true of other big cities in China.
   A) 上海的交通问题相当严重，中国的其他大城市也都是这样。
   B) 上海的交通安全还有问题，中国的其他大城市也是如此。
   C) 上海的交通问题有待改进，要向中国其他大城市学习。

67. We are glad to welcome our Chinese friends to this special business training program. Here, you will have a variety of activities and a chance to exchange ideas with each other. We hope that all of you will benefit a lot from this program. During your stay, please do not hesitate to speak to us with questions or concerns. We believe this will be an educational and enjoyable program.

_____

_____

_____

Part V Writing   (25 minutes)

Directions: *This part is to test your ability to do practical writing. You are required to write a memo according to the instructions given in Chinese below. Remember to write it on the Translation/Composition Sheet.*

说明：根据所给信息完成以下备忘录。

送达：全体员工

发自：经理

主要内容：关于奖金

发件日期：2018年6月14日

内容：公司去年取得很大业绩。每位员工下月将收到奖金$500，与下月工资一起发放。希望大家继续努力工作，为公司发展做出新的贡献。祝愿公司明年取得更大的成绩。

签名: John Blackburn
Words for reference
奖金: bonus
业绩: achievement
做贡献: make contributions

MEMO
Date: _____(1)_____
From: _____(2)_____
To: _____(3)_____
Re: _____(4)_____
Message:
Signature: _____(5)_____

2018年12月A级考试全真试题

Part I Listening Comprehension   （20 minutes）

Directions: *This part is to test your listening ability. It consists of 4 sections.*

Section A

Directions: *This section is to test your ability to understand short dialogues. There are 5 recorded dialogues in it. After each dialogue, there is a recorded question. Both the dialogues and questions will be spoken **only once**. When you hear a question, you should decide on the correct answer from the 4 choices marked A), B), C) and D) given in your test paper. Then you should mark the corresponding letter on the Answer Sheet with a single line through the center.*

Example: *You will hear:*

You will read: A) New York City.   B) An evening party.
              C) An air trip.   D) The man's job.

From the dialogue we learn that the man is to take flight to New York. Therefore, **C) An air trip** *is the correct answer. You should mark C) on the Answer Sheet with a single line through the center.*

[A] [B] [C̶] [D]

Now the test will begin.

1. A) The brand image.   B) The marketing strategy.
   C) The sales plan.   D) The company culture.
2. A) Telephone bills.   B) Online shopping.
   C) Telephone banking.   D) Credit cards.
3. A) On the third floor.   B) On the fifth floor.
   C) On the sixth floor.   D) On the eighth floor.
4. A) She doesn't like the new house.   B) She can't help the man.
   C) She will go to the concert.   D) She will be away on business.
5. A) Write a report.   B) Book a flight.
   C) Attend a meeting.   D) Meet an engineer.

Section B

Directions: *This section is to test your ability to understand short conversations. There are 2 recorded conversations in it. After each conversation, there are some recorded questions. Both the conversations and questions will be spoken **two times**. When you hear a question, you should decide* on the correct answer from the 4 choices marked A), B), C) and D) given in your test paper. Then you should mark the corresponding letter on the Answer Sheet with a single line through the center.

Now listen to the conversations.

Conversation 1

6. A) Selling sports cars. B) Working in a news agency.
   C) Doing logistics. D) Writing computer programs.
7. A) Interesting. B) Challenging.
   C) Tiring. D) Rewarding.
8. A) A fashion designer. B) A bank clerk.
   C) A TV host. D) A sales manager.

Conversation 2

9. A) His water bill. B) His gas bill.
   C) His phone bill. D) His electricity bill.
10. A) He has already paid the bill.
    B) He has moved to a new house.
    C) He has been away for two weeks.
    D) He has been abroad for the whole month.

Section C

Directions: *In this section you will hear a recorded short passage. The passage is printed in the test paper, but with some words or phrases missing. The passage will be read* **two times**. *You are required to put the missing words or phrases on the Answer Sheet in order of the numbered blanks according to what you hear.*

Now the passage will begin.

Good afternoon passengers. This is the pre-boarding announcement for flight 89B to Moscow. We are now __11__ those passengers with small children, and any passengers requiring special assistance, to begin boarding at this time. Please have your __12__ and identification ready. Regular boarding will begin in approximately ten minutes time. Thank you.

...

This is the final boarding call for passengers Eric and Fred Collins booked on flight 89B to Moscow. Please proceed to __13__ immediately. The final checks are being __14__ and the captain will order for the doors of the aircraft to close in approximately five minutes time. I __15__. This is the final boarding call for Eric and Fred Collins. Thank you.

Section D

Directions: *This section is to test your ability to comprehend short passages. You will hear a recorded passage. After that you will hear five questions. Both the passage and questions will be read*

two times. When you hear a question, you should complete the answer to it with a word or a short phrase (***in no more than 3 words***). The questions and incomplete answers are printed in your test paper. You should write your answers on the Answer Sheet correspondingly.

Now listen to the passage.

16. What is the purpose of the party?
    To _____ to Mr. Smith.
17. What new position is Mr. Smith going to take?
    The _____ of New York's branch.
18. How long has Mr. Smith been working in the present office?
    For _____.
19. What has impressed the speaker and his colleagues most?
    Mr. Smith's _____ and kindness.
20. What does the speaker say at the end of the speech?
    He hopes to _____ with Mr. Smith regularly.

Part II   Vocabulany & Structure   (10 minutes)

Directions: *This part is to test your ability to construct grammatically correct sentences. It consists of 2 sections.*

Directions: *In this section, there are 10 incomplete sentences. You are required to complete each one by deciding on the most appropriate word or words from the 4 choices marked A), B), C) and D). Then you should mark the corresponding letter on the Answer Sheet with a single line through the center.*

21. Consumers _____ complaints are handled well by a company will become loyal customers.
    A) who   B) which   C) whose   D) that

22. A good plan provides your employees with a clear direction on how _____ their skills and advance their careers.
    A) increase   B) to increase   C) increased   D) increasing

23. When _____ why they are looking for jobs at new companies, some of them say they want more challenges.
    A) asked   B) ask   C) asking   D) to ask

24. Online retailers could track not only what customers bought, _____ what else they looked at.
    A) so that   B) and thus   C) rather than   D) but also

25. If people don't like _____ by titles, you can ask them how they prefer to be addressed.
    A) are called B) being called C) be called   D) called

26. Companies understandably ask: why should I train you _____ you'll leave and work for my competitors?

A) if B) unless C) until D) although

27. After the bargaining process _____, a final agreement was signed.
    A) is completed B) had been completed
    C) has completed D) had completed

28. Only by being open-minded and willing to try new things _____ happy in Arts and Sciences.
    A) a student truly can be B) a student can truly be
    C) truly a student can be D) can a student be truly

29. No doubt, robots are having a dramatic effect _____ the labor market in this country.
    A) on B) over C) about D) with

30. If I _____ in your position, I would contact the HR department directly by email or text.
    A) am B) will be C) were D) had been

Section B

Directions: *There are 5 incomplete statements here. You should fill in each blank with the proper form of the word given in brackets. Write the word or words in the corresponding space on the Answer Sheet.*

31. I believe the city can improve its condition by (offer)_____ more options of transportation.

32. Career development (general)_____ refers to personal efforts by an employee to learn and develop new skills.

33. I am writing to convey my warm congratulations on your (appoint)_____ to the head of the board.

34. According to the report (publish)_____ yesterday, more young people are pouring into the city to look for a job.

35. The contract won't come into effect until it (sign)_____ by the legal representatives of both parties.

Part III Reading Comprehension (40 minutes)

Directions: *This part is to test your reading ability. There are 5 tasks for you to fulfill. You should read the reading materials carefully and do the tasks as you are instructed.*

Task 1

Directions: *After reading the following passage, you fill find 5 questions or unfinished statements, numbered 36 to 40. For each question or statement, there are 4 choices marked A), B), C) and D). You should make the correct choice and mark the corresponding letter on the Answer Sheet with a single line through the center.*

Clarion Response provides repairs and maintenance services to more than 125,000 homes and is part of Clarion Housing Group, the largest housing association in the UK. We complete over 1,000 repairs every day and are committed to providing a high quality service for all our residents.

Now we are looking for a number of skilled electricians（电工）to deliver a first class repairs service across a variety of our properties within London.

We can offer regular work, an attractive and steady salary, standard working hours and generous employee benefits. Working in occupied properties, you will be carrying out planned electrical testing and associated repair works.

As a qualified electrician, you will be able to understand and interpret work instructions, drawings and diagrams. You must have a good knowledge of testing and inspection along with fault finding.

Ideally, you hold a minimum of NVQ Level 3. Experience of working in social housing is desirable but not essential.

You will be given full training, protective clothing, a van（货车）to get you there as well as the specialist power tools you'll need. We also offer:
- At least 25 days paid holiday
- Company sick pay dependent on your length of service
- Generous pension scheme
- Ongoing training

If you are interested in the job, please send your resume to Clarion Response.

36. Being part of Clarion Housing Group, Clarion Response _____.
    A) sells household appliances in the neighborhood
    B) provides home repairs and maintenance services
    C) offers express delivery services in the UK
    D) develops user-friendly building materials

37. In order to offer a first class service, Clarion Response _____.
    A) is importing machines from overseas
    B) is modifying its service standard
    C) is hiring skilled electricians
    D) is training its employees

38. What is required of the candidates for the job position?
    A) They should have strong communication skills.
    B) They should be good at testing and inspection.
    C) They should be willing to work at weekends.
    D) They should have overseas working experiences.

39. Once they are hired, the candidates will _____.
    A) be offered ongoing training   B) be paid a competitive salary
    C) be asked to buy life insurance   D) be given a two-week paid holiday

40. Those who want to apply for the position should _____.

A) make an appointment with the HR Department

B) visit the company's website for details

C) take part in the company's volunteer program

D) send their resumes to the company

Task 2

Directions: *This task is the same as Task 1. The 5 questions or unfinished statements are numbered 41 to 45.*

Follow Reporting Structure: During the course of your employment, follow the reporting structure when reporting a problem or bringing up a new idea, starting with your immediate supervisor and moving up. If you violate (违反) the accepted practices, you will be marked as unprofessional. When you start a job, ask about the chain of command and commit it to memory.

Be respectful: No matter which job you hold in a company, it's important to be respectful of others. Show respect for their lifestyle choices, personal property and work styles. In any given office or situation, respectful behavior helps establish a professional reputation.

Minimize Personal Communications: With the popularity of smartphones, it can be tempting to spend a disproportionate (不成比例的) amount of time participating in personal communication during work hours. Limit your use of your smartphone to avoid the perception (看法) that you waste company time or do not get enough work done.

Follow Company Policies: In most business, company policies exist for a reason, from safety to legal protection. Get to know your company policy and make every effort to follow it. If a situation arises that requires you to break your company policy, speak to supervisor and ask for suggestions.

41. If you fail to follow the accepted practices of the reporting structure, you will _____.

   A) risk losing your present job

   B) have to take a training course

   C) be considered as unprofessional

   D) be transferred to another department

42. According to paragraph 2, to establish a professional reputation, you are advised to _____.

   A) change your work style

   B) show respect to others

   C) follow the lifestyle of other people

   D) stop using a cell phone at a workplace

43. What will other people think of you spending too much time using your smartphone at work?

   A) You are a lazy person.

   B) You are tired of your job.

   C) You do not get enough work done.

   D) You do not get along well with others.

44. What should you do if you have to break your company policy?

A) Give an excuse to your supervisor.　　B) Promise not to do it next time.
C) Consult the company's lawyer.　　D) Ask your supervisor for suggestions.

45. The passage is mainly about _____.
    A) workplace rules　　B) reporting structures
    C) professional reputations　　D) personal communications

Task 3

Directions: *Read the following passage. After reading it, you are required to complete the outline below it (No. 46 to No. 50). You should write your answers briefly (**in no more than three words**) on the Answer Sheet correspondingly.*

SEEK is a diverse group of companies that have a purpose to help people live more fulfilling and productive working lives and help organizations succeed.

SEEK was founded by brothers Paul and Andrew Bassat and Matthew Rockman, essentially as an online version of print employment advertisements. The website, www.seek.com.au, was launched in 1998.

SEEK is the global leader in the creation and operation of online employment markets. SEEK makes a positive contribution to people's lives through connecting more people to relevant job opportunities using its marketplace scale and technology to build more efficient and effective employment marketplaces.

SEEK owns leading job board in Australia, New Zealand, China, Brazil, Mexico, Africa and across South East Asia and has exposure to 4 billion people and relationships with over 800,000 hirers and 180 million candidates.

Core to delivering on SEEK's purpose is Education. SEEK's education business are focused on helping working adults achieve their career goals via online learning and providing independent education and career insights.

SEEK

Purpose:
　1) to help people live more fulfilling and productive working lives
　2) to help organizations ___46___

Founders: Paul and Andrew Bassat and Matthew Rockman

Website: www.seek.com.au launched in ___47___

Contribution: connecting ___48___ to relevant job opportunities

Job boards: having exposure to 4 billion people and relationships with over 800,000 hires and ___49___ candidates

Education businesses:
　1) to help working adults achieve their ___50___
　2) to provide independent education and career insights

Task 4

Directions: *The following is a list of terms used in postal service. After reading it, you are required to find the items equivalent to those given in Chinese in the table below. Then you should mark the corresponding letters with a single line through the center in order of the numbered blanks, 51 through 55, on the Answer Sheet.*

A—Courier Services Company
C—Insured mail
E—China Post
G—Package Service
I—Printed Matter
K—Commemorative Stamp
M—Self Pick-up Express Item
O—Letter Box
Q—Registered Mail

B—Express Service
D—International Express Service
F—Return Address
H—Postal Code
J—Money Order
L—Greeting card
N—Postal Parcel
P—Freight Collect

Examples: (A) 快递公司   (P) 到付件

51. ( ) 保价邮件		( ) 中国邮政	
52. ( ) 邮政包裹		( ) 纪念邮票	
53. ( ) 国际快递服务		( ) 邮政编码	
54. ( ) 自取卡		( ) 汇票	
55. ( ) 贺卡		( ) 回复地址	

Task 5

Directions: *Read the following passage. After reading it, you should give brief answers to the 5 questions (No.56 to No.60) that follow. The answers (**in no more than 3 words**) should be written after the corresponding numbers on the Answer Sheet.*

We are glad that you are interested in joining our Volunteer Fire Department!

Any person is eligible to apply for membership provided that he or she is at least sixteen years of age.

Previous Fire/EMS experience is NOT required to apply, but we also encourage and welcome those with previous experience to join.

There are three types of membership:

Active Member: Active membership is for those applicants who are interested in becoming a firefighter and/or EMT and participating in fire/rescue activities. All applicants over the age of eighteen are eligible for active membership. All active members in the department are required to attend fifty percent of scheduled department meetings and training each calendar year.

Students Member: Applicants who are sixteen years of age or older and are currently enrolled in high school are eligible to become student members.

Associate Member: The department also accepts applications for Associate Members. Associate Members are those who are interested in assisting the department with fundraising（筹款）functions and special events. Associate Members DO NOT participate in firefighting and rescue activities, nor will they be required to receive any Fire/EMS training.

PLEASE NOTE: All applicants are required to indicate which type of membership they are applying for.

56. What is the age requirement of applying for the membership of the Volunteer Fire Department?

    Applicants must be _____ of age or older.

57. Who are encouraged to join the Volunteer Fire Department?

    Those with _____.

58. What are active members in the department required to do?

    To attend fifty percent of scheduled department _____ each calendar year.

59. What is the main function of Associate Members?

    Assisting the department with _____ and special events.

60. What are all applicants asked to do when applying for the membership?

    To indicate which _____ they are applying for.

Part IV Translation—English into Chinese   (25 minutes)

Directions: *This part, numbered 61 through 65, is to test your ability to translate English into Chinese. After each of the sentences numbered 61 to 64, you will read three choices of suggested translation marked A), B) and C). You should choose the best translation and mark the corresponding letter on your Answer Sheet with a single line through the center. And for the paragraph numbered 65, write your translation in the corresponding space on the Translation/Composition Sheet.*

61. When an employee learns these skills and responsibilities, he becomes better equipped to take on higher-work and leadership roles in the future.

    A）当员工学会这些技能和职责时，他将来就更有能力承担更高层次的工作和领导职务。

    B）只有当员工进入领导层，担任了重要的工作时，他才能体会到责任担当的重要性。

    C）当员工有了高超的技能和强烈的责任感时，他将来就能承担重要的任务和领导工作。

62. Rents are due on the first of every month and will be considered late if not received by the 5th of the month by 5p.m.

    A）租金需一月一缴，最迟不超过每月5日下午5点，否则被视为违反合同。

    B）租金需每月第一天缴纳，如果5日下午5点前尚未收到，将被视为迟缴。

    C）租金须每年一次性缴纳，1月5日下午5点前须缴清，否则不保证续租。

63. When we are not satisfied with a purchase, the vast majority of us fail to complain to the company or business in question.

A）对所购的物品感到不满意时，我们绝大多数人都没有向有关公司或企业投诉。

B）当我们发现收到的商品没有达到标准时，我们就会向这些公司提出全额退款。

C）我们大多数人对买到的商品感到不满意时，都会要求有问题的公司或企业赔偿。

64. Humans will be affected by technology in many aspects of daily life, with some jobs potentially threatened by robots.

A）机器人已经逐步代替人类，正在从事许多繁重枯燥的工作，并且大大地提高了生产率。

B）机器人将会影响到人类生活的方方面面，并很有可能威胁到人类现在从事的许多工作。

C）人类在日常生活的许多方面将会受到技术的影响，有些工作会受到机器人的潜在威胁。

65. Drunk driving has been a problem in this country. People have long been showing concern about the car accidents caused by drunk drivers. In the first half of this year, there were more than 220,000 cases of drunk driving nationwide. Drunk driving has become increasingly serious in some cities. If you drink, do not drive. Call a taxi or use public transportation. This App can help you find a driver to drive you home.

Part V Writing   (25 minutes)

Directions: *This part is to test your ability to do practical writing. You are required to write an email according to the following information given in Chinese. Remember to do the task on the Translation/Composition Sheet.*

说明：假定你是公司采购部经理王斌。请根据以下内容给 ABC 公司销售部经理 Hoffman 先生写一封电子邮件。

内容：

1. 两周前本公司与 ABC 公司签订合同，订购床头灯 1 000 台。订单号：HP3456236；
2. 按照合同，ABC 公司在合同签订后一周内发货，10 日内到货；
3. 但是到目前为止，本公司尚未收到所定货物或任何相关消息；
4. 要求对方查询，并回信告知。

Words for reference

签订合同：sign a contract

床头灯：bedside lamp   采购部：purchasing department

2018年6月A级考试全真试题

Part I   Listening Comprehension (20 minutes)

Directions: *This part is to test your listening ability. It consists of 4 sections.*

Section A

Directions: *This section is to test your ability to understand short dialogues. There are 5 recorded dialogues in it. After each dialogue, there is a recorded question. Both the dialogues and the questions will be spoken **only once**. When you hear a question, you should decide on the correct answer from the 4 choices marked A), B), C) and D) given in your test paper. Then you should mark the corresponding letter on the Answer Sheet with a single line through the center.*

Example: *You will hear*:

    You will read: A) New York City.

                      B) An evening party.

                      C) An air trip.

                      D) The man's job.

*From the dialogue we learn that the man is to take a flight to New York. Therefore, **C) An air trip** is the correct answer. You should mark C) on the Answer Sheet with a single line through the center.*

[A] [B] [C̶] [D]

Now the test will begin

1. A) A training course.   B) A work plan.
   C) Computer skills.   D) Business management.

2. A) He attended a summer school.
   B) He worked as a volunteer.
   C) He travelled around the country.
   D) He made a survey in a local hospital.

3. A) He has been writing a paper.
   B) He has been studying all night.
   C) He has been playing games all night.
   D) He has been working on the night shift.

4. A) Very clear.   B) Too simple.
   C) Too long.   D) Very good.

5. A) He is having a meeting.　　　　　　B) He is in his office now.
　　C) He is available next week.　　　　D) He is on sick leave.

Section B

Directions: *This section is to test your ability to understand short conversations. There are 2 recorded conversations in it. After each conversation, there are some recorded questions. Both the conversations and questions will be spoken* **two times.** *When you hear a question, you should decide on the correct answer from the 4 choices marked A), B), C) and D) given in your test paper. Then you should mark the corresponding letter on the Answer Sheet with a single line through the center.*

Now listen to the conversations.

Conversation 1

6. A) He broke his leg.　　　　　　　　B) He has caught a cold.
　　C) He has a stomach ache.　　　　　D) He has a toothache.
7. A) At 2 o'clock this afternoon.　　　　B) At 3 o'clock this afternoon.
　　C) At 10 o'clock this morning.　　　D) At 10 o'clock tomorrow morning.

Conversation 2

8. A) A construction company.　　　　　B) An engineering company.
　　C) A clothing making company.　　　D) A website design company.
9. A) In the suburbs.　　　　　　　　　B) Near the airport.
　　C) In the downtown area.　　　　　　D) In a small town.
10. A) On foot.　　　　　　　　　　　　B) By bus.
　　 C) By car.　　　　　　　　　　　　D) By subway.

Section C

Directions: *In this section you will hear a recorded short passage. The passage is printed in the test paper, but with some words or phrases missing. The passage will be read* **two times.** *You are required to put the missing words or phrases on the Answer Sheet in order of the numbered blanks according to what you hear.*

Now the passage will begin.

Good Evening Everyone!

Thank you for this wonderful farewell party for me. When I'm leaving, nothing is __11__ than to learn that I am so special. I want everyone here to know that this is the place where I have become the person I am today. I have learned everything that I needed to learn, and more, from this __12__ job. I want to thank this organization, particularly my director, Mr. Anderson, for giving me the space __13__, for allowing me to make my own decisions, and then learning from my own __14__.

As I move on to a world with __15__, I can only say "Thank you, my dear friends", and I will always cherish everything this company has given to me.

Section D

Directions: *This section is to test your ability to comprehend short passages. You will hear a recorded passage. After that you will hear five questions. Both the passage and the questions will be read **two times**. When you hear a question, you should complete the answer to it with a word or a short phrase (**in no more than 3 words**). The questions and incomplete answers are printed in your test paper. You should write your answers on the Answer Sheet correspondingly.*

Now listen to the passage.

16. What ceremony is the speaker addressing?
    The _____ ceremony of the International Arts Contest.
17. What opportunity does the contest provide for young people?
    A good opportunity to _____ their creativity.
18. How many countries and regions participate in the contest now?
    _____.
19. What is the theme of the contest for this year?
    The theme is _____.
20. In what way are the photographic works submitted from overseas?
    Through the _____.

Part II Vocabulany & Structure (10 minutes)

Directions: *This part is to test your ability to construct grammatically correct sentences. It consists of 2 sections.*

Section A

Directions: *In this section, there are 10 incomplete sentences. You are required to complete each one by deciding on the most appropriate word or words from the 4 choices marked A), B), C) and D). Then you should mark the corresponding letter on the Answer Sheet with a single line through the center.*

21. He stayed patient and answered every single question, _____ obvious the answer was.
    A) no matter when   B) no matter whether
    C) no matter what   D) no matter how
22. Generally speaking, you should arrive at the airport with plenty of time _____.
    A) sparing   B) to spare   C) spare   D) spared
23. In most cases, panel interviews were _____ than those held by single interviewers.
    A) more reliable   B) reliable
    C) most reliable   D) least reliable
24. They opened a new store in our city, but not until last week _____ it.
    A) we visited   B) we would visit

  C) did we visit   D) have we visited

25. If I were you, I _____ job-hunting by visiting the websites of these companies.

  A) will start   B) had started   C) start   D) would start

26. Each worker puts in nearly 2,200 hours a year, _____ average, and contributes about $30 to GDP per hour.

  A) with   B) in   C) on   D) under

27. If you have difficulty _____ your bills, tell your utility company as soon as possible.

  A) pay   B) paid   C) to pay   D) paying

28. _____ most students own a smartphone, the school does not allow them to use it in the classroom.

  A) Even though   B) In case   C) Now that   D) If only

29. The airport is usually your first stop before _____ on your vacation or trip.

  A) leave   B) leaving   C) left   D) to leave

30. It was at yesterday's meeting _____ I misunderstood what you had said.

  A) that   B) where   C) which   D) who

Section B

Directions: *There are 5 incomplete statements here. You should fill in each blank with the proper form of the word given in brackets. Write the word or words in the corresponding space on the Answer Sheet.*

31. Training new staff should (conduct) _____ as soon as possible after they are hired.

32. Thank you very much in advance for (consider) _____ my application and I look forward to hearing from you soon.

33. I would be willing to attend an interview at any time (suit) _____ for you.

34. I do believe that you can be a good manager by (slight) _____ adapting your behaviors.

35. Today working for an established company is no longer a guarantee of lifetime (employ) _____.

Part Ⅲ   Reading Comprehension   (40 minutes)

Directions: *This part is to test your reading ability. There are 5 tasks for you to fulfill. You should read the reading materials carefully and do the tasks as you are instructed.*

Task 1

Directions: *After reading the following passage, you will find 5 questions or unfinished statements, numbered 36 to 40. For each question or statement, there are 4 choices marked A), B), C) and D). You should make the correct choice and mark the corresponding letter on the Answer Sheet with a single line through the center.*

  Now you and your family are eligible for ABSOLUTELY FREE pharmacy saving cards. Never pay full price at the pharmacy again.

Your EasyCare cards are ready to use immediately. They entitle you—and every member of your family——to savings on every FDA-approved Prescription Medication（处方药）sold. EasyCare has secured preferred rates on medications by partnering with the largest pharmacy chains in the United States. EasyCare passes those savings along to you for FREE—and we will continue to work with our pharmacy retail partners to bring more affordable healthcare to you.

With these cards you can save up to 75% off all prescriptions（an average of $150 annually per card user）, regardless of your medical history.

Every time you fill a prescription, simply bring your card to one of EasyCare's partner pharmacies and save up to 75% on more than 50,000 prescription medications. See a list of participating pharmacies in the right column on the reverse side of your card.

These cards are not insurance. There are—no monthly fees—no deductibles（自付额）—no eligibility requirements. EasyCare can be used by anyone. No one is excluded from this program for any reason.

If your friends want to request their own card, they can visit us at www.easycare.com.

36. With an EasyCare card, people can _____.
   A) buy valuable medicines at half price
   B) enjoy free medical care all over the country
   C) make an appointment with a well-known doctor
   D) pay less for all FDA-approved Prescription Medications

37. EasyCare can enjoy preferred rates on medications by _____.
   A) working closely with the local pharmacy retailers
   B) being a partner with the largest pharmacy chains
   C) passing its profits to customers
   D) obtaining approval from FDA

38. Where can you find a participating pharmacy in your EasyCare card?
   A) In its left column.
   B) At its bottom.
   C) On its back.
   D) At its top.

39. By saying "No one is excluded from this program for any reason", the writer means _____.
   A) you may be denied for no reason at all
   B) anyone can be an EasyCare card holder
   C) you don't have to pay to join the program
   D) EasyCare is designed to serve professionals

40. The main purpose of this passage is to _____.
   A) ask people to apply for EasyCare cards
   B) tell when EasyCare was approved by FDA
   C) explain why EasyCare operates efficiently
   D) inform people of the cost of EasyCare cards

Task 2

Directions: *This task is the same as Task 1. The 5 questions or unfinished statements are numbered 41 to 45.*

Working to a clear plan during an emergency will help to ensure that you are effectively prioritizing（优先选择）many demands upon your attention.

Do not allow yourself to become distracted by non-vital activities. Always bear in mind the main steps of emergency action—Assess, Make Safe, Give Emergency Aid, and Get Help.

Your approach should be brisk（轻快的）, but calm and controlled, so that you can quickly take in as much information as possible. Your priorities are to identify any risks to yourself, to the casualty（伤亡人员）, and to any other people around, then to access the resources available to you and the kind of help you may need. State that you have first-aid skills when offering your help. If there are no doctors, nurses, or more experienced people present, calmly take charge. First ask yourself these questions: Is there any continuing danger? Is anyone's life in immediate danger? Are there any other people who can help? Do I need specialist help?

The conditions that caused the accident may still present further danger. Remember that you must put your own safety first. You can't help others if you become a casualty yourself.

Often, very simple measures, such as turning off an electric switch, are enough to make the area safe. Sometimes more complicated procedures are required. Never put yourself and the casualty at further risk by attempting to do too much; be aware of your limitations.

41. In order to act effectively during an emergency, you are advised to _____.
    A) ask for help from a hospital
    B) seek an expert's advice
    C) turn to police for help
    D) follow a clear plan

42. To obtain the greatest amount of information in an emergency, you should _____.
    A) identify whether you yourself are safe or not
    B) take a quick, calm and controlled approach
    C) get to the emergency spot immediately
    D) possess some first-aid skills

43. When offering your help in an emergency, you should tell others that you _____.
    A) teach in a medical school
    B) are a medical student
    C) have first-aid skills
    D) work in a hospital

44. What does the writer ask you to keep in mind when offering help to others?
    A) Putting your own safety first.
    B) Turning off all electric devices.
    C) Giving as much help as you can.
    D) Adopting simple measures if possible.

45. The passage is mainly about _____.
    A) whom to turn to during an emergency
    B) how to act properly in an emergency
    C) where to get emergency help
    D) when to offer first-aid help

Task 3

Directions: *Read the following passage. After reading it, you are required to complete the outline below it (No. 46 to No. 50). You should write your answers briefly (**in no more than three words**) on the Answer Sheet correspondingly.*

After months of intense training and preparation, our WorldSkills competitors are ready to make their presence on the world's stage. In the coming October, Singapore will be sending 21 competitors to the 44th WorldSkills Competition, in Abu Dhabi, United Arab Emirates. This competition, also known as the Olympics of Skills, will be held from Oct. 15 to 18. Some 77 countries or regions will compete in 51 skill areas.

Of the 21 competitors from Singapore, 11 of them are NYP students. They conquered (征服) the Singapore version of the competition in July 2016, and have been training since for their nine skills areas which include robotics, IT, healthcare, graphic design and visual merchandising (推销).

NYP has traditionally done well in the global WorldSkills competition. Since first participating in 1997, we've obtained two Albert Vidal Awards (given to the competitor with the overall highest score), 11 Golds, one Silver, five Bronzes and 22 Medal (奖章) for Excellence.

NYP's WorldSkills Competitors

Participation: the 44th WorldSkills Competition (also known as the __46__)
Time: from Oct. 15 to 18
Place: __47__, United Arab Emirates
Number of countries or regions participating: about __48__
Number of skill areas competed: 51
Singapore competitors:
　　Total number: 21
　　Number of NYP students: __49__
　　Skill areas being trained: robotics, IT, healthcare, __50__ and visual merchandising, etc.

Task 4

Directions: *The following is a list of terms related to workplace safety. After reading it, you are required to find the items equivalent to those given in Chinese in the table below. Then you should mark the corresponding letters with a line through the center in order of the numbered blanks, 51 through 55, on the Answer Sheet.*

　　A—Accident Prevention　　　　　　B—Personal Protective Equipment
　　C—Health and Safety Risk　　　　　 D—Corrective Actions
　　E—Dangerous Goods　　　　　　　 F—Job Safety Analysis
　　G—Safety Strategy　　　　　　　　 H—Job Stress

I—Unsafe Acts
K—Worker's Compensation
M—First Aid
O—Medical Treatment
Q—Employee Health Survey

J—Emergency Response Plan
L—Qualified Person
N—Certified Safety Professional
P—Cancer Screening

Examples：（J）急救反应计划　　　　（G）安全策略

51.（　）工作压力		（　）非安全行为	
52.（　）事故预防		（　）癌症筛查	
53.（　）员工健康普查		（　）危险物品	
54.（　）健康与安全风险		（　）急救	
55.（　）工作安全分析		（　）个人防护设备	

Task 5

Directions：*Read the following passage. After reading it, you should give brief answers to the 5 questions (No.56 to No.60) that follow. The answers (**in no more than 3 words**) should be written after the corresponding numbers on the Answer Sheet.*

Part Time Transporter

Hertz Local Edition is seeking professionals to drive our vehicles to various locations while providing our first-class customer service. As a Transporter you will pick up and drop off customers and deliver vehicles from the Hertz Local Edition office to various locations.

The general responsibilities will include but are not limited to：

- Transport vehicles from Hertz Local Edition offices to various locations.
- Will pickup and dropoff customers as required.
- Maintain courteous and professional behavior & appearance.
- Follow all company safety policies procedures and protect company assets.

Requirements

Educational Background：
- High School Diploma, GED or Equivalent Experience

Skills：
- Valid driver's license
- Must be at least 20 years of age
- Flexibility in scheduling which may include nights, weekends and holidays

Professional Experience：
- Previous experience in a related field
- Previous customer service experience
- Satisfactory driving record

Preferred Requirements: Hertz is a Drug-Free Workplace. All employment is contingent（取决于）on successful completion of drug and background screening.

56. What job position is Hertz Local Edition offering according to the advertisement?

    Professionals to _____ to various locations.

57. What are the job responsibilities in terms of behavior & appearance?

    To maintain _____ behavior & appearance.

58. What educational background is required to apply for the job?

    Applicants should have a _____, GED or Equivalent Experience.

59. What is the age requirement for the job?

    Applicants must be at least _____ years old.

60. What professional experience is required when people apply for the job?

    Previous experience in a related field, previous customer service experience and a _____.

Part IV　Translation—English into Chinese　（25 minutes）

Directions: *This part, numbered 61 through 65, is to test your ability to translate English into Chinese. After each of the sentences numbered 61 to 64, you will read three choices of suggested translation marked A), B) and C). You should choose the best translation and mark the corresponding letter on your Answer Sheet with a single line through the center. And for the paragraph numbered 65, write your translation in the corresponding space on the Translation/Composition Sheet.*

61. The agreement will come into force on the date when it is approved by the board of the company and it will continue for five years.

    A）本协议五年期限已满，经全体董事投票后可适当延期。

    B）本协议需得到董事会批准方可生效，有效期最多五年。

    C）本协议自公司董事会批准之日起生效，并将延续五年。

62. Please note that no package should weigh more than 35 kilos, in accordance with UK Health &Safety Regulations.

    A）请注意，根据英国的安保惯例，超过 35 公斤的包裹均必须标明。

    B）请注意，根据英国健康和安全条例，包裹重量不得超过 35 公斤。

    C）请注意，根据英国运输的规定，包裹的净重都不得多于 35 公斤。

63. Various studies and surveys have shown that the heavy usage of smartphones and social media negatively affects children's mental and physical health.

    A）各种研究表明，智能手机和社交媒体的大量使用对儿童的身心健康有负面影响。

    B）所有的研究结果都证明，儿童在成长时期不应该使用智能手机或参与社交媒体活动。

    C）所有的研究和数据都说明，儿童使用智能手机和社交媒体将会影响他们智力的发展。

64. We have a special surprise for you—a seven-day online promotion of all the electronic products we manufactured last year.

A）我们有个特大的喜讯——我们将在七天之内上网展出去年生产的所有电器产品。

B）我们给你一个特别的惊喜——在线促销我们去年生产的所有电子产品,为期七天。

C）我们为你准备了礼物——你可凭去年购买我们公司产品的发票在七天内上网申领。

65. The customer's sense of satisfaction in a restaurant is, in most cases, determined by its waiters' service. If you are a waiter, your primary responsibility is to ensure that all your customers are happy and their needs are met. So you must be ready to respond to a variety of demands from your customers. However, your most important duty is to ensure that you accurately take your customer's order, so he receives the dish exactly the way he likes.

Part V Writing   (25 minutes)

Directions: *This part is to test your ability to do practical writing. You are required to write **a report** according to the following information given in Chinese. Remember to do the task on the Translation/Composition Sheet.*

说明：假定你是公司销售部经理 John Smith，根据以下情况向公司总经理写一份会议汇报。内容如下：

1. 我们于 2018 年 6 月 17 日下午 2 点在公司办公楼第一会议室召开了一次会议，出席会议人员有销售部全体员工；

2. 会议内容：

1）销售部经理在会上做了上半年公司在全国销售情况的发言；

2）会议讨论了下半年的销售部工作，大家一致认为下半年重点是开发新产品和开拓海外市场；

3）请示是否有必要召开各部门经理会议，通报以上情况。

2017年12月A级考试全真试题

Part I Listening Comprehension   （20 minutes）

Directions: *This part is to test your listening ability. It consists of 4 sections.*

Section A

Directions: *This section is to test your ability to understand short dialogues. There are 5 recorded dialogues in it. After each dialogue, there is a recorded question. Both the dialogues and questions will be spoken **only once**. When you hear a question, you should decide on the correct answer from the 4 choices marked A), B), C) and D) given in your test paper. Then you should mark the corresponding letter on the Answer Sheet with a single line through the center.*

Example: *You will hear:*

You will read: A) New York City.　　　　B) An evening party.
　　　　　　　　C) An air trip.　　　　　　D) The man's job.

*From the dialogue we learn that the man is to take a flight to New York. Therefore, **C) An air trip** is the correct answer. You should mark C) on the Answer Sheet with a single line through the center.*

[A] [B] [C̶] [D]

Now the test will begin

1. A) Applying for a visa.　　　　　　　B) Making a reservation.
   C) Checking out in the airport.　　　 D) Filling in an application form.
2. A) In an office.　　　　　　　　　　B) In a club.
   C) In a hospital.　　　　　　　　　　D) In a restaurant.
3. A) From a TV ad.　　　　　　　　　B) From a friend.
   C) From a newspaper.　　　　　　　D) From the radio.
4. A) Check the statistics.　　　　　　　B) Visit some clients.
   C) Draw some charts.　　　　　　　D) Conduct a survey.
5. A) Mr. Brown isn't fit for the job.　　 B) Mr. Brown can do the job well.
   C) She doesn't know Mr. Brown.　　 D) She can do the job herself.

Section B

Directions: *This section is to test your ability to understand short conversations. There are 2 recorded conversations in it. After each conversation, there are some recorded questions. Both the* conversations and questions will be spoken *two times*. When you hear a question, you should decide on the correct answer from the 4 choices marked A), B), C) and D) given in your test paper. Then you should mark the corresponding letter on the Answer Sheet with a single line through the center.

Now listen to the conversations.

Conversation 1

6. A) To make a complaint.　　　　　　　B) To ask about the services.
   C) To rent a meeting room.　　　　　　D) To book a hotel room.
7. A) On April 25.　　　　　　　　　　　B) On April 26.
   C) On April 27.　　　　　　　　　　　D) On April 28.
8. A) The hotel website.　　　　　　　　B) The check-in time.
   C) The way of payment.　　　　　　　D) The room rate.

Conversation 2

9. A) To confirm her flight.　　　　　　　B) To arrange for a party.
   C) To say goodbye.　　　　　　　　　D) To make an appointment.
10. A) She will take a shuttle bus.　　　　B) She will go there by subway.
    C) Linda will book a taxi for her.　　　D) Linda will drive her to the airport.

Section C

Directions: *In this section you will hear a recorded short passage. The passage is printed in the test paper, but with some words or phrases missing. The passage will be read **two times**. You are required to put the missing words or phrases on the Answer Sheet in order of the numbered blanks according to what you hear.*

Now the passage will begin.

Good evening, ladies and gentlemen! On behalf of our company, I'd like to thank you for coming to ___11___ the opening of our new branch office in Hattiesburg. This branch is the 10th office we have ___12___ in the country. I'm glad we finally opened a branch in the southeast area. Now, I would like to ___13___ to thank all the staff here for your efforts to establish the branch. In order to successfully operate the branch, we need the ___14___ of customers like you being present. We will do our best to provide you with the ___15___. Thank you very much.

Section D

Directions: *This section is to test your ability to comprehend short passages. You will hear a recorded passage. After that you will hear five questions. Both the passage and the questions will be read **two times**. When you hear a question, you should complete the answer to it with a word or a short phrase (**in no more than 3 words**). The questions and incomplete answers are printed in your test paper. You should write your answers on the Answer Sheet correspondingly.*

Now listen to the passage.

16. What does the speaker say about college life?

    It is an _____ experience in our life.

17. What will you get in college?

    You will get better _____ of yourself and of your capabilities.

18. What does the speaker say about study in college?

    It is going to be _____.

19. What entertainment events does the speaker mention?

    Plays, festivals, debates, _____ and many more fun activities.

20. What does the speaker tell the students at the end of the speech?

    They are going to make a decision of their _____.

Part II Vocabulany & Structure   (10 minutes)

Directions: *This part is to test your ability to construct grammatically correct sentences. It consists of 2 sections.*

Section A

Directions: *In this section, there are 10 incomplete sentences. You are required to complete each one by deciding on the most appropriate word or words from the 4 choices marked A), B), C) and D). Then you should mark the corresponding letter on the Answer Sheet with a single line through the center.*

21. I am interested in the training course, which _____ at Hilton Hotel in Beijing from March 8 to 12, 2018.

    A) held   B) was held   C) will hold   D) will be held

22. In his paper, John is trying to identify _____ determines the final result of the project.

    A) what   B) whether   C) when   D) how

23. I feel I am entitled to a full refund in addition to an apology for the inconvenience _____.

    A) to cause   B) causing   C) cause   D) caused

24. Recent studies show that employees who take vacation time and leave are _____ than those who do not.

    A) efficient   B) most efficient C) more efficient D) least efficient

25. Only by adopting the highest standards of integrity _____ the trust of our clients and the companies we work with.

    A) we earn   B) can we earn   C) we can earn   D) we will earn

26. If I _____ the challenges at that time, I might not have started my own business.

    A) would know   B) have known   C) had known   D) will know

27. It was not until last July _____ we started to distribute e-readers and launched an e-book store.

A) that   B) who   C) which   D) whom

28. _____ the library for hours without finding anything useful, I turned to my professor for help.

A) To search   B) Having searched

C) Have searched   D) Searching

29. _____ some degree, all managers who supervise people are involved in HR activities.

A) On   B) To   C) For   D) With

30. Our online computer repair and tech support is a convenient way to have your computer _____ without having to leave your home.

A) to fix   B) fixing   C) fix   D) fixed

Section B

Directions: There are 5 incomplete statements here. You should fill in each blank with the proper form of the word given in brackets. Write the word or words in the corresponding space on the Answer Sheet.

31. This chapter will assist you in preparing and writing memos that allow you to communicate (effective) _____ in today's workplace.

32. Thank you for your email, and your feedback on the (attach) _____ proposal would be appreciated.

33. There is no (different) _____ in the brains of those who exercise with light intensity as compared with those who do not exercise at all.

34. When they entered the area, the visitors (require) _____ to turn off their smartphones.

35. When it comes to shopping habits, he suggested (buy) _____ products that are made from recycled materials.

Part III Reading Comprehension (40 minutes)

Directions: This part is to test your reading ability. There are 5 tasks for you to fulfill. You should read the reading materials carefully and do the tasks as you are instructed.

Task 1

Directions: After reading the following passage, you will find 5 questions or unfinished statements, numbered 36 to 40. For each question or statement, there are 4 choices marked A), B), C) and D). You should make the correct choice and mark the corresponding letter on the Answer Sheet with a single line through the center.

To be a good manager, you must be careful to distinctly define the proper boundary (界限) between yourself and your staff. Here are some points to remember.

1. Be clear about the relationship. To maintain the respect of your employees while being friends with them, you must be direct about the nature of your business relationship. This means

being clear about what the goals are, how your employees are to help you reach them, and what they can expect from you. By communicating these things clearly, you avoid the risk that an employee can misinterpret your friendship and behave in an unprofessional manner.

2. Be social—to a degree. In most offices, there's usually a lot of social networking, whether it's a Friday lunch or drinks after work. It's natural for managers to be a part of that. Just remember to socialize（交际）with everyone, be careful with the alcohol, and don't be the last one at the party. Also, keep socializing at the office to a minimum. You want to ensure that you are respected as well as liked.

3. Don't fake it. Maybe you want to try to be friends with all your employees, because you think that would strengthen your team. While some management training courses stress that bosses should ask their staff about their personal lives, such as their weekend plans, their families, or their children, such efforts can backfire if the manager is viewed as not being sincere. It's okay to ask occasional questions of staff, but don't make a big production out of it. Getting to know people takes time.

36. To prevent employees from behaving unprofessionally, managers should _____.

　　A）show respect to their employees' individual needs

　　B）let them know about their future career development

　　C）set short-term and long-term goals for their business

　　D）make them clear about the nature of business relationship

37. According to Paragraph 3, managers are advised _____.

　　A）to create a friendly work environment for their staff

　　B）to keep socializing with the employees to a degree

　　C）to avoid socializing with their employees after work

　　D）to be the first person to a party or to a gathering

38. Some managers believe they can strengthen their team by _____.

　　A）making friends with all their employees

　　B）attending a management training course

　　C）providing a free Friday lunch to the staff

　　D）encouraging their staff to exercise regularly

39. The word "backfire" in the last paragraph most probably means "_____".

　　A）strengthen the relationship

　　B）start a fire in the backyard

　　C）produce an undesired result

　　D）improve management skills

40. The passage is mainly about the importance of _____.

　　A）management training courses for employers

　　B）proper relationship between managers and staff

　　C）setting business goals for both managers and staff

　　D）being a part of social networking for a good manager

Task 2

Directions: *This task is the same as Task 1. The 5 questions or unfinished statements are numbered 41 to 45.*

Before renting the equipment from U-Haul, be clear about the following information.

1. I understand that this equipment must be returned to the same U-Haul location where it was rented. I understand that the minimum rental charge for equipment returned to a different location is twice the amount of the current rate.

2. I understand that the equipment rented is water resistant and not water proof.

3. I acknowledge that I have received the appropriate User Instructions and acknowledge my responsibility to fully read and understand these User concerns or requirement that I have about my rental.

4. I understand that I can also contact U-Haul Customer Service at uhaul.com/contact/email.aspx.

5. I agree that distracted driving is dangerous and that driving while distracted is likely to lead to an accident/crash causing serious injury or death. I agree not to use a hand-held mobile phone (other than for an emergency call). My agreement not to do so is material to U-Haul decision to enter this Agreement. My failure to comply is material breach of this Agreement.

6. I acknowledge that I have received and agreed to the terms and conditions of this Rental Contract and Rental Contract Addendum (附录).

41. Where are you asked to return the equipment rented from U-Haul?

    A) To a free parking lot.
    B) To any U-Haul location.
    C) To where it was rented from.
    D) To the nearest U-Haul location.

42. According to Item 3, it is the renter's responsibility _____.

    A) to fully read and understand the User Instructions
    B) to buy insurance before renting the equipment
    C) to confirm the receipt of the User Instructions
    D) to repair the equipment when necessary

43. The phrase "distracted driving" in Item 5 means _____.

    A) changing lanes without signaling
    B) driving without wearing a seatbelt
    C) running a red light by over-speeding
    D) carrying out other activities while driving

44. While driving, you are allowed to use your hand-held mobile phone to _____.

    A) chat with your assistant
    B) make an emergency call
    C) look for a U-Haul location
    D) receive and send messages

45. This passage is most probably taken from _____.

A) an announcement   B) an advertisement
C) an agreement   D) a notice

Task 3

Directions: *The following is an ad asking people to provide food to hungry people. After reading it, you are required to complete the outline below it (No. 46 to No. 50). You should write your answers briefly (**in no more than three words**) on the Answer Sheet correspondingly.*

Could you look into the eyes of children and tell them they will have nothing to eat tonight? We can't, either.

That's why we have set up the Mississippi Food Network (MFN), a non-profit organization. As a member of Feeding America, we make sure that children, families and seniors in our service area have food. MFN has been feeding Mississippians since 1984.

At MFN, we partner with 430 food pantries (食品供应站), emergency shelters, and soup kitchens in our community to provide the food needed for our hungry neighbors. Because of friends like you, we distribute more than 18 million pounds of food annually to help feed hungry people in our service area.

What a great way to help neighbors in need and make your blessing really count!

You can help make a difference in the fight against hunger. Send your gift today, every $10 you donate helps provide food for 70 meals.

If you have any questions, please use our contact form, call 601-973-7085, or email cguess@msfoodnet.org.

Mississippi Food Network

Founded: in the year of ___46___
Purpose: to provide food to children, ___47___ in the service area
Partners: food pantries, ___48___ and soup kitchens
Food distributed: more than ___49___ pounds annually
Call for donation: providing food for ___50___ for every $10 received
Contact: call 601-973-7085, or email cguess @ msfoodnet.org

Task 4

Directions: *The following is a list of terms related to environmental protection. After reading it, you are required to find the items equivalent to those given in Chinese in the table below. Then you should mark the corresponding letters with a single letter through the center in order of the numbered blanks, 51 through 55, on the Answer Sheet.*

A—Air Pollution   B—Air Quality
C—Alternative Energy Sources   D—Carbon Emissions

E—Carbon Footprint   F—Climate Change
G—Electric Vehicle   H—Energy Efficiency
I—Fossil Fuels   J—Greenhouse Effect
K—Renewable Energy   L—Sustainable Sevelopment
M—Zero Emissions   N—Environmental Impact
O—Global Warming   P—Environmental Compensation Fee
Q—Solid Waste Management

Examples: （J）温室效应   （P）环境补偿费

51. (　　) 可持续发展   (　　) 气候变化
52. (　　) 替代能源   (　　) 全球（气候）变暖
53. (　　) 碳足迹   (　　) 固体废弃物管理
54. (　　) 零排放   (　　) 可再生能源
55. (　　) 能源效率   (　　) 矿物燃料

Task 5

Directions: *Read the following passage. After reading it, you should give brief answers to the 5 questions (No.56 to No.60) that follow. The answers (**in no more than 3 words**) should be written after the corresponding numbers on the Answer Sheet.*

Dear Mr. Hughes,

It is with great pleasure that I write to invite you to the opening of our new production plant in Barnsley Avenue on Friday, January 12, 2018. You have been our regular and loyal customer over the last seven years, so it will be an honor for us if you could attend the opening ceremony of this new plant.

We have been operating as one of the best flour mills（面粉厂）in the country over the past ten years, which would not have been possible without the help and support of our loyal customers. The aim of our company is to remain at the top for years to come, and your contributions towards our success are highly appreciated.

The ribbon（彩带）cutting ceremony is scheduled to take place at 11 p.m. Please make arrangements to arrive on time so that our organizers can find you a comfortable seat. We will also be acknowledging our loyal clients by name, and would like you to be present when we do so. Kindly confirm your availability for the event by January 5, so that we can make the necessary arrangements. We are looking forward to seeing you.

Yours sincerely,
John Smith

56. What event is Mr. Hughes invited to attend?
    The opening ceremony of a＿＿＿＿＿＿＿＿＿＿＿＿＿＿＿＿＿＿＿＿＿＿＿＿＿＿.
57. Why is Mr. Hughes invited by the company?

Because he has been their _____ customer.

58. What is the aim the company wants to achieve?
To remain _____ for years to come.

59. Why is Mr. Hughes asked to arrive on time for the ceremony?
For the organizers to find him _____.

60. When should Mr. Hughes confirm his availability?
By _____.

Part IV Translation—English into Chinese   (25 minutes)

Directions: *This part, numbered 61 through 65, is to test your ability to translate English into Chinese. After each of the sentences numbered 61 to 64, you will read three choices of suggested translation marked A) , B) and C). You should choose the best translation and mark the corresponding letter on your Answer Sheet with a single line through the center. And for the paragraph numbered 65, write your translation in the corresponding space on the Translation/Composition Sheet.*

61. The key to regaining a customer's confidence is to respond promptly to a customer's complaint, whether the problem has been solved or not.

　　A) 及时答复客户的投诉，认真解决他们的问题，这样才可以提高客户信心。

　　B) 重获客户信心的关键是及时回应客户的投诉，不论问题是否已得到解决。

　　C) 取得客户信赖的途径是经常听取他们的意见，不断提高自己的服务质量。

62. If Party A decides to cancel this agreement, he may do so as long as Party B is given 30 days' written notice.

　　A) 如果甲方不同意本协议条款内容，可在 30 天后与乙方一起商定修改条款。

　　B) 如果甲方欲修改本协议，必须在 30 天内将修改内容告知乙方，方可修改。

　　C) 如果甲方决定取消本协议，只要提前 30 天书面通知乙方，就可取消协议。

63. It is our company culture to make sure that employees know how all the jobs in the company work, not just their own.

　　A) 我们的公司文化是让每个员工做好自己所从事的工作，使公司所有的工作都可以有序运行。

　　B) 我们的公司文化是确保员工不仅了解自己的工作，还要了解公司所有的工作是如何运作的。

　　C) 我们的公司文化提倡每个员工都要做好自己的本职工作，同时还要熟悉公司是如何经营的。

64. Once you enroll in the program, we offer you support for six months, during which you should have completed all courses.

　　A) 你只要注册成功，我们这个项目就会给你提供免费支持，但你必须在 6 个月内通过所有课程的考试。

　　B) 你一旦报名参加这个项目，我们就会为你提供 6 个月的支持，在这段时间内你应该完成所有课程。

C）你只要学完了所有的必修课程，并且在6个月内通过所有课程考试，我们就会向你颁发结业证书。

65. Working from home has many advantages, such as flexbility and the ability to take care of your family. However, there are also some disadvantages. For example, if you have not worked in a traditional office, it is difficult for you to understand what office culture is. It is the sense of community（归属感）you get when you are in the office. There are common areas where you can meet your colleagues and talk to them.

Part Ⅴ   Writing   (25 minutes)

Directions: *This part is to test your ability to do practical writing. You are required to write a **Letter of Complaint** according to the following information given in Chinese. Remember to do the task on the Translation/Composition Sheet.*

说明：以顾客王小林的名义给 ABC 商店经理 Johnson 先生写封投诉信，主要内容如下：

1. 你两周前购买了一台洗衣机用了三天后洗衣机出现故障（内容自拟）；
2. 你曾打电话到商店的客户服务中心，他们答应上门维修，但至今未派人来；
3. 要求对方尽快派人上门修理或更换一台新的洗衣机，否则要求全额退款（full refund）；
4. 结束语（自拟）。

2017年6月A级考试全真试题

Part I Listening Comprehension   (20 minutes)

Directions: *This part is to test your Listening ability. It consists of 4 sections.*

Section A

Directions: *This section is to test your ability to understand short dialogues. There are 5 recorded dialogues in it. After each dialogue, there is a recorded question. Both the dialogues and questions will be spoken only once. When you hear a question, you should decide on the correct answer from the 4 choices marked A), B), C) and D) given in your test paper. Then you should mark the corresponding letter on the Answer Sheet with a single line through the center.*

Example: You will hear:

You will read: A) New York City.   B) An evening party.
                C) An air trip.   D) The man's job.

*From the dialogues we learn that the man is to take flight to New York. Therefore, **C**) **An air trip** is the correct answer. You should mark C) on the Answer Sheet with a single line through the center.*

[A] [B] [C̶] [D]

Now the test will begin.

1. A) There is no paper.   B) The man can use the printer.
   C) The printer doesn't work.   D) The man has to pay first.
2. A) He has got a new job.   B) He has got a pay rise.
   C) He has been promoted.   D) He has bought an apartment.
3. A) Sell a car.   B) Rent a car.
   C) Repair a car.   D) Buy a used car.
4. A) He doesn't like the color.   B) He doesn't like the style.
   C) It is too small.   D) It is of poor quality.
5. A) The chief engineer.   B) The receptionist.
   C) The office secretary.   D) The sales manager.

Section B

Directions: *This section is to test your ability to understand short conversations. There are 2 recorded conversations in it. After each conversation, there are some recorded questions. Both the conversations and questions will be spoken **two times**. When you hear a question, you should decide* *on the correct answer from the 4 choices marked A), B), C) and D) given in your test paper. Then you should mark the corresponding letter on the Answer Sheet with a single line through the center.*

Now listen to the conversations.

Conversation 1

6. A) The goods are out of stock.　　　　B) She is moving to another city.
　　C) The sales season is coming soon.　　D) She is afraid the price will go down.
7. A) By train.　　B) By air.　　C) By ship.　　D) By truck.
8. A) In three weeks.　　B) In two weeks.　　C) Next week.　　D) Next month.

Conversation 2

9. A) HR manager assistant.　　　　B) Sales manager.
　　C) Office secretary.　　　　　　D) Software engineer.
10. A) 3 weeks.　　B) 6 weeks.　　C) 3 months.　　D) 6 months.

Section C

Directions: *In this section you will hear a recorded short passage. The passage is printed in the test paper, but with some words or phrases missing. The passage will be read **two times**. You are required to put the missing words or phrases on the Answer Sheet in order of the numbered blanks according to what you hear.*

Now the passage will begin.

I think we'll begin now. First I'd like to welcome you all and thank you for your coming, especially at such short notice. I know you are all very busy and it's difficult to take time away from your __11__ for meetings.

As you can see on the agenda, today we will focus on the upcoming __12__. First, we'll discuss the groups that will be coming in from Germany. After that, we'll discuss the North American Tours, __13__ by the Asian tours. If time __14__, we will also discuss the Australian tours which are booked for early September. Finally, I'm going to request some feedback from all of you __15__ last year's tours and where you think we can improve.

Section D

Directions: *This section is to test your ability to comprehend short passages. You will hear a recorded passage. After that you will hear five questions. Both the passage and the questions will be read **two times**. When you hear a question, you should complete the answer to it with a word or a short phrase (**in no more than 3 words**). The questions and incomplete answers are printed in your test paper. You should write your answers on the Answer Sheet correspondingly.*

Now listen to the passage.

16. What product does the company produce?

17. When was the company set up?
    _____ ago.
18. Where are their products sold?
    Both _____ and abroad.
19. According to the speaker, why do their products have a good reputation?
    Because of the high quality and good _____ they provide.
20. What does the speaker promise to give for a large order?
    A _____ .

Part II Vocabulary & Structure (10 minutes)

Directions: *This part is to test your ability to construct grammatically correct sentences. It consists of 2 sections.*

Directions: *In this section, there are 10 incomplete sentences. You are required to complete each one by deciding on the most appropriate word or words from the 4 choices marked A), B), C) and D). Then you should mark the corresponding letter on the Answer Sheet with a single line through the center.*

21. 62% of the people surveyed said they always avoided _____ their smartphones during meals.

    A) use   B) using   C) to use   D) used

22. The HR department is a critical part of employee well-being in any business, no matter _____ small it is.

    A) how   B) what   C) where   D) which

23. According to the regulation, inspections _____ to ensure that the systems are in good condition.

    A) demanded   B) have demanded   C) be demanded   D) are demanded

24. Before you think about asking for a promotion, make sure that either a position opening exists _____ a new position is needed to be created.

    A) and   B) nor   C) or   D) but

25. The traffic was making so much noise that I couldn't hear what he _____ .

    A) is saying   B) was saying   C) has said   D) will say

26. Our company culture is _____ makes us successful in creating a friendly and exciting environment.

    A) where   B) how   C) what   D) why

27. Most people were greatly shocked by the news _____ the IT company had gone bankrupt.

    A) what   B) how   C) why   D) that

28. I would probably try to find a better job if I _____ in your position.

    A) am   B) were   C) have been   D) be

29. If you are _____ busy to attend the meeting, you can send your assistant to take your place.

　　A) very　　　　　B) so　　　　　C) too　　　　　D) more

30. I had to wait for another two months to be able to have the car _____.

　　A) fixing　　　　B) fix　　　　　C) to fix　　　　D) fixed

Section B

Directions: *There are 5 incomplete statements here. You should fill in each blank with the proper form of the word given in brackets. Write the word or words in the corresponding space on the Answer Sheet.*

31. Our team will meet with each person to learn about his or her (person)_____ and vocational goals.

32. These questions enable the interviewer (know)_____ how you previously reacted or behaved in certain types of situations.

33. Before (ask)_____ for a promotion, try to find out how the decision makers in your company feel about you.

34. They are under the (impress)_____ that their communication ability is the most important factor in whether or not they will be hired.

35. We believe that e-learning can be (effective)_____ than traditional instructions in the future.

Part III　Reading Comprehension　　　　（40 minutes）

Directions: *This part is to test your reading ability. There are 5 tasks for you to fulfill. You should read the reading materials carefully and do the tasks as you are instructed.*

Task 1

Directions: *After reading the following passage, you fill find 5 questions or unfinished statements, numbered 36 to 40. For each question or statement, there are 4 choices marked A), B), C) and D). You should make the correct choice and mark the corresponding letter on the Answer Sheet with a single line through the center.*

Dear Sir/Madam,

　　I am pleased to write a letter of recommendation on behalf of *Sand River* and its CEO, Mrs. Jane King. I am very familiar with the company. My next book deals with it in detail, which is to be published in autumn of 2018. I am also familiar with European consumer. As a Dutch citizen, I have lived in Europe for 46 years and studied European consumer behavior for decades.

　　I believe that *Sand River* offers something unique to the European market. It has established long-term supply relations with herdsman (牧民) families and owns advanced German machinery. Thus it combines natural resources with modern manufacturing techniques. But equally important,

Sand River works with modern fashion designers to create truly contemporary and appealing designs. The result is a newly-established cashmere（羊绒）brand that appeals to a target group of high-income women.

I met Mrs. king the first time in 2013. Since then, we have met several times and talked about *Sand River*'s philosophy, strategy, and appeal to both Chinese and international consumers. I was struck by her deep knowledge about knitting（针织）technology, her enthusiasm for the brand, and her deep understanding of the cashmere shopper. I regard her as a "woman of her word."

To summaries, I believe *Sand River* products deserve a place in luxurious European department stores and Mrs. king is a reliable partner.

If you have any questions, please do not hesitate to contact me.

Sincerely,
Joan Smith

36. Joan Smith wrote the recommendation letter on behalf of _____.
   A) a Dutch citizen
   B) herdsman families
   C) the European consumer
   D) *Sand River* and its CEO

37. From the letter we can learn that *Sand River* _____.
   A) has long-term links with herdsman
   B) employs many herdsman workers
   C) manufactures advanced machines
   D) sells hand-made products

38. The target consumers of the newly-established cashmere brand are _____.
   A) college students
   B) blue-color workers
   C) high-income women
   D) average herdsman families

39. By saying "a woman of her word"（Para. 3）, the writer means that Mrs. King _____.
   A) always keeps her promise
   B) is a good public speaker
   C) knows customers well
   D) is well educated

40. As far as the European market is concerned, the writer thinks that *Sand River* products _____.
   A) are fit for supermarket in big cities
   B) are likely to enjoy a big market share
   C) will appeal to different kinds of customers
   D) deserve a place in luxurious department stores

Task 2

Directions: *This task is the same as Task 1. The 5 questions or unfinished statements are numbered 41 to 45.*

The challenge of writing a powerful cover letter（附信）can lead job candidates to search endlessly for advice, but be careful. While you likely will find some valuable advice, you may come across a few tips that could mislead you.

"You need a lengthy cover letter." This probably is one of the "bad cover letter tips." Think about it: hiring managers have piles of resumes and cover letters to review. If yours is longer than the rest, it might not get read at all. Aim to get all of your points across in three brief paragraphs: a clear introduction that lets employers know which job you are applying for and why you are interested in the position; a paragraph that includes a few specific examples of how you have excelled (擅长) in past roles that are relevant to the open position; and a concluding paragraph that tells employers how you will benefit company and requests a future meeting.

"Your cover letter is less important than your resume." Some hiring managers shove (随手扔) cover letter to the side, but most do not. Because you never know what type of hiring manager you are dealing with, it is best to submit a nice cover letter. While some employers place less emphasis on cover letters, other decide who to interview based on them. Remember that the point of cover letter is to tell employers something that makes them want to meet you.

41. Why should job candidates be careful when searching for advice to write a cover letter?

    A) Some tips are not practical.
    B) Some tips could be misleading.
    C) It is impossible to get useful tips.
    D) It is difficult to find valuable tips.

42. Why shouldn't you write a lengthy cover letter?

    A) Hiring managers may not read it at all.
    B) Well-written cover letters may be read first.
    C) It is difficult to write a good long cover letter.
    D) You are unable to express your points clearly.

43. According to the passage, the introductory paragraph of a cover letter should include _____.

    A) you request for a job interview
    B) the position you are interested in
    C) some examples of your achievements
    D) your education background and degree

44. Which of the following should be included in the concluding paragraph of a cover letter?

    A) Your expected salary.
    B) Your hobbies and interests.
    C) Your request for a meeting.
    D) Your professional background.

45. According to the writer, the purpose of a cover letter is to _____.

    A) urge the employer to read your resume
    B) please your potential employer
    C) get the employer to meet you
    D) show off your achievements

Task 3

Directions: *Read the following passage. After reading it, you are required to complete the outline below it (No. 46 to No. 50). You should write your answers briefly (**in no more than three***

words) *on the Answer Sheet correspondingly.*

Parking Ticket（罚单）Payment System

Parking tickets issued by the City of Toronto can be paid online. All you have to do is:

Enter your Parking Ticket Infraction（违规）number（Top right of the ticket）.

Enter your credit card number（VISA, MasterCard or American Express）and expiry date.

Print a confirmation for your records.

If you have difficulties paying your ticket online, you may call our customer service staff at 416-397-8247, Monday to Friday, between the hours of 8:30 a.m. and 4:30 p.m. for assistance, or contact us by email.

To protect the secured exchange of information between you and this secure site, you may be asked to download and install the latest version of your browser（浏览器）.

Please note that your payment session will end automatically if your computer is left idle（空闲）for more than 2 minutes. We suggest that you have your parking ticket and credit ready before you begin the payment session.

Parking Ticket Payment System

Steps to pay:

1) enter your Parking Ticket Infraction number

2) enter your ___46___

3) print a ___47___ of your records

Customer service:

1) phone number: ___48___

2) service time: ___49___, from 8:30 a.m. to 4:30 p.m.

Information exchange security: download and install the ___50___ of your browser

---

Task 4

Directions: *The following is a list of terms often used in hospitals. After reading it, you are required to find the items equivalent to those given in Chinese in the table below. Then you should mark the corresponding letters with a single letter through the center in order of the numbered blanks, 51 through 55, on the Answer Sheet.*

A—Plastic Surgery   B—Medical Student

C—Registered Nurse   D—Emergency Department

E—Intensive Care Unit（ICU） F—Operating Room

G—Physical Examination   H—Red Blood Cells

I—Blood Pressure   J—White Blood Cells

K—Outpatient Treatment   L—Yellow Fever

M—Skin Test N—Over-the-counter Drug
O—Occupational Disease P—Food Poisoning
Q—Brain Death

Example：（C）注册护士　　　　　　　　　　（L）黄热病

51. ( ) 脑死亡		( ) 急诊部	
52. ( ) 食物中毒		( ) 皮试	
53. ( ) 手术室		( ) 职业病	
54. ( ) 重症监护室		( ) 体检	
55. ( ) 门诊治疗		( ) 血压	

Task 5

Directions: *Read the following passage. After reading it, you should give brief answers to the 5 questions (No.56 to No.60) that follow. The answers (**in no more than 3 words**) should be written after the corresponding numbers on the Answer Sheet.*

Steps in Starting a Used Baby Equipment Business

1. Just like any other business, you have to know the market first. This will help choose a suitable location.

2. Decide on what kind of second-hand baby equipment business you want to specialize in. This will help you advertise your store more effectively.

3. Gather the baby equipment that is still useful from your old collections. You can add to these collections by gathering the used baby equipment from other households with fair pricing. You can also collect items that are not so good, just fix it and sell.

4. Also consider the safety of the babies using the equipment, though you intent to make profit from this business.

5. Finally, your marketing strategy is also important. You can put your store online. Advertise online or you can plan promotional activities involving parents and babies such as contest that will earn them certain baby equipment at the end if they turn out to be the winner.

In addition to these steps, you can think of many other steps to this business dependent on the kind of used baby equipment business you plan to start.

56. What is the first thing you should know in order to start a used baby equipment business?

The _____.

57. Why should you decide on the kind of business you want to specialize in?

To help _____ more effectively.

58. How can you increase your collections of the used baby equipment?

By gathering it from _____ with fair pricing.

59. What should you also pay attention to when starting a used baby equipment business?

The _____ of the babies using the equipment.

60. What examples are mentioned as the marketing strategy in the passage?

Putting your store online, advertising online and planning _____ activities.

Part IV　Translation—English into Chinese　　　（25 minutes）

Directions: *This part, numbered 61 through 65, is to test your ability to translate English into Chinese. After each of the sentences numbered 61 to 64, you will read three choices of suggested translation marked A), B) and C). You should choose the best translation and mark the corresponding letter on your Answer Sheet with a single line through the center. And for the paragraph numbered 65, write your translation in the corresponding space on the Translation/Composition Sheet.*

61. Please write to us or just see the customers service manager if you are not satisfied with any aspect of the service we offer.

A）如果你对我们服务的任何方面不满意，请函告我们或直接找客服经理。

B）如果你不满意我们提供的服务，你可以直接到我们店里找客服经理。

C）如果可能，我们应常给顾客写信，征求他们对本店提供服务的意见。

62. By asking appropriate questions, you are showing the employer that you're interested in being part of their company.

A）你向雇主提出一些恰当的问题，这表明你有兴趣成为他们公司的一员。

B）你向雇主提出的问题与其公司有关，你才有可能获得你所渴望的工作。

C）如果你想要成为他们公司的一分子，你可以向雇主提出一些相关的问题。

63. Due to increased costs for materials used in our manufacturing process, we have to increase the wholesale price of our products.

A）产品价格的高低取决于我们在研发和生产制造过程中所需投入的人力和成本。

B）我们提高了产品的价格，这是因为在制造过程中我们投入了大量的人力和财力。

C）由于我们在生产过程中的材料成本上涨，为此我们不得不提高产品的批发价。

64. When returning products to us, you must take care to see that they are received by us and not damaged in transit.

A）退还货物的时候，你要保证收件人的地址准确无误，并保证货物完好无损。

B）将产品退还给我们时，你必须确保货物已被我们收到，且未在传输中受损。

C）寄送货品时你必须正确地填写收件人的姓名和地址，以及该地的邮政编码。

65. Welcome to our hotel. We wish you a pleasant stay. It is very important to us that your stay be comfortable and enjoyable. We take great pride in providing our guests with the highest levels of professional service. This Guest Information Guide tells you about the services and amenities（娱乐设施）we offer at the hotel. If you should have any more questions, please give us a call at the Front Desk.

Part V Writing   (25 minutes)

Directions: *This part is to test your ability to do practical writing. You are required to write a Notice according to the following information given in Chinese. Remember to do the task on the Translation/Composition Sheet.*

说明：根据下列内容，以小区志愿者团队的名义拟一份通知。

内容：
1. 根据气象预报，台风将在两天后影响本市，并有暴风雨。
2. 请注意安全，尽量减少外出，并采取预防措施。
3. 如果需要帮助，请联系我们。
4. 服务中心备有沙袋，一楼居民可免费领取。
5. 联系电话：656××793。

Notice

Words for reference:

台风 typhoon

沙袋 sandbag

Model Test One (Level A)

Part I Listening Comprehension   (20 minutes)

Directions: *This part is to test your listening ability. It consists of 4 sections.*

Section A

Directions: *This section is to test your ability to understand short dialogues. There are 5 recorded dialogues in it. After each dialogue, there is a recorded question. Both the dialogues and questions will be spoken **only once**. When you hear a question, you should decide on the correct answer from the 4 choices marked A), B), C) and D) given in your test paper. Then you should mark the corresponding letter on the Answer Sheet with a single line through the center.*

Example: *You will hear*:

    You will read: A) New York City.

                      B) An evening party.

                      C) An air trip.

                      D) The man's job.

From the dialogue we learn that the man is to take a flight to New York. Therefore, **C) An air trip** *is the correct answer. You should mark C) on the Answer Sheet with a single line through the center.*

Now the test will begin.

1. A) Teacher and student.   B) Employer and employee.
   C) Waiter and customer.   D) Doctor and patient.
2. A) In a travel agency.   B) In a bank.
   C) In a hotel.   D) In a shop.
3. A) A sense of achievement.   B) High risks.
   C) Self-employment.   D) Young people.
4. A) The company culture.   B) The fierce competition.
   C) The international business.   D) The strong leadership.
5. A) A university teacher.   B) An assistant.
   C) An accountant.   D) A lawyer.

Section B

Directions: *This section is to test your ability to understand short conversations. There are 2* recorded conversations in it. After each conversation, there are some recorded questions. Both the conversations and the questions will be spoken **two times**. When you hear a question, you should decide on the correct answer from the 4 choices marked A), B), C) and D) given in your test paper. Then you should mark the corresponding letter on the Answer Sheet with a single line through the center.

Now listen to the conversations.

Conversation 1

6. A) A wine seller. B) A big client.
   C) A restaurant owner D) A magazine editor.
7. A) A restaurant in France. B) A restaurant called Gourment.
   C) La Place. D) Les Parisians.
8. A) At 4 p.m. today. B) At 7 p.m. today.
   C) At 4 p.m. tomorrow. D) At 7 p.m. tomorrow.

Conversation 2

9. A) He is wise and honest. B) He is kind and humorous.
   C) He is helpful and careful. D) He is diligent and loyal.
10. A) Nine percent. B) Ten percent.
    C) Twelve percent. D) Twenty percent.

Section C

Directions: *In this section you will hear a recorded short passage. The passage is printed in the test paper, but with some words or phrases missing. The passage will be read* ***two times****. You are required to put the missing words or phrases on the Answer sheet in order of the numbered blanks according to what you hear.*

Now the passage will begin.

Ladies and Gentlemen,

The main difference between Chinese and Western ___11___ is that unlike the West, where everyone has his own plate of food, in China the dishes are placed on the table and everybody ___12___. Chinese are very proud of their culture of food and will ___13___ to give you a taste of many different types of cuisine. Among friends, they will just order enough for the people there. If they are taking somebody out for dinner, they will usually order ___14___ than the number of guests. If it is a business dinner or a very formal ___15___, there is likely to be a huge amount of food that will be impossible to finish.

Section D

Directions: *This section is to test your ability to comprehend short passages. You will hear a recorded passage. After that you'll hear five questions. Both the passage and the questions will be read two times. When you hear a question, you should complete the answer to it with a word or a short* phrase (***in no more than 3 words***). The questions and incomplete answers are printed in your test paper. You should write your answers on the Answer Sheet correspondingly.

Now listen to the passage.

16. What do hobbies have according to the speaker?
    Undoubtedly hobbies have _____.

17. What do hobbies offer after a day's work or study?
    Hobbies offer _____ and help people relax.

18. Who may be more energetic?
    Someone who _____ during weekends.

19. What are available for those sharing the same hobbies?
    A lot of clubs and _____.

20. Why does a football fan always join a club?
    To _____ other fans.

Part II Vocabulary & Structure   (10 minutes)

Directions: *This part is to test your ability to construct grammatically correct sentences. It consists of 2 sections.*

Section A

Directions: *In this section there are 10 incomplete sentences. You are required to complete each one by deciding on the most appropriate word or words from the 4 choices marked A), B), C) and D). Then you should mark the corresponding letter on the Answer Sheet with a single line through the center.*

21. This ATM has been out of service for a few days. It should _____ last week.
    A) fix   B) be fixed   C) have fixed   D) have been fixed

22. We will inform you of the result _____ the program is approved by the board.
    A) in order that   B) as if   C) even though   D) as soon as

23. Anyone _____ works in the retail business need to be good at calculating and communicating.
    A) which   B) whom   C) who   D) what

24. _____ that Bob had got promoted, his friends came to congratulate him.
    A) Heard   B) Having heard   C) Hear   D) To hear

25. It wasn't such a good job _____ she had read about in the advertisement.
    A) like   B) which   C) as   D) what

26. They regard _____ as their duty to provide the best service for their customers.
    A) this   B) what   C) it   D) that

27. They will not start the project until the board chairman _____ back from South Africa.
    A) will come   B) is coming   C) came   D) comes

28. The company _____ its sales by an average of 10% per year since its establishment in 1993.
    A) increases   B) increased
    C) is increasing   D) has increased

29. Only when we had finished all the work _____ that it was too late to take a bus home.
    A) did we realize   B) will we realize   C) we did realize   D) we will realize

30. The sales manager had his secretary _____ a press conference for their new products.
    A) arrange   B) to arrange   C) have arranged   D) arranged

Section B

Directions: *There are 5 incomplete statements here. You should fill in each blank with the proper form of the word given in brackets. Write the word or words in the corresponding space on the Answer Sheet.*

31. Today, as natural resources become scarcer and manufacturing costs rise, recycling is (important)_____ than ever.

32. It is (reason)_____ for parents to pay for their children's education.

33. Before the flight takes off, all passengers (ask)_____ to fasten their seat belts.

34. After the flood, life was (extreme)_____ difficult for the farmers in this area.

35. The company has taken several steps to speed up the (move)_____ of goods from the seller to the customer.

Part III Reading Comprehension   (40 minutes)

Directions: *This part is to test your reading ability. There are 5 tasks for you to fulfill. You should read the reading materials carefully and do the tasks as you are instructed.*

Task 1

Directions: *After reading the following passage, you will find 5 questions or unfinished statements, numbered 36 to 40. For each question or statement there are 4 choices marked A), B), C) and D). You should make the correct choice and mark the corresponding letter on the Answer Sheet with a single line through the center.*

In many countries in the process of industrialization, overcrowded cities present a major problem. Poor conditions in these cities, such as lack of housing, inadequate sanitation (卫生) and lack of employment, bring about an increase in poverty, disease and crime.

The over-population of towns is mainly caused by the drift of large numbers of people from the rural areas. These people have become dissatisfied with the traditional life of farming, and have come to the towns hoping for better work and pay.

One possible solution to the problem would be to impose registration on town residents. Only officially registered residents would be allowed to live in the towns and the urban population would thus be limited. In practice, however, registration would be very difficult to enforce (推行); it would cause a great deal of resentment (不满), which would ultimately lead to violence.

The only long-term solution is to make life in the rural areas more attractive, which would encourage people to stay there. This could be achieved by providing encouragement for people to go and work in the villages. Facilities in the rural areas, such as transport, health and education services should be improved. Education should include training in improved methods of farming and other rural industries, so as to develop a more positive attitude towards rural life. The improvement of life in the villages is very important, because the towns themselves cannot be developed without the simultaneous or previous development of the rural area.

36. What does the word "urban" (Line 2, Para. 3) mean?
   A) Of the city.　　　　　　　　　　B) Out of work.
   C) In a bad condition.　　　　　　　D) Of enormous size.

37. Large numbers of farmers have poured into towns because _____.
   A) they can hardly support their families on farms
   B) they are unhappy with their life in the country
   C) the rural areas are too crowded with people
   D) they hope to have their own business

38. In the author's view, solving the cities' problem of overcrowding by strict registrations is _____.
   A) practical　　　B) possible　　　C) not realistic　　　D) not sufficient

39. According to the writer, the problem with crowded cities will be solved if _____.
   A) traditional methods of farming are well kept
   B) conditions in rural areas are much improved
   C) the government can provide more jobs
   D) violence could be controlled in cities

40. Which factor is most important for people to be attracted to live in the country?
   A) Their expectations.　　　　　　B) Their interests.
   C) Their income.　　　　　　　　　D) Their attitude.

Task 2

Directions: *This task is the same as Task 1. The 5 questions or unfinished statements are numbered 41 to 45.*

The human body has developed its millions of nerves to be highly aware of what goes on both inside and outside of it. This helps us adjust to the outside world. Without our nerves and our brain, which is a system of nerves, we couldn't know what's happening. But we pay for our sensitivity. We can feel pain when the slightest thing is wrong with any part of our body. The history of torture (折磨) is based on the human body being open to pain.

But there is a way to handle pain. Look at the Indian fakir (苦行僧) who sits on a bed of nails. Fakirs can put a needle right through an arm, and feel no pain. This ability that some humans have developed to handle pain should give us ideas about how the mind can deal with pain.

The big thing in withstanding pain is our attitude toward it. If the dentist says, "This will hurt a little," it helps us to accept the pain. By staying relaxed, and by treating the pain as an interesting sensation (感觉), we can handle the pain without falling apart. After all, although pain is an unpleasant sensation, it is still a sensation, and sensations are the stuff of life.

41. The human body has developed a system of nerves that enables us to _____.
   A) stay relaxed   B) avoid pain   C) stand torture   D) feel pain
42. What does the writer mean by saying "we pay for our sensitivity" in the first paragraph?
   A) We have to take care of our sense of pain.
   B) We suffer from our sense of feeling.
   C) We should try hard to resist pain.
   D) We are hurt when we feel pain.
43. When the author mentions the Indian fakir, he shows that _____.
   A) fakirs possess magic power
   B) Indians are not afraid of pain
   C) people can learn to cope with pain
   D) some people are born without a sense of pain
44. What is essential for people to stand pain according to the writer?
   A) Their relaxation.   B) Their interest.
   C) Their nerves.   D) Their attitude.
45. The author believes that _____.
   A) feeling pain is part of our life   B) pain should be avoided at all costs
   C) feeling pain can be an interesting thing   D) magic power is essential for reducing pain

Task 3

Directions: *The following is a memo to all employees. After reading it, you are required to complete the outline below it (No. 46 to No. 50). You should write your answers briefly (**in not more than three words**) on the Answer Sheet correspondingly.*

Memo

To: All Employees
From: Berry E. Silver, President
Date: Oct. 22, 2004
Subject: Our goals for the next year

Marketing and Sales

Our present sales program has helped us to improve our sales by slightly over 15%, but I am setting a goal of a 25% increase in sales for the next year. To help make this goal possible, I am announcing today the expansion (扩大) of our Marketing Department.

Research and Development (R&D)

Any company in our business must make great efforts to develop new and better products. Our R&D will certainly make us more competitive. But creative ideas do not come from only R&D departments; they also come from the creative thinking and participation of all employees. One way we have begun to collect the suggestions of our employees is through our new computerized network.

Human Resources

Our company's most valuable resources are its employees. In the years ahead I would like to see our efforts doubled in on-the-job training. To achieve this goal I have asked Barbara Johnson to head a new department, Human Resources and Employee Development, which will coordinate (协调) a company-wide effort.

Memo

Subject Goals for the next year

Marketing and Sales

    1) Goal set to reach a ___46___ in sales;

    2) Measure to be taken to expand the ___47___;

Research and Development R&D

    1) Goal set to encourage the employees, participation;

    2) Channel to collect suggestions: the new ___48___;

Human Resources

    1) Requirement set to double the efforts in ___49___;

    2) Measure to be taken: to appoint Barbara Johnson to head ___50___.

Task 4

Directions: *The following is a list of terms used in the Internet. After reading it, you are required to find the items equivalent to*（与……等同）*those given in Chinese in the table below. Then you should put the corresponding letters in the brackets on the Answer Sheet, numbered 51 through 55.*

A—Abbreviated Dialing Code   B—Off-peak Hours

C—Charging Period   D—Access Code

E—Identity Number   F—Video Conference

G—Operational Status   H—Information Subscription Service

I—Network User Address   J—Audio Signal

K—Local User Terminal   L—File Management

M—Response Signal   N—Operating Instructions

O—Change of the Battery Unit   P—Function Indicator

Q—Entry Rejected   R—External Control

Example:（ A ）缩位拨号码   （ H ）预定信息业务

51. (	) 计费时间	(	) 非高峰时间
52. (	) 网络用户地址	(	) 标识码
53. (	) 本地用户终端	(	) 音频信号
54. (	) 文件管理	(	) 操作指令
55. (	) 外部控制	(	) 功能指示

Task 5

Directions: *The following is an introduction to sunburst Hotel. After reading it, you should give brief answers to the 5 questions (No. 56 to No. 60) that follow. The answers (**in not more than 3 words**) should be written after the corresponding numbers on the Answer Sheet.*

Sunburst Hotel

Location: On Waikiki Beach facing the ocean on one of the main beaches on the island of Oahu.

Accommodation: A large complex including 32 houses, two 12-storey towers with 245 rooms and a 16-storey tower with 300 rooms. Room choices include one or two king or queen size beds or 2 double beds. Each room has a shower, hair-dryer, coffee maker, mini-fridge, in-room safe, phone, TV with pay movies and radio.

Facilities: Two restaurants, three bars and four lounges (休息厅) provide excellent food, relaxation and entertainment 24 hours a day. There are also a tour desk, gift shops, laundry facilities and pay parking. Our room service is prompt and reasonable.

Amusement: Two large swimming pools and a very large fitness (健身) center with three full-time staff.

Special features: Children under 16 stay free when sharing with an adult (one adult per child). More than one child per adult is half price. Coupon (优惠券): All guests receive a coupon book upon check-in. It offers discounts on dining, shopping, entertainment and other activities.

56. Where is the hotel located on the island of Oahu?
    On _____.

57. How many rooms are there altogether in the tower buildings?
    There are altogether _____ rooms.

58. How is the room service in the hotel?
    _____.

59. How much will you pay for your second child if you take two children along?
    _____.

60. What's the use of the coupon book?
    With the coupon book, guests can get _____ on dining, shopping, etc. in the hotel.

Part IV　Translation—English into Chinese　　（25 minutes）

Directions: *This part, numbered 61 through 65, is to test your ability to translate English into Chinese. After each of the sentences numbered 61 to 64, you will read four choices of suggested translation marked A), B), C) and D). You should choose the best translation and mark the corresponding letter on your Answer Sheet. And for the paragraph numbered 65, write your translation in the corresponding space on the Translation/Composition Sheet.*

61. During the meeting held in Brazil last month the supporters of free trade argued that these economic policies could benefit all nations.

　　A）支持者上个月在巴西召开自由贸易会议，他们辩称这些经济政策有利于所有的国家。

　　B）上月在巴西召开的会议上自由贸易的支持者辩称，这些经济政策会使所有国家都受益。

　　C）自由贸易的支持者在上个月召开巴西会议时提出了这些经济政策，以帮助所有国家。

　　D）在上个月的会议上，巴西的支持者就自由贸易政策是否有利于所有国家展开了辩论。

62. Women would double their risk of suffering from lung cancer if they were exposed to 40 or more years of household tobacco smoke.

　　A）妇女在家里吸烟长达 40 年或更长时间，她们患肺癌的痛苦就会加倍。

　　B）家庭妇女接触油烟长达 40 年或更长时间，她们患肺癌的痛苦就会加倍。

　　C）妇女在家里吸烟的时间长达 40 年或更长时间，她们患肺癌的危险就会加倍。

　　D）妇女在吸烟的家庭环境中生活 40 年或更长时间，她们患肺癌的风险就会加倍。

63. If you require funding for tuition costs, your application should be in the Student Financial Aid Services at least three weeks before your registration date.

　　A）如果你需要资助学费，应向助学办公室提出申请，并至少提前三周办理注册。

　　B）如果你需要申请贷款交纳学费，你应该至少在三周内到助学办公室登记注册。

　　C）如果你需要减免学费，应到助学办公室提出申请，并至少提前三周办理注册手续。

　　D）如果你需要学费资助，最迟应该在注册日期三周前将你的申请交到助学办公室。

64. The purchaser will not be responsible for any cost or expenses in connection with the packing or delivery of the above goods.

　　A）卖主并非没有责任解决上述货物在包装和运输方面出现的问题。

　　B）对于上述货物的包装和运输有关费用的任何事宜卖主概不负责。

　　C）以上货物在包装和运输方面所产生的有关费用买主均不予过问。

　　D）买主概不承担与上述货物的包装和运输有关的任何成本或费用。

65. On July 10 the company will hold its first worldwide video conference (电视会议). All twenty facilities will be linked by a satellite broadcasting system so that employees can see and speak with each other. Mr. Black will begin the conference by telling us about our goals for the next five years. Next, each manager will speak about current challenges. The last hour will be devoted to questions from all locations. If it proves successful, we hope to schedule worldwide video conferences annually.

Part V   Writing   (25 minutes)

Directions: *This part is to test your ability to do practical writing. You are required to write a business letter according to the following information given in Chinese. Remember to do the task on the Translation/Composition Sheet.*

说明：假设你是公司总经理 Smith 先生，给市场部经理 Johnson 先生写一封电子邮件，告诉对方以下内容：

1. 已经收到上半年公司的营销报告；

2. 近几个月来公司的产品销售量下降了 20%，有些地区甚至达到了 50%。原因是……（原因自拟）；

3. 下周一上午召开部门经理会议，要求市场部提出具体改进措施，提高产品的销售量。

Model Test Two (Level A)

Part I Listening Comprehension   (20 minutes)

Directions: *This part is to test your listening ability. It consists of 4 sections.*

Section A

Directions: *This section is to test your ability to understand short dialogues. There are 5 recorded dialogues in it. After each dialogue, there is a recorded question. Both the dialogues and questions will be spoken **only once**. When you hear a question, you should decide on the correct answer from the 4 choices marked A), B), C) and D) given in your test paper. Then you should mark the corresponding letter on the Answer Sheet with a single line through the center.*

Example: *You will hear:*

You will read: A) New York City.

B) An evening party.

C) An air trip.

D) The man's job.

From the dialogue we learn that the man is to take a flight to New York. Therefore, **C) An air trip** *is the correct answer. You should mark C) on the Answer Sheet with a single line through the center.*

Now the test will begin.

1. A) Professor and student.   B) Employer and employee.
   C) Salesman and customer.   D) Business partners.
2. A) By plane.   B) By train.   C) By bus.   D) By ship.
3. A) Four.   B) Five.   C) Six.   D) Seven.
4. A) Visit places of interest.   B) Enjoy Peking Opera.
   C) Have Chinese food.   D) Do some shopping.
5. A) Monday.   B) Tuesday.   C) Wednesday.   D) Thursday.

Section B

Directions: *This section is to test your ability to understand short conversations. There are 2 recorded conversations in it. After each conversation, there are some recorded questions. Both the conversations and the questions will be spoken **two times**. When you hear a question, you should decide on the correct answer from the 4 choices marked A), B), C) and D) given in your test paper. Then* *you should mark the corresponding letter on the Answer Sheet with a single line through the center.*

Now listen to the conversations.

Conversation 1

6. A) Paris. B) Vancouver. C) London. D) Tokyo.
7. A) One. B) Two. C) Three. D) Four.
8. A) At 6:15 a.m. B) At 8:15 a.m. C) At 6:15 p.m. D) At 8:15 p.m.

Conversation 2

9. A) On business. B) Visiting clients.
   C) Signing a contract. D) Taking a holiday.
10. A) Mr. Green who is the Import Manager.
    B) Mr. Brown who is the Import Manager.
    C) Mr. Green who is the Export Manager.
    D) Mr. Brown who is the Export Manager.

Section C

Directions: *In this section you will hear a recorded short passage. The passage is printed in the test paper, but with some words or phrases missing. The passage will be read **two times**. You are required to put the missing words or phrases on the Answer sheet in order of the numbered blanks according to what you hear.*

Now the passage will begin.

We have asked you to come to our "Thank You Party" today to show our heartfelt gratitude to all of you for being our reliable __11__.

As you all know, doing business is not an easy thing. There may be different purposes of doing business: Some do it for an __12__ pursuit of profit, and others, __13__ of the well-being of the society. One thing, however, that we should not __14__ in doing business is to have a sense of appreciation. A sense of regret or resentment will not help us in any way. Having a sense of appreciation for all the people will keep us __15__ in business.

Section D

Directions: *This section is to test your ability to comprehend short passages. You will hear a recorded passage. After that you'll hear five questions. Both the passage and the questions will be read **two times**. When you hear a question, you should complete the answer to it with a word or a short phrase (**in no more than 3 words**). The questions and incomplete answers are printed in your test paper. You should write your answers on the Answer Sheet correspondingly.*

Now listen to the passage.

16. Which kind of job should you choose?
    You should choose a job that you _____.

17. What may happen if you don't like your job?

   It may result in another _____ finally.

18. What is another important aspect?

   Another important aspect is _____ or training.

19. What is also necessary according to the speaker?

   The _____ for future promotion is also necessary.

20. Why does everyone want to get promoted?

   Because it means higher _____ and higher position.

Part II Vocabulary & Structure   (10 minutes)

Directions: *This part is to test your ability to construct grammatically correct sentences. It consists of 2 sections.*

Section A

Directions: *In this section there are 10 incomplete sentences. You are required to complete each one by deciding on the most appropriate word or words from the 4 choices marked A), B), C) and D). Then you should mark the corresponding letter on the Answer Sheet with a single line through the center.*

21. Although he did not feel well, he insisted _____ going there together with us.

   A) on   B) to   C) at   D) for

22. Only by adopting more creative approaches _____ to overcome present-day challenges.

   A) we can hope   B) hope we can
   C) can we hope   D) can hope we

23. My brother brought me a few reference books, but _____ of them was of any use for my report.

   A) neither   B) none   C) either   D) all

24. I think that the Great Wall is worth _____ hundreds of miles to visit.

   A) to travel   B) traveling   C) traveled   D) travel

25. Would you please pass me the book _____ cover is black?

   A) which   B) whose   C) that   D) its

26. I was almost asleep last night when I suddenly heard someone _____ at the door.

   A) be knocking B) knocking   C) to knock   D) having knocked

27. You can't get a driver's license _____ you are at least sixteen years old.

   A) if   B) unless   C) when   D) though

28. Though he _____ well prepared before the job interview, he failed to answer some important questions.

   A) will be   B) would be   C) has been   D) had been

29. I felt so embarrassed that I couldn't do anything but _____ there when I first met my

present boss.

  A) to sit   B) sitting   C) sat   D) sit

  30. This website may contain links to other websites _____ privacy practices may be different from ours.

  A) that   B) which   C) who   D) whose

Section B

Directions: *There are 5 incomplete statements here. You should fill in each blank with the proper form of the word given in brackets. Write the word or words in the corresponding space on the Answer Sheet.*

  31. Working from home is flexible and beneficial not only to the employees but also to the (employ) _____.

  32. After an (introduce) _____ by the chairperson, we'll go on with the day's discussion.

  33. James (work) _____ for this company since 2008 and is now in charge of the company's sales department.

  34. Finally the woman found her (lose) _____ child with the help of the police.

  35. The lecture was so (bore) _____ that many of the students in the classroom fell asleep.

Part Ⅲ   Reading Comprehension   (40 minutes)

Directions: *This part is to test your reading ability. There are 5 tasks for you to fulfill. You should read the reading materials carefully and do the tasks as you are instructed.*

Task 1

Directions: *After reading the following passage, you will find 5 questions or unfinished statements, numbered 36 to 40. For each question or statement there are 4 choices marked A), B), C) and D). You should make the correct choice and mark the corresponding letter on the Answer Sheet with a single line through the center.*

  We don't have beds in the spacecraft, but we do have sleeping bags. During the day, when we are working, we leave the bags tied to the wall, out of the way. At bedtime we untie them and take them wherever we've chosen to sleep.

  On most spacecraft flights everyone sleeps at the same time. No one has to stay awake to watch over the spacecraft; the craft's computers call us on the radio.

  On the spacecraft, sleep-time doesn't mean nighttime. During each ninety-minute orbit（轨道）the sun "rises" and shines through our windows for about fifty minutes, then it "sets" as the spacecraft takes us around the dark side of the Earth. To keep the sun out of our eyes, we wear black sleep masks.

  It is surprisingly easy to get comfortable and fall asleep in space. Every astronaut（宇航员）

sleeps differently: some sleep upside down, some sideways, and some right side up. When it's time to sleep, I take my bag, my sleep mask and my tape player with earphones and float (漂浮) up to the flight deck (驾驶舱). Then I get into the bag, and float in a sitting position just above a seat, right next to a window. Before I pull the mask down over my eyes, I relax for a while, listening to music and watching the Earth go by under me.

36. When the astronauts are working, sleeping bags are fastened _____.
    A) on the wall   B) to their seats
    C) onto the flight deck   D) anywhere they like

37. Why can all the astronauts sleep at the same time?
    A) They have to follow the same timetable.
    B) The radio will take care of the aircraft for them.
    C) There are enough sleeping bags in the spacecraft.
    D) There is no need for them to watch over the spacecraft.

38. To relax himself before sleep, the writer often _____.
    A) makes a bed   B) gets into his bag
    C) listens to music   D) wears a sleep mask

39. How long does it take the spacecraft to go round the Earth?
    A) Forty minutes.   B) Fifty minutes.
    C) Ninety minutes.   D) Twenty-four hours.

40. The best title for this passage is _____.
    A) Traveling in Space   B) Sleeping in the Spacecraft
    C) Equipment Used by Astronauts   D) The Earth Seen from Outer Space

Task 2

Directions: *This task is the same as Task 1. The 5 questions or unfinished statements are numbered 41 to 45.*

Everybody has an opinion about telecommuting (远程办公). "It won't work in most jobs," "It costs too much," "It reduces air pollution," "It helps people balance family and work responsibilities," and "Most people are doing it."

In reality, researchers continue to find strong growth and acceptance of telecommuting. Nearly two thirds of the top 1,000 companies in the world have a telecommuting program, and 92 percent say it reduces cost and improves worker productivity (生产力). The days of everyone commuting to the office five days a week are quickly disappearing.

Telecommuting involves a non-traditional work arrangement enabling workers to work at home or elsewhere, some or all of the time. This is not a new, novel, or untested way of working.

But is it for you? Telecommuting is not a panacea (万能药). Whether you are a manager, or an HR (Human Resources) specialist, there are decisions to make and actions to take before you begin a telecommuting arrangement.

Join us for any or all of the following meetings to get answers, information, and resources to develop and carry out a successful telecommuting arrangement. Each meeting offers you an informative presentation followed by the opportunity for a discussion with a panel of "experts" who have made telecommuting work for them.

41. How do people look at telecommuting according to the first paragraph?
    A) They are against it.　　　　　　　B) They don't care about it.
    C) They share the same view.　　　D) They differ in their opinions.

42. According to the response of most of the top 1,000 companies, telecommuting _____.
    A) increases worker productivity　　B) will disappear in the near future
    C) cannot be accepted by the public　D) is practiced in all the top companies

43. Which of the following statements is TRUE of telecommuting?
    A) It is up to the employees to accept it or not.
    B) It is getting popular in different companies.
    C) It is a new untested way of working.
    D) It is a traditional work arrangement.

44. Before beginning a telecommuting arrangement, the management should _____.
    A) appoint a new HR specialist
    B) provide the facilities and conditions
    C) improve the company's productivity first
    D) decide whether it is suitable for the company

45. According to the last paragraph, meetings are held to _____.
    A) appreciate the efforts of the telecommuting companies
    B) discuss the employment of telecommuting experts
    C) help introduce the practice of telecommuting
    D) train people before they start telecommuting

Task 3

Directions: *The following is an application letter. After reading it, you are required to complete the outline below it (No. 46 to No. 50). You should write your answers briefly (**in not more than three words**) on the Answer Sheet correspondingly.*

Dear Mr. Williams:

　　Your advertisement in this morning's paper for manager of public relations appeals to me. I found the wording of your advertisement quite attractive with emphasis on leadership, initiative, and flexibility. And my experience and qualifications indicate that I am the person you are seeking.

　　The enclosed résumé indicates my experience in the area of public relations and management communications. I am quite familiar with the kinds of issues and problems that you have to deal with.

　　I'd like to draw your attention to page 2 of my résumé, on which I describe my concept of public relations. And I am most eager to put this concept into practice to prove it to you.

　　Although I have been very happy with my present employer and colleagues, I am more willing to join your company where I can assume even broader responsibility.

I am free to travel and open to relocation. I would welcome the opportunity to meet you and to further discuss how I may benefit your organization. Please call me at 0411-89726374 to arrange an interview at your earliest convenience.

Sincerely yours,
Stephen Smith

An Application Letter

Applicant: __46__
Position applied for: the manager of __47__
Requirements emphasized in the ad: leadership, initiative, and __48__
Expectation of the applicant: to assume __49__
Contact telephone number: 0411-89726374
Purpose of the letter: asking for __50__

Task 4

Directions: *The following is a list of terms related to college courses. After reading it, you are required to find the items equivalent to（与……等同）those given in Chinese in the table below. Then you should put the corresponding letters in the brackets on the Answer Sheet, numbered 51 through 55.*

A—Advanced Mathematics　　　　　　B—Experiment in College Physics
C—Fundamentals of Laws　　　　　　　D—Theory of Circuitry
E—Circuit Measurement Technology　　F—Optimum Control
G—Signal & Linear Systems　　　　　　H—Electrical Engineering Practice
I—Experiment in Electronic Circuitry　　J—Principles of Microcomputers
K—Motor Elements and Power Supply　L—Auto-measurement Techniques
M—Automatic Control Systems　　　　N—Microcomputer Control Technology
O—Basis of Software Techniques　　　P—Principles of Mechanics
Q—Digital Image Processing

Example：（ A ）高等数学　　　　　（ J ）微机原理

51. (　　) 自动控制系统　　　　　(　　) 法律基础
52. (　　) 数字图像处理　　　　　(　　) 电路测量技术
53. (　　) 软件技术基础　　　　　(　　) 信号与线性系统
54. (　　) 自动检测技术　　　　　(　　) 大学物理实验
55. (　　) 电工实习　　　　　　　(　　) 微机控制技术

Task 5

Directions: *The following is part of an introduction to life insurance. After reading it, you should give brief answers to the 5 questions (No. 56 to No. 60) that follow. The answers (**in not more than 3 words**) should be written after the corresponding numbers on the Answer Sheet.*

When you buy life insurance, you want a policy that fits your needs at a reasonable cost. Your first step is to determine how much life insurance you need. Next, you need to decide how much money you can afford to pay. Finally, you must choose the type of policy that meets your coverage(保险类别) goals and fits into your financial plan. Once you have completed these steps, you will be able to move ahead and contact several life insurance companies through an agent who will shop for the right type of policy for you.

There are many reasons for purchasing life insurance, among which are the following:

Insurance to provide family protection and financial security to surviving family members upon the death of the insured person.

Insurance to cover a particular need upon the insured's death such as paying off a mortgage or other debts.

56. What should you take into consideration when choosing a life insurance policy?
    Both your needs and the _____.
57. What's the relationship between the type of policy and your financial plan?
    The type of policy should meet your _____.
58. Who can help you buy the right type of policy from an insurance company?
    _____.
59. Who will benefit from the life insurance upon the death of the insured person?
    Surviving _____.
60. What is the second goal for buying life insurance?
    To pay off a mortgage or _____ after death.

Part IV Translation—English into Chinese (25 minutes)

Directions: *This part, numbered 61 through 65, is to test your ability to translate English into Chinese. After each of the sentences numbered 61 to 64, you will read three choices of suggested translation marked A), B) and C). You should choose the best translation and mark the corresponding letter on your Answer Sheet. And for the paragraph numbered 65, write your translation in the corresponding space on the Translation/Composition Sheet.*

61. We are honored to be invited to the seminar on computer technology to be held in Beijing next month.

    A) 我们很高兴下月将参加在北京举行的计算机研讨会，相信会受益匪浅。

    B) 受邀参加下个月在北京举行的计算机技术研讨会，我们感到十分荣幸。

    C) 根据公司的要求，我们将于下月访问北京，并参观计算机技术研讨会。

62. If you are truly ambitious, you should be moving up every 2-3 years, either in the form of a promotion or a change of company.

　　A）如果你不断努力，我相信2～3年以后你一定能够找到一家心仪的大公司。
　　B）假如你真有理想，每2～3年该换一次工作，争取到一家大公司继续发展。
　　C）如果你真有抱负，每2～3年就该有进步，要么升职，要么就换一家公司。

63. Email application is closely related to the education level: the higher the education level, the more frequent the use of email.

　　A）普及电邮就要从提高受教育程度入手，提高高等教育普及率是关键一步。
　　B）电邮的使用与受教育程度密切相关：教育程度越高，电邮使用频率越高。
　　C）使用电邮与否是与学历高低相关联的，受过高等教育的人使用电邮最多。

64. Industrial robots are used for handling a variety of products for complex processes that are hard to realize by means of conventional machines.

　　A）工业机器人可用于处理各种产品的复杂加工，使用传统机器很难实现这些加工。
　　B）工业机器人会使用复杂的工艺制造大量产品，这些产品用传统机器则无法制造。
　　C）工业机器人具有各种各样的类型与功能，它们的优势是传统机器所无法比拟的。

65. Good morning, ladies and gentlemen, I would like to welcome you the annual meeting of our company. Mr. Smith will give a report on business developments in the first half of the year, and Dr. Black will then explain the sales for the second half of the year. Mr. Green will give us a report on the current situation in the home market that could have an impact on our business in the future. At the end of the meeting, we will be delighted to answer questions. Now, let's welcome Mr. Smith.

_____
_____
_____
_____

Part V　Writing　　　　　　　　　　　　　　（25 minutes）

Directions: *This part is to test your ability to do practical writing. You are required to write a letter of invitation according to the following information given in Chinese. Remember to do the task on the Translation/Composition Sheet.*

说明：以 ABC 公司市场部经理的名义用英语写一封邀请函。

内容如下：

1. 定于 2015 年 12 月 18 日在东方宾馆举行产品发布会；
2. 发布会上将展示本公司的新产品，并邀请有关专家做相关报告；
3. 会后将举行业务洽谈；
4. 感谢对方多年的合作，并邀请对方参加；
5. 请在 11 月月底前回函确认。

Words for reference：

产品发布会：New Product Release

Model Test Three (Level A)

Part I Listening Comprehension (20 minutes)

Directions: *This part is to test your listening ability. It consists of 4 sections.*

Section A

Directions: *This section is to test your ability to understand short dialogues. There are 5 recorded dialogues in it. After each dialogue, there is a recorded question. Both the dialogues and questions will be spoken **only once**. When you hear a question, you should decide on the correct answer from the 4 choices marked A), B), C) and D) given in your test paper. Then you should mark the corresponding letter on the Answer Sheet with a single line through the center.*

Example: *You will hear:*

You will read: A) New York City.
B) An evening party.
C) An air trip.
D) The man's job.

*From the dialogue we learn that the man is to take a flight to New York. Therefore, **C) An air trip** is the correct answer. You should mark C) on the Answer Sheet with a single line through the center.*

Now the test will begin.

1. A) In a corn field.   B) At a bus station.
   C) On a farm.   D) On a bus.
2. A) Two years.   B) Three years.
   C) Four years.   D) Five years.
3. A) Tim is learning to repair jeep.   B) It is difficult to find Tim lately.
   C) Tim is too busy to help them now.   D) Tim finds it difficult to pass his exams.
4. A) There was something wrong with her car.
   B) She got up too late.
   C) There was no parking place nearby.
   D) She got lost on her way to Andrew's home.
5. A) Ask her mother.   B) Buy the ingredients.
   C) Read the recipe.   D) Cook the soup.

Section B

Directions: *This section is to test your ability to understand short conversations. There are 2 recorded conversations in it. After each conversation, there are some recorded questions. Both the conversations and the questions will be spoken* **two times**. *When you hear a question, you should decide on the correct answer from the 4 choices marked A), B), C) and D) given in your test paper. Then you should mark the corresponding letter on the Answer Sheet with a single line through the center.*

Now listen to the conversations.

Conversation 1

6. A) She will be picked up at the station.
   B) She will be picked up at her own house.
   C) She will take a train there.
   D) She will take a bus.

7. A) Around 6 p.m.　　　　　　　　　B) Around 7 p.m.
   C) Around 8:30 a.m.　　　　　　　D) Around 8:30 p.m.

Conversationv 2

8. A) Friends.　　　　　　　　　　　B) Colleagues.
   C) Boss and staff.　　　　　　　　D) Husband and wife.

9. A) She is going to stay in the city.
   B) She is going to work with her father at the workshop.
   C) She'll read books.
   D) She'll go to the park with her family.

10. A) None.　　　　　　　　　　　　B) Once.
    C) Twice.　　　　　　　　　　　　D) Four times.

Section C

Directions: *In this section you will hear a recorded short passage. The passage is printed in the test paper, but with some words or phrases missing. The passage will be read two times. You are required to put the missing words or phrases on the Answer sheet in order of the numbered blanks according to what you hear.*

Now the passage will begin.

If you are ___11___ at a fancy place, you might find a mint or some little candy on your pillow. These are free and nice. Some of the channels on the TV will be free, including probably a "movie" channel or two. These channels ___12___ movies all the time, but there will also be "pay for TV" channels which are not free and the cost of using them will be added to your bill. The phones will call ___13___ in the hotel or motel for free. ___14___, be careful of the refrigerator. Frequently the refrigerator is stocked with all sorts of delicious things to eat and drink, ___15___ snacks and beer.

Section D

Directions: *This section is to test your ability to comprehend short passages. You will hear a recorded passage. After that you'll hear five questions. Both the passage and the questions will be read* ***two times.*** *When you hear a question, you should complete the answer to it with a word or a short phrase (**in not more than 3 words**). The questions and incomplete answers are printed in your test paper. You should write your answers on the Answer Sheet correspondingly.*
Now the passage will begin.

16. What is the passage talking about?
    _____.
17. What's the first advantage of little cars?
    There will be less _____.
18. What about the cost of owning and driving such cars?
    The little cars will cost _____ to own and to drive.
19. What's the speed of little cars?
    These little cars can only go _____ per hour.
20. What's the disadvantage for little cars?
    They will not be useful for _____.

Part II Vocabulary & Structure   (15 minutes)

Directions: *This part is to test your ability to use words and phrases correctly to construct meaningful and grammatically correct sentences. It consists of 2 sections.*

Section A

Directions: *There are 10 incomplete statements here, each with a blank. You are required to complete each statement by choosing the appropriate answer from the 4 choices marked A), B), C) and D). You should mark the corresponding letter on the Answer Sheet with a single line through the center.*

21. It was your recommendation _____ enabled me to be an engineer in this world-famous company.
    A) when   B) who   C) what   D) that
22. It wasn't such a good TV set _____ she had promised us.
    A) that   B) as   C) which   D) what
23. _____ for your advice, we'd never have been able to overcome the difficulties.
    A) Had it not   B) If it were not
    C) Had it not been   D) If we had not been
24. As long as you keep on _____ hard, you'll get promoted sooner or later.
    A) work   B) be working

C) worked D) working

25. _____ such a good chance, he planned to learn more.
   A) To be given B) Having been given
   C) Having given D) Giving

26. Mark often attempts to escape _____ whenever he breaks traffic regulations.
   A) having been fined B) to have been fined
   C) to be fined D) being fined

27. The atmosphere is as much a part of the earth as _____ its soils and the water of its lakes, rivers and oceans.
   A) are B) is C) do D) has

28. Finally, the thief handed everything _____ he had stolen to the police.
   A) which B) what C) whatever D) that

29. _____ the temperature, _____ water turns into steam.
   A) The high, the fast B) Higher, faster
   C) The more higher, the faster D) The higher, the faster

30. Our company is _____ of other makers of spare parts for the airplane.
   A) in advance B) ahead C) advance D) in front

Section B

Directions: *There are 5 incomplete statements here. You should fill in each blank with the proper form of the word given in the brackets. Write the word or words in the corresponding space on the Answer Sheet.*

31. Lily enjoys (talk) _____ with him because he has a good sense of humor.
32. Mr. John wouldn't see you unless you have an (appoint) _____.
33. Professor Wang is a man much (respect) _____ by the people.
34. If he (study) _____ hard, he would have passed the examination.
35. The building is a (memory) _____ to those killed in the war.

Part III Reading Comprehension   (40 minutes)

Directions: *This part is to test your reading ability. There are 5 tasks for you to fulfill. You should read the reading materials carefully and do the tasks as you are instructed.*

Task 1

Directions: *After reading the following passage, you will find 5 questions or unfinished statements, numbered 36 to 40. For each question or statement there are 4 choices marked A), B), C) and D). You should make the correct choice and mark the corresponding letter on the Answer Sheet with a single line through the center.*

"Depend on yourself" is what nature says to every man. Parents can help you. Teachers can help you. Others still can help you. But all these only help you to help yourself.

There have been many great men in history. But many of them were very poor when they were young, and had no uncles, aunts or friends to help them. Schools were few and not very good. They could not depend upon them for education. They saw how it was, and set to work with all their strength to know something. They worked their own way till they became well-known. One of the most famous teachers in England used to tell his pupils, "I cannot make worthy men of you, but I can help make men of yourselves."

Some young men do not try their best to make themselves valuable to society. They never can gain achievements unless they see their weak points and keep improving themselves. They are nothing now and will be nothing as long as they live, unless they accept the advice of their parents and teachers, and depend on their own efforts.

36. Which of the following titles fits this passage best?

　　A) How to become famous　　　　B) What helps to make a good teacher
　　C) Men must help each other　　　D) Depend on your own efforts

37. Many great men succeeded because _____.

　　A) they were anxious to become rich
　　B) they had received good education
　　C) they had made great efforts to learn and work
　　D) they wanted very much to become well-known

38. One of the most famous teachers in England said that he wanted to _____.

　　A) make his pupils rich men
　　B) make his pupils great men
　　C) help his pupils find a way to win honor
　　D) help his pupils make themselves useful men

39. If young people depend on their own efforts, _____.

　　A) they are sure to be famous in the world
　　B) they can be successful in their lives
　　C) they can live without support from their families
　　D) they will no longer need help

40. From this passage we can see that the writer _____.

　　A) is a man with a strong will
　　B) shows great respect for teachers
　　C) is in favor of those who struggle for success
　　D) feels it important to accept the advice of others

Task 2

Directions: *This task is the same as Task 1. The 5 questions or unfinished statements are numbered 41 to 45.*

What is your favorite color? Do you like yellow, orange or red? If you do, you must be an optimist, a leader, or an active person who enjoys life, people and excitement. Do you prefer grays and blues ? Then you are probably quiet, shy and you would rather follow than lead. If you love green, you are strong-minded and determined. You wish to succeed and want other people to see you are successful. At least this is what psychologists tell us, and they should know, because they have been seriously studying the meaning of color preference, and the effect that colors have on human beings. They tell us that we don't choose our favorite color as we grow up. If you happen to love brown, you did so as soon as you opened your eyes, or at least as soon as you could see clearly.

A yellow room makes us feel more cheerful and more comfortable than a dark green one, and a red dress brings warmth and cheer to the saddest winter day. On the other hand, black is depressing. Light and bright colors make people not only happier but also more active. It is a fact that factory workers work better, harder, and have fewer accidents when their machines are painted orange rather than black or dark gray.

Remember, then, that if you feel low, you can always brighten your day or your life with a new shirt or a few colorful things. Remember also that you will know your friends and your enemies better when you find out what colors they like and dislike. And don't forget that anyone can guess about your character when you choose a piece of handkerchief or a lampshade.

41. The author believes in the passage that _____.

   A) anyone can choose his color preference in his life

   B) no one can choose his color preference in his life

   C) anyone is born with his color preference

   D) no one is born with his color preference

42. According to the passage, _____.

   A) if you enjoy life, you must like yellow, orange and red

   B) when you are quiet, you must prefer grays and blues

   C) if you love green, you usually do what you have decided

   D) if you love pink, you often go to flower shops

43. Psychologists study the meaning of color preference because _____.

   A) colors may affect the emotional states of the people

   B) colors may decide the results of our work and study

   C) color preference can tell you who your friends are

   D) color preference can help you to see through your enemies

44. Which of the following statements is TRUE according to the passage ?

   A) It is not proper to wear a red dress in summer.

   B) We feel happier and more active if we see light and bright colors.

   C) All the machines in a factory are painted orange.

   D) No machines in a factory are painted black.

45. The main idea of this passage is _____.

   A) color preference has something to do with one's character

   B) colors have effects on human psychological states

C) you will know your friends or your enemies by knowing the colors they like
D) all of the above

Task 3

Directions: *The following is an introduction to some of the famous inventors and their inventions. After reading it, you should complete the information by filling in the blanks marked 46 to 50 (**in not more than 3 words**) in the table below.*

New inventions are appearing every day to make our lives easier, longer, warmer, speedier and so on. But only a few inventors design a new machine or product that becomes so well-known that the invention, named after its creator, becomes a household word. Here are four famous inventors and the invention that are named after them:

1. John Bowler, a London hatter who designed the hard round hat known as the bowler in about 1850. It has become the symbol of a respectable British man.

2. Louis Braille (1809—1952), born in France. He was blinded as a child. In 1924 he developed his own alphabet patterns known as Braille by which the blind could read by touch.

3. Rudolf Diesel (1858—1913), a German engineer who invented the diesel engine in 1897 and so began a transport revolution in cars, lorries and trains.

4. Charles Rolls, a car salesman who with the engineer Henry Royce created the world-famous Rolls-Royce car.

Inventors and their Inventions

Our lives are made easier, longer, warmer and speedier by __46__. A few inventions were named after their inventors.
Here are some inventors and their inventions:
John Bowler: The __47__ of hat bowler
Louis Braille: His own __48__ by which the blind could read
Rudolf Diesel: An engine that began a transport revolution __49__ and trains
Charles Rolls: The world-famous __50__ car

Task 4

Directions: *The following is a list of commercial terms. After reading it, you are required to find the items equivalent to (与……等同) those given in Chinese in the list below. Then you should put the corresponding letters in brackets on the Answer Sheet, numbered 51 through 55.*

A—Domestic Trade B—International Trade
C—Terms of Trade D—Free-trade Area
E—Importer F—Exporter

G—Commercial Channels   H—Commercial Transaction
I—Middleman   J—Stocks
K—Bulk Sale   L—Retail Trade
M—Unfair Competition   N—Dumping Profit Margin
O—Registered Trademark   P—Head Office

Examples:（D）自由贸易区   （P）总部

51.（　）国内贸易		（　）零售业	
52.（　）商业渠道		（　）进口商	
53.（　）注册商标		（　）不公平竞争	
54.（　）贸易条件		（　）中间商	
55.（　）整批销售		（　）交易	

Task 5

Directions: *Read the following letter carefully. After reading it, you are required to complete the statements that follow the questions（No. 56 to No. 60）. You should write your answers（**in no more than 3 words**）on the Answer Sheet correspondingly.*

July 20, 2004

Dear Sirs,

　　Today we have received your bill for 150 name-bearing（刻有名字的）crystal vases（花瓶）which you sent us the other day.

　　We had ordered these vases on condition that they should reach us by the end of June. But they arrived here 15 days behind the schedule.

　　The customers refused to accept the goods because they arrived too late. Since the vases bear their names, we cannot sell them to other customers. So we asked the customers again and again to take the vases, and finally they agreed to accept them, but at a price cut of 30%.

　　You may understand how we have lost the customer's confidence in us. In this situation, we have to ask you to compensate for the loss we have suffered. We are looking forward to hearing from you soon.

Yours faithfully,
G. Pastry

56. What was the problem with the delivery of the vases?
　　They arrived 15 days _____.
57. When did the vases actually arrive?
　　In the middle of _____.
58. Why couldn't the vases be sold to other customers?
　　Because they were bearing _____ of those who ordered the vases.
59. In what condition did the customers accept the goods?
　　At a price cut of _____.

60. What was the purpose of this letter?

To ask the supplier to _____ for the loss they have suffered.

Part IV Translation—English into Chinese   (25 minutes)

Directions: *This part, numbered 61 through 65, is to test your ability to translate English into Chinese. After each of the sentences numbered 61 to 64, you will read three choices of suggested translation marked A), B) and C). You should choose the best translation and mark the corresponding letter on your Answer Sheet. And for the paragraph numbered 65, write your translation in the corresponding space on the Translation/Composition Sheet.*

61. To confirm the reservation, please visit our office during business hours with a deposit of 75% of the total tour fare per person.

   A) 要想确保能够如期旅行，请在工作时间来我们办公室并交足旅行全款的 75%。

   B) 请在营业时间来办公室确认预订，并支付每人旅行费用总额的 75% 作为押金。

   C) 为了证实你已经预定了座位，请向办公人员出示车票及所交 75% 的押金收据。

62. The company has appointed more than one hundred agents in various important cities in over 50 countries throughout the world.

   A) 该公司已与 100 多家海外经销商合作，将产品推销到 50 多个国家。

   B) 在世界 50 多个国家的主要城市中有 100 多家企业承接该公司业务。

   C) 该公司在全球 50 多个国家的许多重要城市指定了 100 多家代理商。

63. We ensure that there is an environment in which differences are respected and different solutions and ideas are welcome.

   A) 我们保证有这样的氛围：差异得到尊重，不同的解决方案和想法受到欢迎。

   B) 我们正在营造的环境是：差异尽管存在，欢迎提出解决问题的方案和主意。

   C) 我们要努力创造出一种状态：人人受到重视，个个能提出不同的创新思想。

64. Once your application has been processed, the details of the benefits and services will be sent to you within 5 workdays.

   A) 当你的申请输入电脑后，福利和服务的详细情况将在 5 个工作日后送达你处。

   B) 假如你需要了解有关福利和服务的情况，请你提前 5 个工作日提出书面申请。

   C) 你的申请一旦处理完毕，有关福利和服务的详情将在 5 个工作日内发送给你。

65. Today you can do nearly all your banking by using your smart phone. Many of the major banks allow you to pay bills or transfer funds with a smart phone. Experts say that about 70% of Americans will use a mobile banking service in the near future. But some of them are worried about the safety of the mobile banking service, if you are to do banking frequently with your smart phone, you should get anti-virus（防病毒）software and set a password on your phone.

Part V　Writing　　　　　　　　　　　　　　　（25 minutes）

Directions: *This part is to test your ability to do practical writing. You are required to write an email for room reservations according to the following information given in Chinese. Remember to do the task on the Translation/Composition Sheet.*

某公司销售部经理William Taylor先生与其秘书James Rogers先生将去新宁市，要向Starry Night Hotel预定2018年5月29日至6月2日的套房一间、单人房一间，并有以下特别要求：

1. 因Taylor先生要与一些外国客户会面并可能签订合同，因此希望所订的套间环境安静，并配有足够的座位和茶具；

2. Rogers先生的单人间要配备电话和传真机。

以该公司职员李军的身份于5月8日写一封电子邮件，预订房间。Starry Night Hotel预订处的电子邮箱是bookingservice@snh.net.cn，李军的电子邮箱是lj0534@ttyc.com.cn。

Words for reference：

套房 suite　　单人房 single room　　传真机 fax machine

注意：按电子邮件的格式写明时间、收件人、发件人、主题。

Model Test Four (Level A)

Part I Listening Comprehension   (20 minutes)

Directions: *This part is to test your listening ability. It consists of 4 sections.*

Section A

Directions: *This section is to test your ability to understand short dialogues. There are 5 recorded dialogues in it. After each dialogue, there is a recorded question. Both the dialogues and questions will be spoken **only once**. When you hear a question, you should decide on the correct answer from the 4 choices marked A), B), C) and D) given in your test paper. Then you should mark the corresponding letter on the Answer Sheet with a single line through the center.*

Example: *You will hear*:

    You will read: A) New York City.

                    B) An evening party.

                    C) An air trip.

                    D) The man's job.

From the dialogue we learn that the man is to take a flight to New York. Therefore, **C) An air trip** *is the correct answer. You should mark C) on the Answer Sheet with a single line through the center.*

Now the test will begin.

1. A) At a bank.   B) At a restaurant.
   C) At a friend's house.   D) At a hotel.
2. A) Get some changes from Jane.   B) Go to look for a pay phone.
   C) Use the woman's phone.   D) Pay for the phone call.
3. A) Five.   B) Four.
   C) Six.   D) Seven.
4. A) 10:30.   B) 10:00.
   C) 10:50.   D) 10:40.
5. A) Because Henry has no time.
   B) Because someone else decorated the house.
   C) Because there was no instruments in the house.
   D) Because Henry decorated the house himself.

Section B

Directions: *This section is to test your ability to understand short conversations. There are 2 recorded conversations in it. After each conversation, there are some recorded questions. Both the conversations and questions will be spoken **two times**. When you hear a question, you should decide on the correct answer from the 4 choices marked A), B), C) and D) given in your test paper. Then you should mark the corresponding letter on the Answer Sheet with a single line through the center. Now listen to the conversations.*

Conversation 1

6. A) Classical group.   B) Pop group.
     C) Jazz group.   D) Rock group.
7. A) The man will go alone.   B) The woman will go alone.
     C) They will go together.   D) They won't go together.

Conversations 2

8. A) She has caught a cold.   B) She has a headache.
     C) She feel tired and sleepy all the time.   D) She is ill.
9. A) She wants to stop learning the text.   B) She wants to go abroad.
     C) She wants to see a doctor.   D) She wants to rent a small flat.
10. A) Because she is afraid of living by herself and she is short of money.
     B) Because she is afraid of seeing a doctor.
     C) Because she needs to rent a flat.
     D) Because she doesn't know the reason.

Section C

Directions: *In this section you will hear a recorded short passage. The passage is printed in the test paper, but with some words or phrases missing. The passage will be read **two times**. You are required to put the missing words or phrases on the Answer sheet in order of the numbered blanks according to what you hear.*

Now the passage will begin.

Many Chinese students want to __11__ their Master's or PhD's degree in foreign universities, especially in American schools. However, it usually takes much time and __12__ to apply for a Western school, and the chance of getting admitted into a good school is not very high. There are always far more __13__ than the quotas set for the international students. Only the most competitive candidates will be admitted. Therefore, if you dream of studying __14__, you should, first of all, have faith in your intellectual abilities and other talents; secondly, you need to be mentally prepared for a long and sometimes frustrating process of __15__ your dream.

Section D

Directions: *This section is to test your ability to comprehend short passages. You will hear a recorded passage. After that you'll hear five questions. Both the passage and the questions will be read two times. When you hear a question, you should complete the answer to it with a word or a short phrase (**in not more than 3 words**). The questions and incomplete answers are printed in your test paper. You should write your answers on the Answer Sheet correspondingly.*

Now the passage will begin.

16. Where do fish live?
    They live _____ where there is water.

17. How many kinds of fish are there in the world?
    _____.

18. How long does the biggest fish grow up to?
    _____.

19. What is the characteristic of a sea horse?
    It doesn't _____.

20. What does a sea horse do when it wants to stay in one place?
    It takes hold of plants with _____.

Part II Vocabulary & Structure   (10 minutes)

Directions: *This part is to test your ability to construct grammatically correct sentences. It consists of 2 sections.*

Section A

Directions: *In this section there are 10 incomplete sentences. You are required to complete each one by deciding on the most appropriate word or words from the 4 choices marked A), B), C) and D). Then you should mark the corresponding letter on the Answer Sheet with a single line through the center.*

21. _____ he was seriously ill, I wouldn't have told him the truth.
    A) If I knew   B) If I know   C) Had I known   D) Did I know

22. The first question we now discuss is _____ we should go there so early tomorrow.
    A) whether   B) what   C) where   D) whom

23. The car _____ by the side of the road and the driver tried to repair it.
    A) breaks down
    B) was breaking down
    C) has broken down
    D) broke down

24. When he went out, he would wear sunglasses _____ nobody would recognize him.
    A) so that
    B) now that
    C) as though
    D) in case

25. We were all excited at the news _____ our annual sales had more than doubled.

   A) which   B) that   C) it   D) what

26. Some people think _____ about their rights than they do about their responsibilities.

   A) so much   B) too much C) much more D) much too

27. The City of London, _____ repeatedly in 1940 and 1941, lost many of its famous churches.

   A) bombed   B) to bomb   C) bombing   D) having bombed

28. _____ traveling expenses rising a lot, Mrs. White had to change all her plans for the tour.

   A) Since   B) As for   C) By   D) With

29. Allan is looking forward to _____ his American partner at the trade fair.

   A) meet   B) meeting   C) be meeting D) having met

30. With the introduction of the computer, libraries today are quite different from _____ they were in the past.

   A) that   B) what   C) which   D) those

Section B

Directions: *There are 5 incomplete statements here. You should fill in each blank with the proper form of the word given in brackets. Write the word or words in the corresponding space on the Answer Sheet.*

31. It is important that he (be) _____ called back immediately.

32. It's really (wonder) _____ to see you here again in Beijing.

33. At the meeting a (propose) _____ was put forward by John Smith.

34. As a rule, readers (not allow) _____ to take dictionaries out of the reading room.

35. It has been a long winter, and we're (eager) _____ waiting for the coming of spring.

Part III Reading Comprehension   (40 minutes)

Directions: *This part is to test your reading ability. There are 5 tasks for you to fulfill. You should read the reading materials carefully and do the tasks as you are instructed.*

Task 1

Directions: *After reading the following passage, you will find 5 questions or unfinished statements, numbered 36 to 40. For each question or statement there are 4 choices marked A), B), C) and D). You should make the correct choice and mark the corresponding letter on the Answer Sheet with a single line through the center.*

The eight airlines of the One-world Alliance (联盟) have joined forces to give world travelers a simple way to plan and book a round-the-world journey. It's called the One-world Explorer program.

One-world Explorer is the perfect solution for a once-in-a-lifetime holiday or an extended business trip. It's a great way for you to explore the four corners of the earth in the safe hands of the eight One-world airlines.

You can have hundreds of destinations to choose from, because the One-world network covers the globe. And, as you travel around the world, you'll have the support of 260, 000 people from all our airlines, who are devoted to the success of your journey, helping you make smooth transfers and offering support all along the way.

The One-world goal is to make global travel easier and more rewarding for everyone of our travelers. We try our best to make you feel at home, no matter how far from home your journey may take you.

We can offer travelers benefits on a scale beyond the reach of our individual networks. You'll find more people and more information to guide you at every stage of your trip, making transfers smoother and global travel less of a challenge.

36. One-world in the passage refers to _____.
   A) a travel agency   B) a union of airlines
   C) a series of tourist attractions D) the title of a flight program

37. The One-world Explorer program is said to be most suitable for those who _____.
   A) have been to the four corners of the earth
   B) travel around the world on business
   C) want to explore the eight airlines
   D) need support all along the way

38. The advantage of the alliance lies in _____.
   A) its detailed travel information   B) its unique booking system
   C) its longest business flights   D) its global service network

39. We can learn from the last paragraph that One-world _____.
   A) offers the lowest prices to its passengers
   B) keeps passengers better informed of its operations
   C) offers better services than any of its member airlines alone
   D) is intended to make round-the-world trips more challenging

40. The purpose of the advertisement is to _____.
   A) promote a special flight program   B) recommend long distance flights
   C) introduce different flights   D) describe an airlines group

Task 2

Directions: *This task is the same as Task 1. The 5 questions or unfinished statements are numbered 41 to 45.*

Do you know how to use a mobile phone (手机) without being rude to the people around you?

Talking during a performance irritates (激怒) people. If you are expecting an emergency call, sit near the exit doors and set your phone to vibrate (振动). When your mobile phone vibrates, you can leave quietly and let the others enjoy the performance.

Think twice before using mobile phones in elevators, museums, churches or other indoor public places—especially enclosed spaces. Would you want to listen to someone's conversation in these places? Worse yet, how would you feel if a mobile phone rang suddenly during a funeral! It happens more often than you think. Avoid these embarrassing situations by making sure your mobile phone is switched off.

When eating at a restaurant with friends, don't place your mobile phone on the table. This conveys the message that your phone calls are more important than those around you.

Mobile phones have sensitive microphones that allow you to speak at the volume you would on a regular phone. This enables you to speak quietly so that others won't hear the details of your conversations. If you are calling from a noisy area, use your hand to direct your voice into the microphone.

Many people believe that they can't live without their mobile phone. Owning a mobile phone definitely makes life more convenient, but limit your conversations to urgent ones and save the personal calls until you are at home.

41. What should you do when you need to answer a phone call during a performance?
    A) Call back after the performance.   B) Answer it near the exit door.
    C) Talk outside the exit door.   D) Speak in a low voice.

42. Putting your mobile phone on a restaurant table may make your friends think _____.
    A) you prefer to talk to your friends at the table
    B) you value your calls more than your friends
    C) you are enjoying the company of your friends
    D) you are polite and considerate of your friends

43. When you are calling in a noisy area, you are advised to _____.
    A) use a more sensitive microphone
    B) shout loudly into your microphone
    C) go away quietly to continue the phone call
    D) use your hand to help speak into the phone

44. The author implies that the use of mobile phones in such places as museums should be _____.
    A) limited   B) expected   C) discouraged   D) recommended

45. Which of the following is TRUE according to the passage?
    A) You should limit your mobile phone calls to personal affairs.
    B) You should speak quietly into your phone while in a church.
    C) You are supposed to turn off your mobile phone at a funeral.
    D) You are supposed to use your mobile phone as much as possible.

Task 3

Directions: *The following is a short introduction to The Red cross. After reading it, you are required to complete the outline below it (No. 46 to No. 50). You should write your answers briefly (in* *not more than three words*) *on the Answer Sheet correspondingly.*

The Red Cross is an international organization which cares for people who are in need of help. A man in a Pairs hospital who needs blood, a woman in Mexico who was injured in an earthquake and a family in India that lost their home in a storm may all be aided by the Red Cross.

The Red Cross exists in almost every country around the globe. The World Red Cross organizations are sometimes called the Red Crescent, the Red Mogen Davis, the Sun and the Red Lin. All of these agencies share a common goal of trying to help people in need.

The idea of forming an organization to help the sick and wounded during a war started with Jean Henri Dunant. In 1859, he observed how people were suffering on a battlefield in Italy. He wanted to help all the wounded people regardless of which side they were fighting for. The most important result of his work was an international treaty called the Geneva Convention. It protects prisoners of war, the sick and wounded and other citizens during a war.

The American Red Cross was set up by Clara Barton in 1881. Today the Red Cross in the United States provides a number of services for the public, such as helping people in need, teaching first aid, demonstrating water safety and artificial respiration (人工呼吸), and providing blood.

The Red Cross

The popularity of the Red Cross: It exists in __46__ around the world.

The common goal of its agencies: trying to __47__ in need

The founder of the Red Cross: __48__

The most important result of the founder's work: an international treaty— __49__

The American Red Cross:

1. Set up in 1881 by Clara Barton
2. Provide __50__ to the public

Task 4

Directions: *The following is the contents of a book named public relations. After reading it, you are required to find the items equivalent to (与……等同) those given in Chinese in the table below. Then you should put the corresponding letters in the brackets on the Answer Sheet, numbered 51 through 55.*

A—Research and Analysis
C—Communication Process
E—Dealing with the News Media
G—Reaching the Audience
I—Feedback and Evaluation
K—Social and Cultural Agencies
M—Government and Public Affairs

B—Role of Departments
D—Sampling Public Opinion
F—Planning Actions
H—Opportunities in the Print Media
J—Public Opinion and Persuasion
L—Entertainment and Sports
N—Membership Organizations

O—Legal Problems   P—International Public Relations

Examples: (E) 与新闻媒体打交道   (F) 行动计划

51. ( ) 交流过程		( ) 娱乐与体育
52. ( ) 国际公共关系		( ) 公众意见抽样调查
53. ( ) 政府和公众事务		( ) 研究与分析
54. ( ) 部门职能		( ) 社会与文化机构
55. ( ) 反馈与评价		( ) 法律问题

Task 5

Directions: *The following is a letter. After reading it, you should give brief answers to the 5 questions (No. 56 to No. 60) that follow. The answers (**in not more than 3 words**) should be written after the corresponding numbers on the Answer Sheet.*

We hope that by observing the following points you will enjoy your visit to Christ Church without disturbing the life of the college.

* Please obey all notices and do not enter the areas marked Private.

* Please do not enter any college rooms.

* Please avoid leaving litter (杂物); picnicking within the college is not permitted.

* Please do not smoke.

* Please do not gather so as to obstruct (阻塞) paths or passages, particularly in the Hall.

* Please be as quiet as possible, remembering that this is a college where people are working.

* In the event of a fire or other danger, or if you hear a fire alarm or warning, please leave the building without delay. At all times please follow the advice of the Custodians (保安人员) who are here to help you.

* Closed circuit television surveillance (监视) is in operation. Images are being recorded for purposes of crime prevention and public safety.

* Thank you for visiting Christ Church. If you have any comments please write to:

The Steward, Christ Church, Oxford OX1 1DP

56. What is the name of the place open to tourists?
    It's _____.

57. Which areas are not allowed for tourists to visit?
    The areas _____ and any college rooms.

58. What is not permitted to do during the visit to the college?
    Leaving litter, _____ inside the college or smoking, etc.

59. What should tourists do in the event of a fire or any other danger?
    They should leave the building and _____ of the Custodians.

60. Why is closed circuit television surveillance in operation?
    To _____ and ensure public safety.

Part IV　Translation—English into Chinese　（25 minutes）

Directions: *This part, numbered 61 through 65, is to test your ability to translate English into Chinese. After each of the sentences numbered 61 to 64, you will read four choices of suggested translation marked A), B), C) and D). You should choose the best translation and mark the corresponding letter on your Answer Sheet. And for the paragraph numbered 65, write your translation in the corresponding space on the Translation/Composition Sheet.*

61. Any academic breakthrough, brilliant as it may be, does not automatically ensure that it can be applied to practice.

　　A）学科上的任何成果，除非它辉煌灿烂，否则不能自动用于实践。
　　B）任何学科上的成就，尽管不能自动用于实践，但也可能是灿烂辉煌的。
　　C）学术上的任何成就，无论杰出与否，都不能确保它可以自动地用于实践。
　　D）任何学术上的突破，或许本身卓越，也并非自然而然地就可用于实践。

62. With increasing awareness of the environment, people have realized that the way coal is used is critical and new approaches have to be sought.

　　A）尽管环境意识提高了，人们认为使用煤炭仍然是重要的，并且已经找到了新的方法。
　　B）随着环境意识的增强，人们认识到使用煤炭的方法应该受到批评，必须寻求新的途径。
　　C）随着环境意识的日益增强，人们认识到如何使用煤炭至关重要，因而得寻求新的方法。
　　D）尽管人们对环境越来越了解，他们也认识到使用煤炭应该受到批评，但要寻找到新的能源才行。

63. The global market in these services is likely to touch US$640 billion, a figure comparable with the size of the IT industry.

　　A）整个市场的服务费用已上升到 6 400 亿美元，这个额度有可能会达到 IT 业的规模。
　　B）以总体为 6 400 亿美元服务于市场的目标有望实现，这一目标是相对于 IT 行业而言的。
　　C）这些服务业的全球市场有可能达到 6 400 亿美元，这一数字与 IT 业产值的大小相当。
　　D）整个市场中的服务行业可能要突破 6 400 亿美元，这一数字与 IT 业的规模不相上下。

64. The author suggests that human resources management should be taught as a required subject in this school, along with science courses.

　　A）作者建议，这所学校开设人力资源管理课程或是开设理科课程都是必要的。
　　B）作者建议，除了理科课程之外，这所学校应将人力资源管理作为必修课开设。

C）作者建议，作为学校的一门课程，人力资源管理应该在其他理科课程之后开设。

D）作者建议，把人力资源管理作为这所学校的一门必修课开设，像理科课程一样。

65. We invite you to submit a paper to the 19th World Conference on Business Management. It will take place in Paris, France, on June 29th to July 2nd, 2019. The deadline for submission is on January 21st, 2019. The conference focuses on small business management, which is closely related to your research area. If you need more time, please let us know about a suitable time for you and I will inform you if it is feasible for us.

Part V　Writing　　　　　　　　　　　　　　　　（25 minutes）

Directions: *This part is to test your ability to do practical writing. You are required to write two letters according to the following information given in Chinese. Remember to do the task on the Translation/Composition Sheet.*

说明：以 ABC 公司市场部经理的名义用英语写一封邀请函。

内容如下：

1. 定于 2019 年 12 月 18 日在东方宾馆举行产品发布会；

2. 发布会上将展示本公司的新产品，并邀请有关专家做相关报告；

3. 会后将举行业务洽谈；

4. 感谢对方多年的合作，并邀请对方参加；

5. 请在 11 月月底前回函确认。

Words for reference

产品发布会：New Product Release

B 级参考答案（Keys to the Tests）

2018 年 12 月 B 级考试全真试题答案

Part I　Listening Comprehension（共 24 分）

1. A　2. C　3. D　4. B　5. C　6. A　7. D　8. A　9. C　10. B
11. D　12. C　13. A　14. B　15. C　16. D　17. A　18. B　19. D
20. express　21. be proud of　22. depend on　23. ideas　24. once again

Part II　Vocabulary & Structure（共 15 分）

25. B　26. D　27. A　28. C　29. B　30. C　31. D　32. A
33. B　34. D　35. to see　36. be delivered　37. sending　38. equipment　39. cheaper

Part III　Reading Comprehension（共 31 分）

40. C　41. D　42. A　43. B　44. A　45. B　46. D　47. A
48. return　49. your packaging　50. easily seen　51. detailed information　52. photos
53. C, M　54. K, P　55. J, I　56. A, O　57. Q, E
58. insurance card　59. the policy number　60. insurance provider's website
61. any changes　62. expensive

Part IV　Translation—English into Chinese（共 15 分）

63. B　64. A　65. C　66. A

67.【参考译文】我们希望本页的提示对您很有帮助，并在下一次假期中能够用到它们。不管您是乘坐飞机还是自驾，在交通出行和宾馆住宿的需求上，可以使用我们的旅行对比选择工具。欢迎再次光临并报名获得我们的业务通讯，从而不断获得最好的消费体验和旅行贴心提示。通过酒店价格对比和选择，您可以节省高达 70% 的费用。

Part V　Writing（共 15 分）

【参考范文】

Volunteer Application Form

Thank you for your interest in volunteering with Reading Together

Personal Details

Name：（1）Chen Daming　　　√ Mr.　　□ Mrs.　　□ Ms.
Mobile：（2）177×××8956
Email：（3）chendm999@163.com
Birth Date：（4）December 15th, 1998

College Information

College Name：Dongfang Technical College
Major：Computer Technology　　　Department：（5）Computer Department

Describe why you are interested in working as a volunteer with us.

　　Firstly, I am interested in reading. Secondly, I hope I can help the children in the countryside with the knowledge which I learnt. Thirdly, I would make more friends in the volunteer activity. Lastly, my reading and communication ability will be improved by joining in the reading together.

2018年6月B级考试全真试题答案

Part I　Listening Comprehension（共24分）

1. A　2. C　3. C　4. B　5. A　6. D　7. B　8. B　9. D　10. C
11. A　12. D　13. B　14. A　15. B　16. A　17. C　18. A　19. D
20. local　21. safety training　22. new skills　23. at our offices　24. at least

Part II　Vocabulary & Structure（共15分）

25. D　26. A　27. B　28. C　29. D　30. D　31. A　32. C　33. D　34. B
35. different　36. better　37. creating　38. healthy　39. is expected

Part III　Reading Comprehension（共31分）

40. B　41. A　42. A　43. C　44. D　45. B　46. D　47. C
48. cheaper　49. long-term　50. network　51. member ID　52. full-service delivery
53. H，D　54. F，O　55. P，J　56. A，L　57. Q，M
58. service line　59. arranged an inspection　60. the inspection
61. safe and reliable　62. is not performed

Part IV　Translation—English into Chinese（共15分）

63. B　64. B　65. A　66. C

67.【参考译文】如果你准备好规划下一步的生活了，我们可以帮助您最大限度地利用您的资金。您可以与您的客户经理进行沟通。客户经理将帮助您找到一种方法，使您的资金更好的运转。我们还会帮助您打理信用卡和贷款。预约，请致电 0345-000-888。

Part V　Writing（共15分）

【参考范文】

Memo

To：（1）all department managers
From：（2）Tom Brown
Date：（3）June 18, 2018
CC：（4）John Smith
Subject：（5）Discussion on the sales plan for the second half of the year

　　The Marketing Department has formulated the company's sales plan for the second half of the year which I have sent to you. See Attachment. The General Manager's Office will hold a meeting at the company meeting room at 2p.m. on June 20th to discuss the plan and listen to the opinions of all departments. All department managers should attend the meeting. If you are unable to attend the meeting, please inform General Manager's office in advance.

2017年12月B级考试全真试题答案

Part I　Listening Comprehension（共24分）

1. A　2. C　3. B　4. D　5. C　6. B　7. A　8. D　9. B　10. A
11. B　12. D　13. A　14. C　15. B　16. D　17. A　18. B　19. C
20. manage　21. in high demand　22. possible　23. advantages　24. the right decision

Part II　Vocabulary & Structure（共15分）

25. C　26. B　27. D　28. A　29. D　30. C　31. B　32. A　33. C　34. D
35. to give　36. greatly　37. viewing　38. production　39. is required

Part III　Reading Comprehension（共31分）

40. B　41. C　42. A　43. D　44. C　45. B　46. C　47. A
48. 33　49. $250,000　50. members　51. in force　52. insurance agency
53. B, O　54. D, F　55. P, Q　56. E, H　57. M, L
58. Ground maintenance workers　59. outdoor environment
60. all weather conditions　61. on-the-job　62. 12.90

Part IV　Translation—English into Chinese（共15分）

63. C　64. B　65. A　66. B

67.【参考译文】一些人可能发觉，由于年龄较大，游览公园变得困难了。现在，我们为这类人群提供了免费服务。我们专门培训了志愿者作为园区引导员，他们熟知园区历史。而此项便民服务由社区捐款赞助。在此，我们呼吁大家对此项服务予以支持。

Part V　Writing（共15分）

【参考范文】

Field Trip Report

Report to: Mr./Ms. (1) <u>Wang Xiaolin</u>

Report from: Mr./Ms (2) <u>Li Junjie</u>

Date: (3) <u>December 24th, 2017</u>

Trip destination: (4) <u>JUK Manufactory</u>

Trip period: from <u>December 4th, 2017</u> to (5) <u>December 8th, 2017</u>

Participants: <u>Li Junjie & His team members</u>

Summary

　　In order to know the problem of water pollution, we went to JUK Manufactory to visit for a whole week. We had acquaintance with the source of pollution. The engineer of the factory introduced several ways of dealing with waste water to us. This visit helped us a lot with our research.

2017年6月B级考试全真试题答案

Part I   Listening Comprehension（共 24 分）

1. D   2. B   3. C   4. A   5. B   6. D   7. C   8. A   9. D   10. C
11. A   12. C   13. B   14. D   15. B   16. C   17. A   18. B   19. C
20. inviting   21. lovely   22. talking to   23. good relationship   24. a great time

Part II   Vocabulary & Structure（共 15 分）

25. C   26. A   27. B   28. C   29. D   30. A   31. A   32. C   33. B   34. D
35. suggestion/suggestions   36. longer   37. helpful   38. to smoke   39. was asked

Part III   Reading Comprehension（共 31 分）

40. D   41. B   42. C   43. A   44. C   45. D   46. A   47. C
48. services   49. care   50. confidential   51. postage-paid
52. 541-754-1374   53. K, F   54. A, P   55. I, E   56. C, H   57. O, G
58. turn off   59. non-busy   60. 10-minute   61. damage the printers   62. operation

Part IV   Translation—English into Chinese（共 15 分）

63. B   64. A   65. C   66. B

67.【参考译文】很多物品在邮寄时可能被认为属于危险品并可能引发严重事故。您有责任确保您包裹中的物品属于非危险品。有了您的合作，事故才能得以避免。如果发生事故，您要对此负责。如果您想了解某件物品是否可以邮寄，可以拨打客服电话 1-800-267-1177.

Part V   Writing（共 15 分）

【参考范文】

Guest Experience Card

We value your feedback

Name：(1) Zhang Jianlin

Email address：(2) zhangj1999@163.com

Date of visit：(3) June 15ᵗʰ, 2017

Time of visit：(4) 11:30 a.m.

Did our Team Members exceed your expectations？   Yes   If yes,

Please provide their names：(5) John Chen

Comments：

　　The staff are kind and provide me with good service, especially Mr. John Chen. It's a great experience for me to stay in such a clean and tidy room and I also enjoy the delicious food in the dining hall. However, for the convenience of the guests, I hope a shuttle bus can be arranged between the hotel and the subway station because the hotel is rather far from the downtown area.

　　Thank you for choosing our hotel.

　　If you would like to talk to us about your experience today,

please contact the Guest Services Department at 1-888-601-1616.

B 级参考答案（Keys to the Tests）

Model Test One（Leve B）

Part I　Listening Comprehension（共 24 分）

1. B　2. C　3. C　4. A　5. D　6. B　7. B　8. D　9. B　10. C
11. A　12. B　13. C　14. D　15. C　16. B　17. C　18. C　19. C
20. necessary　21. advice　22. watch　23. growing up　24. battle

Part II　Vocabulary & Structure（共 15 分）

25. A　26. B　27. A　28. B　29. C　30. B　31. B　32. A　33. D　34. D
35. easier　36. Unbelievably　37. tells　38. unable　39. is

Part III　Reading Comprehension（共 31 分）

40. C　41. B　42. A　43. B　44. A　45. C　46. C　47. D
48. St. Martin's College　49. Saturday afternoon　50. Monday，23 September
51. $120　52. Conference organizer/Dr Johnson
53. N，K　54. F，I　55. A，L　56. G，D　57. B，C
58. this week's issue　59. overall hotel work　60. a recent photograph
61. an Assistant Manager　62. on holiday

Part IV　Translation—English into chinese（共 15 分）

63. A　64. B　65. C　66. A
67. 财务管理包括募集充足的资金和管理好已投入的资本，它要求对公司未来运营中所需的现金进行估算，对使用短期还是长期贷款做出决断，选择适当的时机发行股票或出售债券等。

Part V　Writing（共 15 分）

【参考范文】

Notice

　　To help students learn more about computers，we have invited Professor Shen Lan from the Computer Department of Wuhan University to give us a lecture on Saturday，December 26th. He will talk about the use of computer and how to learn through the Internet. The lecture begins at 2：00 p.m. in Room 208 of the Library Building. Any computer lover is welcome to attend the lecture. Please be on time.

The Students'Union
19th，December

Model Test Two（Level B）

Part I　Listening Comprehension（共 24 分）

1. A　2. B　3. A　4. C　5. C　6. D　7. A　8. D　9. A　10. C
11. B　12. A　13. C　14. B　15. A　16. B　17. C　18. C　19. B
20. widely　21. exactly　22. find out　23. strong　24. discovered

Part II Vocabulary & Structure（共 15 分）

25. A 26. B 27. D 28. D 29. A 30. B 31. A 32. B 33. A 34. C
35. uncomfortable 36. be set 37. hadn't prepared 38. was elected 39. widen

Part III Reading Comprehension（共 31 分）

40. C 41. A 42. C 43. D 44. D 45. D 46. B 47. C
48. generating ideas 49. structured written outline 50. first draft
51. the second draft 52. the final draft
53. F, I 54. A, D 55. E, N 56. J, B 57. C, G
58. Transformers 59. Details 60. technical specification 61. More than 10 units
62. pictures

Part IV Translation—Engish into Chinese（共 15 分）

63. C 64. B 65. C 66. A

67. 因为现代通信手段的发展和人口的迁移及增长结束了各民族之间的相互隔绝，所以世界上的很多语言都处于消亡的过程中。专家认为，到 22 世纪，世界上 6 000 种语言中至少有一半可能灭绝，只有 5% 的语言是安全的，所谓"安全"是指这些语言的使用者不低于 100 万人，同时它们的使用得到官方的支持。

Part V Writing（共 15 分）

【参考范文】

Announcement of Removal

Dear Sir or Madam,

　　Due to the development of new business, our company will move to Room 2022 Zhongxin Building No.17 Zhongshan Road from December 10, 2009. Our new telephone and fax numbers are 025-83321145 and 025-83326542 respectively.

　　We are very sorry for the inconvenience brought to you. We would also like to take this chance to thank you for your continued support over the years and hope that we can keep on working together in the future.

Yours faithfully,

Clare Tao

General Secretary

Model Test Three（Level B）

Part I Listening Comprehension（共 24 分）

1. B 2. A 3. A 4. D 5. A 6. C 7. B 8. B 9. C 10. C
11. C 12. D 13. A 14. B 15. C 16. B 17. C 18. D 19. A
20. where 21. leave 22. grow up 23. as if 24. moving

Part II Vocabulary & Structure（共 15 分）

25. C 26. D 27. B 28. A 29. A 30. B 31. C 32. A 33. A 34. D
35. would have come 36. confident 37. equipment 38. to learn 39. is

Part III Reading Comprehension（共 31 分）

40. A 41. C 42. D 43. B 44. D 45. B 46. C 47. B
48. apples 49. little spots 50. a reduced price 51. a credit 52. the right quality
53. C, Q 54. O, J 55. P, K 56. B, F 57. I, E
58. interviewing 59. design engineer 60. XELL Company 61. opportunity
62. 0811-8222-5555

Part IV Translation（共 15 分）

63. A 64. C 65. B 66. C
67. 欢迎订购我们的图书。我们有会员计划，现在你只需要购买我们任意一本书即可成为我们的会员。会费是 100 元，会员有效期为一年。如果你成为会员，将会享受到一定折扣。尤其是当你打算购买很多书时，真的是相当划算。

Part V Writing（共 15 分）

【参考范文】

Manager of Ticket Booking Office

Air southern China，Guangzhou

Sept. 10，2012

Dear sir,

　　I am on an urgent mission and expect to get to Hong Kong as soon as possible.

　　Please reserve a seat for me in the flight leaving Guangzhou for Hong Kong at six a.m. tomorrow. I shall be obliged if you will deliver the ticket to the room 1903 of Baiyun where I am staying.

　　With many thanks!

Yours sincerely,

David Smith

Model Test Four（Level B）

Part I Listening Comprehension（共 24 分）

1. A 2. B 3. A 4. A 5. D 6. C 7. C 8. D 9. B 10. C
11. B 12. B 13. D 14. A 15. C 16. C 17. D 18. A 19. C
20. a number of 21. heavy 22. well-developed 23. lakes 24. probably

Part II Vocabulary & Structure（共 15 分）

25. A 26. D 27. A 28. C 29. B 30. A 31. C 32. A 33. A 34. C
35. laughing 36. made/should make 37. Having completed 38. go 39. to look

Part III Reading Comprehension（共 31 分）

40. A 41. B 42. C 43. B 44. C 45. B 46. D 47. B
48. beautiful weather 49. wonderful scenery 50. 71.9 ℉ 51. only 23 inches
52. warm sunshine
53. H, D 54. L, C 55. J, N 56. E, A 57. I, F
58. look after children 59. English and French 60. uninteresting

61. less important 62. a gardener

Part IV　Translation（共 15 分）

63. C   64. C   65. B   66. A

67. 我们非常高兴地欢迎中国朋友参加这次商务培训项目。在这里，你们将参加各类活动并且有机会相互交流。我们希望，你们都会从培训项目中获益匪浅。在各位逗留期间，如有问题和困难，请告知我们。我们相信这次培训既有教育意义又轻松愉快。

Part V　Writing（共 15 分）

【参考范文】

MEMO

Date：　June 14th, 2018

From：　manager

To：　all staff

Re：　about bonus

　Message：Every employee will receive a bonus of $500 issued together with next month's salary. I hope you can continue to work hard and make new contributions to the company's development. Wish our company a greater success next year.

　　Signature：John Blackburn

· 166 ·

A级参考答案（Keys to the Tests）

2018年12月A级考试全真试题答案

Part I Listening comprehension（共20分）

1. A   2. C   3. B   4. B   5. D   6. B   7. C   8. A   9. D   10. C
11. inviting   12. boarding pass   13. Gate 3   14. completed   15. repeat
16. say goodbye   17. manager   18. five years   19. working ability   20. keep in touch

Part II Vocabulary & Structure（15分）

21. C   22. B   23. A   24. D   25. B   26. A   27. B   28. D   29. A   30. C
31. offering   32. generally   33. appointment   34. published   35. is signed

Part III Reading Comprehension（35分）

36. B   37. C   38. B   39. A   40. D   41. C   42. B   43. C   44. D   45. A
46. succeed   47. 1998   48. more people   49. 180 million   50. career goals
51. C, E   52. N, K   53. D, H   54. M, J   55. L, F
56. sixteen years   57. previous experience   58. meetings and training
59. fundraising function   60. type of membership

Part IV Translation—English into Chinese（15分）

61. A   62. B   63. A   64. C

65. 酒驾一直是这个国家的一个问题，人们长期以来一直关注酒驾造成的交通事故。今年上半年，全国有22万多起酒驾案件。在一些城市，酒驾变得越来越严重。如果喝了酒，不要开车，叫辆出租车或乘坐公共交通工具。这个应用程序可以帮助你找到司机开车送你回家。

Part V Writing（15分）

【参考范文】

To: Mr. Hoffman, Sales manager, ABC Company
From: Wang Bin, Purchasing Department Manager
Date: December 16, 2018
Subject: Order number: HP3456236

Dear Hoffman,

　　I'm writing to complain about the poor service in your company. Two weeks ago, our company signed a contract with your company to order 1,000 bedside lamps. Order number is HP3456236.

　　According to the contract, you shall deliver the goods within one week after the signing of the contract and deliver the goods within 10 days. However, up to now, we have not received the goods or any relevant information.

Please put the matter right at once. We are looking forward to your early reply.

Yours sincerely,

Wang Bin

2018年6月A级考试全真试题答案

Part I　Listening comprehension（共20分）

1. A　2. B　3. B　4. D　5. C　6. B　7. A　8. D　9. C　10. D

11. more exciting　12. wonderful　13. to grow　14. mistakes

15. different opportunities　16. prize presentation　17. develop and express　18. 41

19. Our Mother Earth　20. online system

Part II　Vocabulary & Structure（15分）

21. D　22. B　23. A　24. C　25. D　26. C　27. D　28. A　29. B　30. A

31. be conducted　32. considering　33. suitable　34. slightly　35. employment

Part III　Reading Comprehension（35分）

36. D　37. B　38. C　39. B　40. A　41. D　42. B　43. C　44. A　45. B

46. Olympics of Skills　47. Abu Dhabi

48. 77　49. 11　50. graphic design

51. H, I　52. A, P　53. Q, E　54. C, M　55. F, B

56. drive our vehicles　57. courteous and professional　58. High School Diploma

59. 20　60. satisfactory driving record

Part IV　Translation—English into Chinese（15分）

61. C　62. B　63. A　64. B

65. 在大多数情况下，顾客对餐厅的满意度是由服务员的服务决定的。如果你是服务员，你的主要责任是确保你所有的顾客满意，他们的需求能得到满足。因此，你必须准备好应对来自客户的各种需求。然而，你最重要的职责是确保准确地为客人点单，这样他才能按照自己喜欢的方式享用食物。

Part V　Writing（15分）

【参考范文】

Dear General Manager,

We held a meeting at 2 p.m. on June 17, 2018 in the first meeting room of the company's office building, and all the staff of the sales department attended the meeting.

The main points of the meeting are as follows: Firstly, the sales manager made a speech on the national sales situation of our company's first half year. Secondly, the staff discussed the sales department's work in the second half of the year. It was agreed that the focus of the second half year was to develop new products and exploit overseas markets. Last but not the least, we would like to know whether it is necessary to hold a meeting to inform all department managers of the above messages.

Yours,
Sales Department Manager
John Smith

2017年12月A级考试全真试题答案

Part I　Listening comprehension（共20分）

1. A　2. D　3. C　4. A　5. B　6. D　7. A　8. B　9. C　10. D

11. celebrate　12. set up　13. take this opportunity　14. support　15. best service

16. exciting　17. understanding　18. more difficult　19. sports competitions

20. future career

Part II　Vocabulary & Structure（15分）

21. D　22. A　23. D　24. C　25. B　26. C　27. A　28. B　29. B　30. D

31. effectively　32. attached　33. difference　34. were required　35. buying

Part III　Reading Comprehension（35分）

36. D　37. B　38. A　39. C　40. B　41. C　42. A　43. D　44. B　45. C

46. 1984　47. families and seniors　48. emergency shelters　49. 18 million　50. 70 meals

51. L, F　52. C, O　53. E, Q　54. M, K　55. H, I

56. new production plant　57. regular and loyal　58. at the top　59. a comfortable seat

60. January 5

Part IV　Translation—English into Chinese（15分）

61. B　62. C　63. B　64. B

65. 在家工作有许多优点，比如时间灵活，能照顾家庭。但是，同样也有一些缺点。例如，如果你不在传统的办公室工作，你就很难理解办公室文化。这是一种在办公室才能感知的归属感。你可以在办公室的公用区和你的同事见面聊天。

Part V　Writing（15分）

【参考范文】

Dear Mr. Johnson,

I bought a washing machine from your shop two weeks ago, but I regret to tell you that it went down three days later. After checking, I assumed that the machine couldn't work due to the improper packing. I called the Customer Service Center and they promised to offer on-site repair. However, they haven't sent anyone yet. Therefore, I would like to ask you to repair the machine as soon as possible or to replace a new one. Otherwise, I demand that a full refund be made to me.

Thank you for your consideration and I will be looking forward to your reply.

Yours,
Wang Xiaolin

2017年6月A级考试全真试题答案

Part I　Listening comprehension（共20分）

1. C　2. A　3. B　4. C　5. D　6. C　7. B　8. C　9. A　10. D

11. daily tasks　12. tourist season　13. followed　14. permits　15. concerning

16. Bicycles / Bikes　17. 50 years　18. at home　19. after-sales service

20. special discount

Part II　Vocabulary & Structure（15分）

21. B　22. A　23. D　24. C　25. B　26. C　27. D　28. B　29. C　30. D

31. personal　32. to know　33. asking　34. impression　35. more effective

Part III　Reading Comprehension（35分）

36. D　37. A　38. C　39. A　40. D　41. B　42. A　43. B　44. C　45. C

46. credit card number　47. confirmation　48. 416-397-8247　49. Monday to Friday

50. latest version

51. Q, D　52. P, M　53. F, O　54. E, G　55. K, I

56. market　57. advertise your store　58. other households　59. safety　60. promotional

Part IV　Translation—English into Chinese（15分）

61. A　62. A　63. C　64. B

65. 欢迎下榻我们的酒店。希望您拥有一个愉快的住宿体验。您的舒适及愉快是我们的首要责任。能为您提供最高品质的服务是我们的荣幸。这份顾客信息指南介绍了酒店提供的所有服务项目及娱乐设施。如果您有任何疑问，请致电酒店前台咨询。

Part V　Writing（15分）

【参考范文】

Notice

　　According to the weather report, the typhoon will attack our city in two days with a storm. Please pay attention to the safety of you and your family, try not to go out and take precautions. If you need any help, please contact us at 656××793.

　　In addition, the service center is equipped with sandbags, which is free for the first floor residents.

Volunteers Team of the neighborhood

Model Test One（Level A）

Part I　Listening Comprehension（共20分）

1. C　2. A　3. C　4. B　5. D　6. B　7. C　8. D　9. D　10. C

11. eating habits　12. shares　13. do their best　14. more dishes　15. occasion

16. many advantages 17. pleasure 18. goes hunting 19. websites 20. communicate with

Part II　Vocabulary & Structure（共 15 分）

21. D 22. D 23. C 24. B 25. C 26. C 27. D 28. D 29. A 30. A

31. more important 32. reasonable 33. are asked 34. extremely 35. movement

Part III　Reading Comprehension（共 35 分）

36. A 37. B 38. C 39. B 40. B 41. D 42. B 43. C 44. D 45. A

46. 25% increase 47. Marketing Department 48. computerized network

49. on-the-job training 50. a new department

51. C, B 52. I, E 53. K, J 54. L, N 55. R, P

56. Waikiki Beach 57. 545 58. prompt and reasonable 59. Half price 60. discounts

Part IV　Translation（共 15 分）

61. B 62. D 63. D 64. D

65. 7月10日，该公司将召开第一届全球电视会议。所有的二十套设备将通过卫星广播系统连接在一起，这样，雇员们就可以互相看得见，并且可以互相对话。布莱克先生将首先致辞，并告诉我们下一个五年的目标。接下来，每一位经理将谈论当前的挑战。最后的一个小时用于反映各地的问题。如果会议成功主办，我们希望安排全球电视年会。

Part V　Writing（共 15 分）

【参考范文】

June 14，2018

Dear Mr. Johnson，

　　I have received the sales report of the first half of the year. In the recent months，the sales of our products fell by 20% and the sales in some areas was even off 50% because of many reasons such as the design of the products，the promotion plan，etc. Department heads meeting will be held on the next Monday morning. Your department is expected to propose specific measures to improve the sales of our products.

　　I'm looking forward to your proposal.

Sincerely yours，

Smith

Model Test Two（Level A）

Part I　Listening Comprehension（共 20 分）

1. D 2. A 3. B 4. C 5. D 6. B 7. B 8. D 9. A 10. D

11. business partners 12. endless 13. for the sake 14. forget 15. going on

16. are interested in 17. career change 18. further study 19. opportunity 20. salary

Part II　Vocabulary & Structure（共 15 分）

21. A 22. C 23. B 24. B 25. B 26. B 27. B 28. D 29. D 30. D

31. employers 32. introduction 33. has worked/has been working 34. lost 35. boring

Part III　Reading Comprehension（共 35 分）

36. A　37. D　38. C　39. C　40. B　41. D　42. A　43. B　44. D　45. C

46. Stephen Smith　47. public relations　48. flexibility　49. broader responsibility

50. an interview

51. M, C　52. Q, E　53. O, G　54. L, B　55. H, N

56. cost　57. coverage goals　58. An agent　59. family members　60. other debts

Part IV　Translation（共 15 分）

61. B　62. C　63. B　64. A

65. 女士们，先生们，早上好，欢迎参加公司年会。史密斯先生将作关于公司上半年业务发展的报告，然后布莱克博士将解读下半年销量。格林先生将做关于国内市场目前形势的报告，国内市场形势将会影响我们将来的业务。最后，我们很高兴解答您提出的问题。现在，我们有请史密斯先生。

Part V　Writing（共 15 分）

【参考范文】

I'm the Marketing Manager of ABC Company. It is scheduled that our company will hold a New Product Release on December 18, 2015 at Orient Hotel. We will display our new products and invite relevant experts to give reports. There will be a business discussion after the meeting.

Thank you for your cooperation for many years. You are cordially invited to attend the Release. Please reply to confirm whether you will join before the end of November. We look forward to your attendance.

Model Test Three（Level A）

Part I　Listening Comprehension（共 20 分）

1. D　2. D　3. C　4. C　5. C　6. A　7. D　8. A　9. D　10. D

11. staying　12. show　13. anywhere　14. Finally　15. including　16. little cars

17. air pollution　18. much lower/less　19. 55 miles　20. long trips

Part II　Vocabulary & Structure（共 15 分）

21. C　22. A　23. C　24. D　25. B　26. D　27. A　28. D　29. D　30. B

31. talking　32. appointment　33. respected　34. had studied　35. memorial

Part III　Reading Comprehension（共 35 分）

36. D　37. C　38. D　39. B　40. C　41. C　42. C　43. A　44. B　45. D

46. new inventions　47. designer　48. alphabet patterns　49. in cars, lorries　50. Rolls-Royce

51. A, L　52. G, E　53. O, M　54. C, I　55. K, H

56. behind the schedule　57. July　58. names　59. 30%　60. compensate

Part IV　Translation（共 15 分）

61. B　62. C　63. A　64. C

65. 今天，你可以用智能手机处理几乎一切你的银行业务。许多主要银行准许顾客使用智能手机支付账单或转账。专家们说将来约有 70% 的美国人会使用手机银行服务。但是有些人担心手机银行服务的安全性。如果你经常使用智能手机的银行服务，你应该安装防病毒软件并给手机设置密码。

Part V Writing（共15分）

【参考范文】

Date：May 8，2018
To：bookingservice@snh.net.cn
From：lj0534@ttyc.com.cn
Subject：Booking a suite and a single room
Dear Sirs，

　　Our Sales Manager, Mr. William Taylor, and his secretary, Mr. James Rogers will be in Xinning from May 29 to June 2. Therefore, kindly reserve us one suite and one single room for four nights beginning May 29.

　　We wish you could satisfy our special requests. As Mr. William Taylor will meet customers from some foreign companies in the hotel, and probably sign contracts with some of them, we hope the suite that we reserve will be quiet and have enough seats and tea sets. What's more, the single room for his secretary should be equipped with telephone and fax machine so that he can connect quickly with our company.

Yours faithfully,
Li Jun

Model Test Four（Level A）

Part I　Listening Comprehension（共20分）

1. B　2. C　3. A　4. A　5. A　6. B　7. C　8. C　9. D　10. A
11. pursue　12. costs much money　13. competitors　14. abroad　15. realizing
16. almost any place　17. 21,000　18. 60 feet　19. swim very well　20. its little tail

Part II　Vocabulary & Structure（共15分）

21. C　22. A　23. D　24. A　25. B　26. C　27. A　28. D　29. B　30. B
31. (should) be　32. wonderful　33. proposal　34. are not allowed　35. eagerly

Part III　Reading Comprehension（共35分）

36. B　37. B　38. D　39. C　40. A　41. C　42. B　43. D　44. A　45. C
46. almost every country　47. help people　48. Jean Henri Dunant
49. The Geneva Convention　50. many services
51. C, L　52. P, D　53. M, A　54. B, K　55. I, O
56. Christ Church　57. marked Private　58. picnicking　59. follow the advice
60. prevent crime

Part IV　Translation（共15分）

61. D　62. C　63. C　64. D
65. 我们谨邀请您向第十九届世界企业管理大会提交论文。大会将于2016年6月29日

· 173 ·

至 7 月 2 日在法国巴黎召开。论文递交截止日期是 2016 年 1 月 21 日。本次会议的重点是小型企业管理，这与您的研究领域密切相关。如果您需要更多时间准备，请告知我们对您合适的时间。如果此时间对我们也合适，我们将会通知您。

Part V　Writing（共 15 分）

【参考范文】

It is scheduled that our company will hold a New Product Release on December 18, 2015 at Orient Hotel. We will display our new products, and invite relevant experts to make reports. There will be a business discussion after the meeting.

Thank you for your cooperation for many years. You are cordially invited to attend the Release. Please reply to confirm whether you will join before the end of November. We look forward to your attendance.

Yours sincerely,
Zhang Wei
Marketing Manager of ABC Company

B级听力文稿（Scripts for the Tests）

2018年12月B级考试全真试题听力文稿

Section A

1. Can I speak to your department manager?
2. Do you know Mr. Green, the chief engineer?
3. How can I start the machine?
4. Do you enjoy traveling on business?
5. How long have you been in the new position?
6. Where did you get the information?
7. What do you think of your boss?

Section B

8. W: Do you know what day is April 22?

    M: It is Earth Day.

    Q: What day is April 22?

9. W: Do you have telephone banking services?

    M: Yes, of course.

    Q: What is the woman asking about?

10. W: Where should I sign my name?

    M: At the bottom of the page.

    Q: What does the woman want to know?

11. M: Where can I learn more about your training program?

    W: From our website.

    Q: How can the man get more information?

12. W: How does our new product sell in the market?

    M: It sells well.

    Q: What are the two speakers talking about?

13: M: When can we get our orders?

    W: You will receive them within three days.

    Q: What is the man asking about?

14: W: When did you start your company?

    M: In 1998. Now it has over 350 employees.

    Q: What do we know about the company from the dialogue?

Section C

Conversation 1

W: You seem quite busy these days.

M: Yes. We're doing a market survey.

W: Really? What's it about?

M: About people's attitudes toward online shopping.

W: What results have you got?

M: Most young people prefer shopping online.

W: How about old people?

M: Some old people also like online shopping.

Q15: What is the man doing these days?

Q16: What can we learn about online shopping from the conversation?

Conversation 2

M: Hi, Jenny. I've found a summer job.

W: That's fine.

M: I will be working at Disneyland.

W: Wow, sounds great.

M: How about you, Jenny?

W: I've got an offer as a tour guide.

M: But a tour guide has to work long hours.

W: That's why I haven't made up my mind yet.

Q17: What do we learn about the man?

Q18: What job is offered to the woman?

Q19: Why hasn't the woman made up her mind to accept the job?

Section D

Good evening, ladies and gentlemen!

First of all, I'd like to express a sincere welcome to you all, the new comers of our company. As you know, our company is one of the top 50 companies in the country and has a history of more than 100 years. I think you must be proud of being a member of such a great company. But we cannot depend on tradition alone. We need new employees with new knowledge and creative ideas.

I would like to welcome you once again, and from today, let's begin to work together.

2018年6月B级考试全真试题听力文稿

Section A

1. May I take your order now?

2. Hi, John, how was your trip to Paris?

3. Could I book a double room for next Friday?

4. May I come in and have a talk with you?

5. Could I make an appointment with Doctor Green?

6. Tom, could you give me the report?

7. Mr. Brown, can you fill in this form now?

Section B

8. M: How shall we go to the city center?

   W: Let's walk there. It's not far from here.

   Q: How will the two speakers go to the city center?

9. M: When can you have the design ready, Mary?

   W: Will tomorrow morning be okay?

   Q: What are the two speakers talking about?

10. W: Have you got any work experience?

    M: Yes, I have been a programmer for two years.

    Q: What can we learn about the man?

11. M: Is your job difficult?

    W: Yes, it's hard to deal with angry customers.

    Q: What is the difficult part of the woman's job?

12. M: You are here on holiday, aren't you?

    W: No, I'm here on business.

    Q: Why does the woman come here?

13. W: What's wrong with your car?

    M: The front window was broken.

    Q: What happened to the man's car?

14. W: I'm trying to look for a new job, any tips?

    M: Why not attend a job fair?

    Q: What does the man advise the woman to?

Section C

Converation1

M: Good morning, can I help you?

W: Morning, sir. I need to report a case.

M: What is it about?

W: My handbag was stolen.

M: When did you find it was stolen?

W: Ten minutes ago.

M: What's in your handbag?

W: My passport.

15. Why did the woman make the phone call?

16. What was in the woman's handbag?

Converation2

M: What's wrong with you?

W: It's my stomach. It's killing me here.

M: How long have you got this pain?

W: Since this morning.

M: Have you ever had stomach pain before?

W: No.

M: I think we have to get you to the emergency room right away.

W: OK.

17. What is the woman's problem?

18. When did the woman begin to have this illness?

19. What is the doctor going to do for the patient?

Section D

Volunteers are our heart and soul. Please come and help us build homes for local low-income families. There is no experience needed and we supply the safety training. Just volunteer for a day. It's fun, rewarding and you can learn some new skills!

If building isn't your thing, come and volunteer for one of our events or at our offices.

You must be at least 14 years of age to volunteer and those 15 years and under must come with a parent.

Come and sign up now to volunteer your time.

2017年12月B级考试全真试题听力文稿

Section A

1. Excuse me, where is the information center?

2. Can you show me how to use this machine?

3. How was your flight, Mr. Smith?

4. It's a new model. Do you want to try it?

5. Would you sign your name here, please?

6. What do you think about our holiday plan?

7. This T-shirt is a little too small. Can I have a larger size?

Section B

8. W: Why do you look so worried?

   M: I'll have a job interview this afternoon.

   Q: What is the man worried about?

9. W: Mr. Smith, here is the new price list.

   M: Thank you. That's what I need.

   Q: What does the woman give to the man?

10. M: Shall we tell John about what's going on?

    W: Yes, of course. I'll call him right now.

    Q: What will the woman do?

11. W: We need to use the meeting room this Friday.
    M: Well, I'm sorry. It has been booked.
    Q: Why can't the woman use the meeting room?
12. W: So how was your presentation?
    M: I've no idea. I was so nervous.
    Q: How did the man feel while making his presentation?
13. W: Jack, you are looking for a new job, aren't you?
    M: Yeah, I've got a job offer.
    Q: What can we learn about the man?
14. M: Have you got the driving license?
    W: Not yet. I've just passed the road test.
    Q: What can we learn from the conversation?

Section C

Conversation 1

W: Hello, Mr. Brown. It's Linda.
M: Hello, Linda.
W: I'm calling to ask whether you've decided to place an order of our products.
M: Not yet.
W: Our products are of high quality. You won't be disappointed.
M: Emm, but we still have to think about the price.
W: We always offer good discounts.
15. Why does the woman call the man?
16. What does the woman say about their products?

Conversation 2

W: Mr. Wang, what's wrong with your car?
M: It wouldn't start this morning.
W: Did you check the battery?
M: Yeah, it was dead again.
W: Perhaps you have to buy a new battery.
M: But I bought it only last month. It's still new.
W: What are you going to do then?
M: I'll return it to the store.
17. What happened to the man's car?
18. What does the man say about the battery?
19. What will the man do with the battery?

Section D

I am Mike Wang, a real estate agent. I manage to sell this home in just 15 days. I would love to help you buy or sell. Properties in this area are in high demand. If you have considered selling your home, I would love to speak with you and help you in any way possible. If you are currently renting a home and would like to buy one, give me a call. Home ownership has many advantages over renting and is not as difficult as many think. Call me today and let me help you make the right decision.

2017年6月B级考试全真试题听力文稿

Section A

1. Can I help you, Madam?
2. May I have your name, please?
3. Would you like a cup of coffee?
4. Shall we meet on Friday?
5. Excuse me, are you Jane Smith from England?
6. Are you interested in this training course?
7. Would you like to attend the sales meeting?

Section B

8. M: This building looks quite old.
   W: Yes, it was built about 150 years ago.
   Q: When was the building built?

9. W: Are you satisfied with your job?
   M: Yes, the boss is nice and the pay is good.
   Q: What does the man think of his job?

10. W: Does your city have a large population?
    M: Yes, about 3 million people.
    Q: What does the woman ask about the city?

11. M: Have you ever been to Shenzhen?
    W: Yes, many times. It's a very modern city.
    Q: What does the woman think of the city?

12. M: Are you planning to study abroad?
    W: I wish I could, but I haven't got enough money.
    Q: What problem does the woman have?

13. M: Excuse me, how can I apply for a membership card?
    W: Please fill in this form first.
    Q: What will the man probably do first?

14. M: Hi, Jane. What's wrong with you?
    W: I've got a headache.
    Q: What can we learn about the woman?

Section C

Conversation 1

W: Good morning.
M: Good morning. I want to rent an apartment.

W: What kind of apartment do you want?
M: A two-bedroom one.
W: Where do you want it to be?
M: Near my office in the downtown.
W: Yes, we have several apartments available.

15. What kind of apartment does the man want to rent?
16. Where does the man want the apartment to be?

Conversation 2

W: Good morning.
M: Good morning.
W: Why are you interested in this job?
M: I want to have more opportunities.
W: Good. How long have you been working at your current position?
M: For five years.
W: What do you expect to be in a few years?
M: I hope I can become a skilled engineer.

17. Why does the man apply for the job?
18. How long has the man been working in his current position?
19. What does the man expect to be in the near future?

Section D

First of all, on behalf of all the people from our company, I would like to say "Thank you for inviting us to such a wonderful party". I think the music is lovely, the food and wine are very nice, and the people here are all very kind. Also we've enjoyed meeting and talking to you, sharing the comfortable time together. We have really enjoyed ourselves. I hope we will be able to maintain the good relationship and make next year another great one together. Thank you again for the party. We've really had a great time.

Model Test One (Level B)

Section A

1. We haven't seen each other for a long time. How are you doing?
2. What's the matter with you?
3. What size does Jane wear?
4. It's hot. Why not go swimming?
5. Do you know how much it costs?
6. I want to buy this T-shirt. Shall I make an offer?
7. Can I charge it on my credit card?

Section B

8. W: I told you that you should not be late for class.

M: Well, I'm sorry. The bus came late and the traffic was heavy.

   Q: What might the man be?

9. M: It's already 7 o'clock. The film will start in 20 minutes.

   W: Don't worry. It only takes us 15 minutes to get there.

   Q: When will the film start?

10. W: Would you please sit down and wait for several minutes?

    M: I can't wait. I have to go right now.

    Q: What can we learn about the man?

11. M: Dear, can you watch the football match with me?

    W: Sorry, I have something to buy.

    Q: Where is the woman going?

12. W: Are you coming with us to Li's birthday party?

    M: I'd love to, but my daughter got a cold and I have to take care of her.

    Q: Why can't the man go to Li's birthday party?

13. W: How much are the potatoes?

    M: Half a pound a kilogram, madam.

    Q: What's the woman?

14. M: How do you like it?

    W: I like it, but the sleeves are too short and it's a little tight around the waist.

    Q: Where did this conversation most likely take place?

Section C

Conversation 1

W: How are you getting on, White? Are you still working for the Merry Lynch Bank?

M: Yes, Kitty, that's right.

W: I suppose you know quite a lot about banking by now, don't you?

M: Oh, yes. To tell you the truth, I'm a bit tired of it.

W: Really? Isn't it good to work in a bank?

M: You know I've been working for the Merry Lynch Bank for over 15 years.

W: So you are thinking of making a change, are you?

M: Yes, I am. Actually, you know, I'm thinking of beginning my own business.

W: That sounds great.

M: Yes, I think it over, but the problem is money. If I had enough money, I'd leave the bank tomorrow.

W: What are you going to do to solve the problem?

M: I'll borrow some money from a bank, of course, but not from the one I've been working for.

Q15. How does White like his work?

Q16. What does White plan to do?

Q17. Where is White going to borrow money?

Conversation 2

M: Good morning. Will you book a plane ticket to London for me?

W: Yes, sir. What time would you like to leave?

M: Next Tuesday, if possible.

W: That'll be the 21st of December.

M: Yes, that's right.

W: There are several flights available.

M: Would you check what flights are available on the 21st of December?

W: All right. Let me check it over.

M: Morning flights will be perfect.

W: Yes, sir. There is a flight available on that day, at 10:00 a.m.

M: Fine. I'll take that flight, then.

W: 10:00 a.m. I'll fix your ticket.

M: When do I check in?

W: You must be there by 9:00 a.m.

M: Thank you.

Q18. What does the conversation talk about?

Q19. What's the relationship between the two speakers?

Section D

Old age has always been thought of as the worst age to be; but is not necessary for the old to be unhappy. With old age should come wisdom and the ability to help others with advice wisely given. The old have the joy of seeing their children making progress in life; they can watch their grandchildren growing up around them; and perhaps best of all, they can, if their life has been a useful one, feel the happiness of having come through the battle of life safely and having reached a time when they can lie back and rest, leaving others to continue the battle.

Model Test Two (Level B)

Section A

1. Would you like to have a cup of coffee?
2. Jeff looks very pale. Do you think he is ill?
3. What does your university look like?
4. I really enjoy classic music. How about you?
5. Will you be free this weekend?
6. Which sport do you like, football or basketball?
7. May I speak to Mr. Li?

Section B

8. M: What have you been doing these past five years?

   W: How time flies! It has been five years since we graduated from this school.

   Q: What is the probable relationship between the two speakers?

9. W: Can you lend me $4.00?

M: I had $10.00, but I just spent $7.00.

　　Q: How much money does the man have?

10. M: Excuse me, can you tell me which bus I should take to the People's park?

　　W: I'm afraid I can't. I've only been here for several days.

　　Q: Why can't the woman give the man directions?

11. W: What did your teacher tell you just now?

　　M: He said that I should have handed in my paper earlier.

　　Q: What can be concluded from the conversation?

12. M: I heard you were moving to a new house next month.

　　W: Yes, my neighbor plays the violin all night long and I can't fall asleep.

　　Q: Why is the woman going to move?

13. M: My flight leaves at 4:30.

　　W: Then you'd better leave for the airport at about 2:30.

　　Q: What can we learn from the conversation?

14. W: Can you tell me how much it costs to send this package by air?

　　M: OK, let me weigh it... three pounds.

　　Q: Where does the conversation probably take place?

Section C

Conversation 1

M: May I speak to Petty?

W: Speaking.

M: Good morning, Petty.

W: Good morning, Steward.

M: I'd like to discuss your suggestion with you as soon as possible. Would Tuesday be all right for you?

W: Tuesday. That's tomorrow?

M: Yes.

W: Let me see. How about tomorrow, say, 8:30?

M: Then suppose I come to your office at 8:30 tomorrow.

W: Good. I'll be expecting you then.

M: Thank you. Good-bye.

W: Good-bye.

Q15. What time do the two speakers agree to meet?

Q16. Why does the man make a call to the woman?

Conversation 2

M: No.11 Police Station. Can I help you?

W: Yes. It's about my son Leech. He went to the school this morning but hasn't been back yet and it's 6:00 p.m. now.

M: Just a moment, please. May I have his name?

W: Leech Smith, 112 Broadway.

M: Thank you. Now Mrs. Smith, what is the matter exactly?

W: Well, Leech left home at 7 o'clock this morning, but just now her teacher called me and asked why Leech didn't go to school.

M: Do you think it's possible that he went to friend's home?

W: I don't think so. I called his friends and our neighbors, but none of them had seen Leech today.

M: I see. Now, Let's move to some details. How old is he?

W: 10 years old. And he is 1.5 meters'tall.

M: What's he wearing?

W: A blue shirt, and white shoes, carrying a green school bag.

M: We'll do our best to find him, Mrs. Smith. Please try not to worry.

Q17. Where does this conversation most probably take place?

Q18. How long has Leech been away from home?

Q19. What's the color of Leech's shirt? And what's the color of his bag?

Section D

The word horsepower was first used two hundred years ago. James Watt had made the world's first widely used steam engine. He had no way of telling people exactly how powerful it was, for at that time there were no units for measuring power. Watt decided to find out how much work one strong horse could do in one minute. He called that unit one horsepower. With this unit he could measure the work his steam engine could do. He discovered that a horse could lift a 3,300-pound weight 10 feet into the air in one minute. His engine could lift a 3,300 pound weight 100 feet in one minute. Because his engine did ten times as much work as the horse, Watt called it a ten-horsepower engine.

Model Test Three (Level B)

Section A

1. Can you tell me the way to the Post Office?
2. You don't like your English teacher, do you?
3. How do you go to work every day?
4. Peter, can you tell me who won the soccer game?
5. How did you learn Italian?
6. Did you call me, Mary?
7. When do you start to serve dinner in the evening?

Section B

8. W: I have a sore throat.

   M: Let me have a look... Well, it's nothing serious.

   Q: What is the probable relationship between the two speakers?

9. M: How long does it take you home by bus?
   W: Only half an hour. But if in rush hour, it will take me 50 minutes.
   Q: How long does it take the woman to go home by bus when it isn't in rush hour?
10. W: If you can help me with this job, I would finish it before 5 o'clock.
    M: I would like to, but Mr. Golden told me to type some letters before I went home.
    Q: What did Mr. Golden ask the man to do?
11. M: When are you leaving for France?
    W: Well, I don't know. It's difficult to get the visa.
    Q: What does the woman mean?
12. W: I'm so excited that I can't sleep the whole night.
    M: I'd be excited too if I had got such a good job as yours.
    Q: Why was the woman excited?
13. M: This is the dining room.
    W: Good. What I want to know is what time they serve breakfast.
    Q: What does the woman mean?
14. M: Can I help you, Madam?
    W: Yeah, please show me the menu.
    Q: What's the relationship between the two speakers?

Section C

Conversation 1

M: Who do you work for?

W: ABC Company.

M: They're in the dress business, aren't they?

W: That's right. I'm the secretary to the General manager. What about you?

M: I work for IBM.

W: So you're in computers.

M: Yes, I'm a product manager.

W: What are you working on at the moment?

M: I can't give you all the details, because it's a secret. But we are developing a new product for the Chinese market.

Q15. Who does the woman work for?

Q16. What does the man deal with?

Conversation 2

M: Do you feel like going to the cinema?

W: Oh, yes, what kind of films do you like?

M: Well, I like all sorts of films, but my favorite sorts are those like Star Wars. You know, the fantasy, special effect ones that you can escape into another world. I also like mystery films, do you like mystery films?

W: Yes, but I don't like horror films because they really give me nightmares.

M: I don't like horror films either. They're sort of stupid and unbelievable. I do like crime films, you know, where you can follow the detective and try to guess who the murderer is.

W: What about a comedy or musical?

M: No, I'm not interested.

W: What about ringing up the ABC and find out what's on? Then we can decide.

M: OK. That's definitely the best thing we ought to do. Because I haven't got an evening paper.

Q17. What films do both the man and the woman like?

Q18. What does the man think of horror films?

Q19. What do they decide to do?

Section D

Fish are animals that live in water. They live in almost any place where there is water. Some are found in lakes, other fish live in the sea. Most fish never leave water. There are about 21,000 kinds of fish. One kind might not look like another. Some fish are very small. The smallest one is no bigger than a fly. Others are very big. The biggest fish can grow up to 60 feet. One kind of fish looks as if it has a little horse's head. It is called a sea horse. It doesn't swim very well. A sea horse is mostly pushed along by the moving water. What does it do when it wants to stay in one place? It takes hold of plants with its little tail.

Model Test Four (Level B)

Section A

1. Would you mind closing the door?

2. How do you like the book?

3. How long will it take you to go home by train?

4. I have no money with me now. How about lending me 100 yuan?

5. How is everything with you, Nancy?

6. I've got a sore throat and a bad cough.

7. I want to go to the shopping mall, but I don't know the way.

Section B

8. M: Make 20 copies for me.

   W: Yes, sir. I will do it right now.

   Q: What is the probable relationship between the two speakers?

9. W: Did you play basketball yesterday?

   M: I planned to. But it rained. So I cleaned the room instead.

   Q: What did the man do yesterday?

10. M: Hurry up, drink your coffee. The train is leaving. We'll be late.

    W: It's too hot for me to drink.

    Q: Where does the conversation probably take place?

11. W: I'm sorry to have kept you waiting.

M: That's all right. I've been here only for five minutes.

Q: Why did the woman apologize to the man?

12. M: Do you know where Diana is? I want her to type this report for me.

W: Well, I don't know. But I can show you how to use this machine.

Q: What's the woman's reply to the man?

13. W: Is the hotel near the bank where I should go?

M: Yes, it's exactly where you should go.

Q: Where should the woman go?

14. M: Are you going to your mother's in the downtown?

W: Yes, we haven't seen each other for a long time.

Q: Where is the woman going?

Section C

Conversation 1

M: Amy, what was your first job?

W: Well, when I graduated from the college in 1998, I worked first as a secretary to the General manager. That lasted for two years. Then I was promoted the personnel Manager.

M: What were your duties?

W: I was responsible for all personnel matters.

M: Did you enjoy it?

W: Well, the people were nice. I liked the people I worked with. But the job was poorly paid.

M: And how long did you stay there?

W: Oh, about a year. I left because I wanted to apply for a position in the Sales Department. That's where I work now.

Q15. What was Amy's first job?

Q16. What was Amy's second job?

Q17. How long did Amy stay in the Personnel Department?

Conversation 2

W: When did you become interested in collecting stamps?

M: Oh, when I was about ten years old. It's an exciting hobby. You know, the first postage stamps were issued in Britain in 1840.

W: Really? I didn't know that. I did know that the charge for mail delivery before the appearance of postage stamps was paid by either the sender or the receiver. How much was the usual charge?

M: Oh, about ten cents for a short distance. But post offices were losing money with that system. Rowland Hill, an Englishman, suggested using postage stamps. Here's a picture of the first two stamps issued.

W: They both bear a picture of Queen Victoria.

Q18. When were the first postage stamps issued?

Q19. Who paid for the mail delivery before the appearance of postage stamps?

Section D

New Zealand is famous for its agriculture. Most of the exports come from the farms. Yet only about 10% of the labor force work in agriculture, 25% of the labor force work in factories. Today the factories make clothes and shoes and a number of other consumer goods. Most of the heavy machinery has to be imported. Mining is not well-developed, but New Zealand has plenty of power. 85% of the electricity is produced by water. There is a lot of rain during the year, and there are many lakes and fast rivers in the mountains. Water power is cheaper than power from coal or oil. New Zealanders probably have the cheapest electricity in the world.

A级听力文稿（Scripts for the Tests）

2018年12月A级考试全真试题听力文稿

Section A

1. W: George, do you have any idea to improve our brand image?
   M: Oh, I've just talked about the brand image with Susan.
   Q: What are the two speakers talking about?

2. M: Hello, Customer Service. How can I help you?
   W: Yes, I'd like some information on your telephone banking service.
   Q: What is the woman asking about?

3. M: Excuse me, how can I get to the manager's office?
   W: Take the lift to the fifth floor. It's the third office on the left.
   Q: Where is the manager's office?

4. M: Would you help me to move into my new house this Saturday?
   W: I'm really sorry. I have an appointment with my doctor.
   Q: What does the woman mean?

5. W: Could you go to the airport to meet Mr. Smith, the new engineer?
   M: Certainly. What's the flight number?
   Q: What does the woman ask the man to do?

Section B

Conversation 1

M: There are many jobs offered in this career fair.
W: Yes. What job do you prefer?
M: Working in a news agency. I'd love to be a sports reporter.
W: Are you joking? A sports reporter? It seems so tiring.
M: And what would you like to do?
W: I want to work as a fashion designer.
M: Why?
W: It's more creative than a sports reporter.
M: Yes. But sports reporting is more exciting.
W: I hope we both can find an ideal job at this fair.

Q6: What job does the man prefer to do?

Q7: What does the woman think of sports reporting?

Q8: What does the woman prefer to be?

Conversation 2

W: Hello. Customer Service. Can I help you?

M: Yes. There seems to be something wrong with my electricity bill.

W: I'm sorry. Can you tell me your account number?

M: Certainly. It's 66767.

W: 66767, Mr. Smith?

M: Yes.

W: What's the problem?

M: I think I've been charged too much last month.

W: Why do you think so?

M: We have been away on vacation for two weeks. But the bill is doubled that of the previous month.

W: Let me have a check. And I'll see what I can do.

Q9: What does the man complain about?

Q10: Why does the man think he has been charged too much?

Section C

Good afternoon passengers. This is the pre-boarding announcement for flight 89B to Moscow. We are now inviting those passengers with small children, and any passengers requiring special assistance, to begin boarding at this time. Please have your boarding pass and identification ready. Regular boarding will begin in approximately ten minutes time. Thank you...

This is the final boarding call for passengers Eric and Fred Collins booked on flight 89B to Moscow. Please proceed to Gate 3 immediately.

The final checks are being completed and the captain will order for the doors of the aircraft to close in approximately five minutes time. I repeat. This is the final boarding call for Eric and Fred Collins. Thank you.

Section D

Today we are here to hold a party to say goodbye to Mr. Smith. We all know that he is going to leave us soon and he will become the manager of New York's branch of the company. I am very happy that he has been promoted. Mr. Smith has been working with us for the past five years. His working ability and kindness have left us a good impression. I think his absence from our office will be a great loss for us. However, it is lucky for the staff in New York's office to have Mr. Smith as their manager. We will be sure to miss you very much, Mr. Smith. We wish you the very best luck in your future work. And we also hope to keep in touch with you regularly.

Q16: What is the purpose of the party?

Q17: What new position is Mr. Smith going to take?

Q18: How long has Mr. Smith been working in the present office?

Q19: What has impressed the speaker and his colleagues most?

Q20: What does the speaker say at the end of the speech?

2018年6月A级考试全真试题听力文稿

Section A

1. M: I attend a computer training course twice a week. Why not join us?
   W: Good, I'm also interested in such a course.
   Q: What are the two people talking about?

2. W: How did you spend your summer vacation, John?
   M: I worked as a volunteer in a local hospital.
   Q: What did the man do in the summer vacation?

3. W: Hi Tom, you look tired. What's up?
   M: It's finals week and I have been up all nights studying.
   Q: Why does the man look tired?

4. W: What do you think of the schedule I've made?
   M: Very good. I can't agree with you more.
   Q: What does the man think of the schedule?

5. M: Excuse me, is the sales manager available now?
   W: Sorry, he is away on business. He won't be back until next week.
   Q: What can we learn about the sales manager?

Section B

Conversation 1

W: Good afternoon. Doctor Smith's office, how may I help you?
M: Hello, I'd like to make an appointment with Doctor Smith, please.
W: What do you need to see the doctor about?
M: Well, I've caught a cold and now I'm running a fever.
W: When do you want to see him?
M: May I see him now?
W: I'm afraid not. He is fully occupied.
M: How about 2 o'clock in the afternoon?
W: Yes, that's OK.
M: Thank you.
W: You are welcome.

Q6. What's wrong with the man?
Q7. When will the man see the doctor?

Conversation 2

M: Jane, have you got an offer?
W: Yes, I have. I will start working in three weeks.
M: Excellent, what company are you going to work for?

W: It's a website design company.

M: Is it a big company?

W: It has about 120 employees.

M: Where is the company?

W: It's in the downtown area.

M: Good, so you can go to work by subway.

W: Yes.

M: Wish you all the best with your new job.

W: Thank you.

Q8. What kind of company is the woman going to work with?

Q9. Where is the company located?

Q10. How will the woman most likely go to work?

Section C

Good Evening Everyone!

Thank you for this wonderful farewell party for me. When I'm leaving, nothing is more exciting than to learn that I am so special. I want everyone here to know that this is the place where I have become the person I am today. I have learned everything that I needed to learn, and more, from this wonderful job. I want to thank this organization, particularly my director, Mr. Anderson, for giving me the space to grow, for allowing me to make my own decisions, and then learning from my own mistakes.

As I move on to a world with different opportunities, I can only say "Thank you, my dear friends", and I will always cherish everything this company has given to me.

Section D

Dear judges, guests, teachers and students,

It is my great honor to attend this prize presentation ceremony of the International Arts Contest. I am happy to share the joy and achievements of the event with all of you. This contest provides young people with a good opportunity to develop and express their creativity. It also enables the public to appreciate different cultures. Since 2010, the number of participating countries and regions has increased from 25 to 41. This year, the theme is Our Mother Earth. It is very encouraging that over 5,000 pieces of photographic works have been submitted through the online system from overseas. I would like to take this opportunity to welcome our guests and prize winners from different parts of the world. Thank you very much!

Q16. What ceremony is the speaker addressing?

Q17. What opportunity does the contest provide for young people?

Q18. How many countries and regions participate in the contest now?

Q19. What is the theme of the contest for this year?

Q20. In what way are the photographic works submitted from overseas?

2017年12月A级考试全真试题听力文稿

Section A

1. M: Susan, do you know how long it takes to apply for a visa for China?

   W: 5 to 7 work days, I'm afraid.

   Q: What are the two people talking about?

2. M: May I take your order, Madam?

   W: Yes, I'd like a vegetable soup and Peking Duck, please.

   Q: Where does the conversation most probably take place?

3. W: I'm calling to ask about the apartment you advertised in yesterday's newspaper.

   M: Yes, it's still available. Would you like to take a look?

   Q: Where does the woman get the information of the apartment?

4. W: When can you finish your project report, David?

   M: At least in two weeks. I have to check all the statistics again.

   Q: What does the man have to do with his report?

5. M: Do you think Mr. Brown is qualified for this position?

   W: Yes, he would be a perfect choice.

   Q: What does the woman mean?

Section B

Conversation 1

W: Good morning, Great Wall Hotel.

M: Good morning. I'd like to make a reservation for one room.

W: No problem. What's the exact day of your arrival?

M: April 25.

W: How long will you be staying?

M: For 3 nights.

W: Your name, please?

M: Charles White.

W: OK, Mr. White. And your phone number, please.

M: It's 55545783. By the way, what's your check-in time?

W: 2:00 in the afternoon.

M: Great, thank you so much.

Q6: Why does the man make the phone call?

Q7: When will the man arrive at the hotel?

Q8: What does the man want to know at the end of the conversation?

Conversation 2

W: Hello, Mr. Johnson. I'm calling to say goodbye to you.

M: Hi, Mary. How time flies! When are you leaving?

W: This Wednesday. I must thank you for what you've done for me during my stay here.

M: We are glad to be working with you. When does the plane leave?

W: 10:00, Wednesday morning.

M: I see. Let me ask Linda to drive you to the airport.

W: Thanks. It's very kind of you. Welcome to visit my country when you have time.

M: I will. Goodbye.

W: Goodbye.

Q9: Why does the woman call the man?

Q10: How will the woman get to the airport?

Section C

Good evening, ladies and gentlemen!

On behalf of our company, I'd like to thank you for coming to celebrate the opening of our new branch office in Hattiesburg. This branch is the 10th office we have set up in the country. I'm glad we finally opened a branch in the southeast area. Now, I would like to take this opportunity to thank all the staff here for your efforts to establish the branch. In order to successfully operate the branch, we need the support of customers like you being present. We will do our best to provide you with the best service. Thank you very much.

Section D

From now on, you are college students. College life is an exciting experience in our life. It is in college that you get better understanding of yourself and of your capabilities. It doesn't matter whether you're attending a community college or a top university. Study is going to be more difficult. Your responsibility and workload would also increase, so you have to get ready for that. College also involves much of entertainment. There would be events like plays, festivals, debates, sports competitions and many more fun activities. No doubt you will be having a great faculty and teachers. This is your time now and you're going to make a decision of your future career.

Q16: What does the speaker say about college life?

Q17: What will you get in college?

Q18: What does the speaker say about study in college?

Q19: What entertainment events does the speaker mention?

Q20: What does the speaker tell the students at the end of the speech?

2017年6月A级考试全真试题听力文稿

Section A

1. M: Excuse me, may I use this printer?

   W: Sorry, it's out of order.

   Q: What does the woman mean?

2. M: Hi, Mary! I've got a new job. The salary is good.

   W: Really, congratulations!

Q: Why does the woman congratulate the man?

3. W: Can I help you, sir?

   M: Yes, I want to rent a car for one week.

   Q: What does the man want to do?

4. W: Good morning. What's the problem?

   M: I'd like to change this shirt for a larger size.

   Q: Why does the man want to change the shirt?

5. W: Hello, sales department.

   M: Hello, I'm John Smith form ABC Company. May I speak to your manager?

   Q: Whom does the man want to speak to?

Section B

Conversation 1

W: Mr. Johnson, can you deliver our goods next week?

M: No, I'm afraid we can't.

W: When is the earliest time we can receive them?

M: Early next month, I think.

W: It's too late. You see, the sales season for this commodity is coming soon.

M: Yes, I understand.

W: Is there anything else you can do?

M: Maybe we can deliver the goods by air instead of by train.

W: Well, the cost would be much higher.

M: That's true. But you can receive them next week.

W: All right. Perhaps that's all we can do now.

Q6: Why does the woman think the delivery is too late?

Q7: What suggestion does the man make to deliver the goods?

Q8: When can the woman receive the goods?

Conversation 2

W: Good afternoon, sir. May I help you?

M: Yes, I'd like to apply for a job at your company.

W: Good, but what position are you applying for?

M: HR manager assistant.

W: What's your major at college?

M: Business management.

W: That's good. And have you got any experience?

M: Yes, I worked part time as an HR manager assistant for six months.

W: Fine. Now, please fill in this form and wait for our further notice.

M: Okay. Thank you very much.

Q9: What position is the man applying for?

Q10: How long did the man work part time as an HR manager assistant?

Section C

I think we'll begin now. First I'd like to welcome you all and thank you for your coming, especially at such short notice. I know you are all very busy and it's difficult to take time away from your daily tasks for meetings.

As you can see on the agenda, today we will focus on the upcoming tourist season. First we'll discuss the groups that will be coming in from Germany. After that, we'll discuss the North American tours, followed by the Asian tours. If time permits, we will also discuss the Australian tours which are booked for early September. Finally, I'm going to request some feedback from all of you concerning last year's tours and where you think we can improve.

Section D

Good morning, Ladies and Gentlemen!

Let me introduce our company to you first. We are one of the leading bicycle manufactures in China. Our company was set up 50 years ago. We produce many brands of bicycles, and they sell very well both at home and abroad. We have agents all over the world and we have an office here in London too. Because of the high quality and good after-sales service we provide, our bicycles enjoy a good reputation. If you're interested in our products, we can send you our catalog and price list. For large orders, we promise to give you a special discount.

Q16. What product does the company produce?

Q17. When was the company set up?

Q18. Where are their products sold?

Q19. According to the speaker, why do their products have a good reputation?

Q20. What does the speaker promise to give for a large order?

Model Test One (Level A)

Section A

1. M: Are you ready to order now?

   W: Yes, I'll have some salad, roast beef, and mashed potatoes.

   Q: What is the probable relationship between the two speakers?

2. M: Hello, I'd like to see some brochures. I'm thinking of taking a trip.

   W: Here are some. Where would you like to go?

   Q: Where does the woman work?

3. W: What's your advice to young people who are thinking about self-employment?

   M: Self-employment can yield a sense of achievement, but it also carries high risks.

   Q: What are they talking about?

4. M: I heard you had accepted an offer from a big corporation.

   W: Yes, the fierce competition is very attractive to me.

   Q: What attracts the woman to work in the big corporation?

   M: I want to study law in the university. What's your ideal job in the future?

W: I want to be an accountant.

Q: What does the man want to be in the future?

Section B

Conversation 1

M: I'll treat Mr. Lee to dinner tomorrow evening.

W: Well, Mr. Lee has a very good taste in wine, and he is one of our biggest clients.

M: Where do you think I should take him?

W: I suggest you take him to a decent French restaurant.

M: That's a good idea.

W: Make sure you make a really good impression.

M: Then which one do you recommend?

W: La Place is great. Ranked No.2 in this year's Gourmet Magazine, it is just second to Les Parisians.

M: We'll go to La Place. Could you book a table for four at 7p.m.?

W: Sure.

Q6: Who is Mr. Lee?

Q7: Which restaurant will the man go to?

Q8: When will their dinner begin?

Conversation 2

M: Excuse me, madam. May I talk to you?

W: Sure, come on in. What can I do for you?

M: Well, madam, as you know. I have been an employee of this company for over nine years.

W: Yes?

M: Madam, I would like a raise.

W: A raise? This is just not the right time.

M: You must take into consideration my hard work and loyalty to this company for nearly a decade.

W: Okay, I'm willing to offer you a twelve percent raise and an extra five days of vacation time.

M: Great! It's a deal! Thank you, madam!

W: You are welcome.

Q9: What are the man's good qualities?

Q10: How much raise does the woman offer the man?

Section C

The main difference between Chinese and Western eating habits is that unlike the West, where everyone has his own plate of food, in China the dishes are placed on the table and everybody shares. Chinese are very proud of their culture of food and will do their best to give you a taste of many different types of cuisine. Among friends, they will just order enough for the people there. If they are taking somebody out for dinner, they will usually order more dishes than the number of guests. If it is a business dinner or a very formal occasion, there is likely to be a huge amount of food that will be impossible to finish.

Section D

Do you have your own hobbies? Do you keep in touch with people through your common hobbies? There is no doubt that hobbies have many advantages. Hobbies offer pleasure and help people relax after a busy day's work or study; they also say things about a person. By asking about and knowing one's hobbies, we can gain certain insight into the person's personality or character. Someone who goes hunting during weekends may be more energetic; someone who prefers reading or writing may be more of a quiet and silent type. Nowadays a lot of clubs and websites are available for those who share the same hobbies. For example a football fan can always join a club or access a website to communicate with other fans.

Model Test Two (Level A)

Section A

1. W: Excuse me, sir, but are you Mr. Brown from Chicago?
   M: Oh, yes. I'm Brown from ABC Company.
   Q: What is the probable relationship between the two speakers?
2. M: Did you enjoy your trip?
   W: Yes, it was a very smooth and pleasant flight.
   Q: How did the woman travel?
3. W: How many people are there in your party?
   M: There are altogether five people in the delegation this time.
   Q: How many people are there in total?
4. W: Now that you are in China, how about trying some Chinese dinner?
   M: That sounds great.
   Q: What are they going to do?
5. W: I'm trying to arrange a meeting for next week, can you come on Monday?
   M: I'm sorry, I can't. Could you make it Thursday instead?
   Q: What time would be suitable for the man?

Section B

Conversation 1

W: UA Reservations. May I help you?

M: I'd like to make reservations for a flight to Vancouver.

W: When will you be departing?

M: Around eight tonight. Are there any flights available around that time?

W: How many tickets do you want?

M: Two seats, please.

W: Two seats, Vancouver, around eight...We have a flight leaving at 8:15 tonight.

M: That will be fine. My name is Li Wei, and I'll be with Mr. Wang Gang.

W: Fine. Check in will be thirty minutes before departure.

M: Thank you.

Q6. What is the man's flight destination?

Q7. How many tickets does the man want?

Q8. When will the flight leave?

Conversation 2

W: Hello, ABC company. May I help you?

M: Hello. This is Li Ming. May I speak to Mr. Green?

W: I'm sorry, but he is in Shanghai on business.

M: Do you have any idea when he will be back?

W: Probably sometime tomorrow.

M: I have a question about the F-325 radio. Is there anyone else who can help me?

W: Of course, Mr. Brown is the Export Manager. Would you like to speak to him?

M: Yes, please.

W: OK, I will just put you through.

M: Thank you.

Q9. What is Mr. Green doing in Shanghai?

Q10. Who will help the man most probably?

Section C

We have asked you to come to our "Thank You Party" today to show our heartfelt gratitude to all of you for being our reliable business partners.

As you all know, doing business is not an easy thing. There may be different purposes of doing business: Some do it for an endless pursuit of profit, and others for the sake of the well-being of the society. One thing, however, that we should not forget in doing business is to have a sense of appreciation. A sense of regret or resentment will not help us in any way. Having a sense of appreciation for all the people will keep us going on in business.

Section D

When considering a career change, there are lots of factors to consider. First of all, you should choose a job that you are interested in. If you don't like your job, you won't do it well, and may result in another career change finally. So personal interest is very important. Another important aspect is further study or training. Further study or training can make us keep up with the latest technology and improve our skills so that we can do the work more easily and quickly. What's more, the opportunity for future promotion is also necessary. Everyone wants to get promoted, because it means higher salary and higher position. And more opportunities encourage the staff to work harder to compete with each other.

Model Test Three (Level A)

Section A

1. W: Look at that big field of corn. And there's a farm with some beautiful houses.

M: You really get to know the country when you go by bus, don't you?

Q: Where did the conversation most probably take place?

2. W: Your spoken English is very good. I like it very much.

   M: Thank you! You see, I've ever stayed in England for five years and during that time my oral English was improved a lot.

   Q: How long did the man stay in England?

3. M: We can ask Tim to help us repair the jeep.

   W: When would he find time? He has exams tomorrow.

   Q: What does the woman mean?

4. M: Morning, Lily. What kept you?

   W: Morning, Stan. Sorry I'm so late, but you know, it's impossible to find a parking place round here.

   Q: Why was the woman late?

5. W: I want to make meat soup for lunch, but I'm not sure what ingredients are needed.

   M: Here is a recipe your mother gave.

   Q: What is the woman going to do next?

Section B

Conversation 1

M: Hello, Amy. Are you coming to my birthday party?

W: Yes, I am. How do I get to your house from the station?

M: Well, call me when you get to the station and I'll come and pick you up in my car.

W: Are you sure it won't be too much trouble?

M: It's no trouble at all. It only takes about 15 minutes.

W: Oh, I want to check your phone number. Is it 82881688?

M: No. It's 81881688.

W: Oh, really? I'm glad I checked.

M: What time do you plan to arrive at the station?

W: I plan to get there around 8:30.

M: OK. See you then.

W: See you. Goodbye.

Q6: How can the woman get to the man's house?

Q7: When does the woman plan to get to this station?

Conversation 2

M: What are you going to do after your return from New York?

W: I'm going to stay in the city.

M: What will you do all day?

W: I'm going to work with my father at the workshop. In the evening, I will read books. On weekends, I'll go to the park with my family.

M: Have you ever worked?

W: No, but I can learn. What are you going to do this summer?

M: I'm going to camp. I've gone to camp for four summers.

W: I've never gone to camp. What do you do there?

M: We do many things. In the morning, we go swimming and boating. In the afternoon, we play volleyball or tennis. We sit around a campfire at night. We sing or tell stories.

W: That sounds wonderful.

M: It is wonderful. What's Wales going to do this Summer?

W: I think he's going to the mountains with his parents.

M: Well, so long, Alice. Have fun.

W: You too, Leslie. Give my regards to Wales. I'll see you in October.

Q8. What is the possible relationship between them?

Q9. What is the woman going to do on weekends?

Q10. How many times has the man gone to camp in summer?

Section C

If you are staying at a fancy place, you might find a mint or some little candy on your pillow. These are free and nice. Some of the channels on the TV will be free, including probably a "movie" channel or two. These channels show movies all the time, but there will also be "pay for TV" channels which are not free and the cost of using them will be added to your bill. The phones will call anywhere in the hotel or motel for free. Finally, be careful of the refrigerator. Frequently the refrigerator is stocked with all sorts of delicious things to eat and drink, including snacks and beer.

Section D

Here are little cars that may someday take the place of today's cars. If everyone drives such a car in the future, there will be less pollution in the air. There will also be more parking spaces in cities, and the streets will be less crowded. Three such cars fit in the space now needed for one car of the usual size. The little cars will cost much less to own and to drive. Driving will be safer, too, as these little cars can only go 55 miles per hour. The cars of the future will be fine for getting around a city, but they will not be useful for long trips.

Model Test Four (Level A)

Section A

1. W: Are you ready to order soup?

   M: Yes, I would like to have some vegetable soup.

   Q: Where are the two speakers?

2. M: Hi, Jane, do you have some changes? I have to make a call on the pay phone.

   W: Pay phone? Why not use my mobile phone? Here you are.

   Q: What does the woman suggest the man doing?

3. W: We have made ten copies.

M: At first it is planned to need ten copies, and now we don't need so many. Five would be enough.

Q: How many unnecessary copies they have made?

4. W: The plane arrives at 10:50. It is already 10:40 now. Be quick!

M: Relax. Your watch must be fast. There are still twenty minutes left.

Q: What time is it now?

5. M: Did Henry decorate the whole house himself?

W: He had it decorated because he has no time.

Q: Why did Henry have his house decorated?

Section B
Conversation 1

M: Helen, can I have a look at your newspaper?

W: Sure, go ahead.

M: I want to know what's on this weekend.

W: Is there anything interesting?

M: The Fools Garden is giving a performance today.

W: They are a pop group. They are said to be very good. What time does the performance start?

M: 7 p.m., will you be free then?

W: Yes, I'd like to go.

M: Let's go together then.

W: All right.

Q6: What does the Fools Garden refer to?

Q7: What have the two speakers decided to do?

Conversation 2

W: I'm losing my sleep. I feel tired and sleepy all the time. I've got to do something about it.

M: I'm so sorry for you. But what are you going to do?

W: I want to move out of the dorm and rent a small flat.

M: That's a good idea. It will be much more convenient for you.

W: But I need your help.

M: How? To find one person for you?

W: Yes.

M: I'll sleep on it tonight and tell you my decision tomorrow, OK?

Q8: What's wrong with the woman?

Q9: What's the woman going to do with the problem?

Q10: Why does the woman need the man's help?

Section C

Many Chinese students want to pursue their Master's or PhD's degree in foreign universities, especially in American schools. However, it usually takes much time and costs much money to apply for a Western school, and the chance of getting admitted into a good school is not very high.

There are always far more competitors than the quotas set for the international students. Only the most competitive candidates will be admitted. Therefore, if you dream of studying abroad, you should, first of all, have faith in your intellectual abilities and other talents; secondly, you need to be mentally prepared for a long and sometimes frustrating process of realizing your dream.

Section D

Fish are animals that live in water. They live almost any place where there is water. Some are found in lakes. Other fish live in the sea. Most fish never leave water.

There are about 21,000 kinds of fish. One kind might not look like another. Some fish are very small. The smallest one is no bigger than a fly. Others are very big. The biggest fish grows up to 60 feet.

One kind of fish looks as if it has a little horse's head. It is called a sea horse. It doesn't swim very well. A sea horse is mostly pushed along by the moving water. What does it do when it wants to stay in one place? It takes hold of plants with its little tail.

参 考 文 献

[1] 白鹭，毕辉，蔡系荣，等.高等学校英语应用能力考试 A 级全真模拟试卷［M］.北京：外文出版社，2018.
[2] 白鹭，毕辉，蔡系荣，等.高等学校英语应用能力考试 B 级全真模拟试卷［M］.北京：外文出版社，2018.